*Mass Deception*

CRITICAL ISSUES IN CRIME AND SOCIETY
*Raymond J. Michalowski, Series Editor*

Critical Issues in Crime and Society is oriented toward critical analysis of contemporary problems in crime and justice. The series is open to a broad range of topics including specific types of crime, wrongful behavior by economically or politically powerful actors, controversies over justice system practices, and issues related to the intersection of identity, crime, and justice. It is committed to offering thoughtful works that will be accessible to scholars and professional criminologists, general readers, and students.

For a list of titles in the series, see the last page of the book.

# Mass Deception

## MORAL PANIC AND THE U.S. WAR ON IRAQ

SCOTT A. BONN

RUTGERS UNIVERSITY PRESS
*New Brunswick, New Jersey, and London*

LIBRARY OF CONGRESS CATALOGING-IN-PUBLICATION DATA

Bonn, Scott A., 1957–
    Mass deception : moral panic and the U.S. war on Iraq / Scott A. Bonn.
      p. cm. — (Critical issues in crime and society)
    Includes bibliographical references and index.
    ISBN 978-0-8135-4788-6 (hardcover : alk. paper)
    ISBN 978-0-8135-4789-3 (pbk. : alk. paper)
    1. Iraq War, 2003– —Deception.   2. Iraq War, 2003– —Causes.
  3. Deception—Political aspects—United States.   4. Rhetoric—Political
aspects—United States.   5. Bush, George W. (George Walker), 1946–  I. Title.
    DS79.76.B657   2010
    956.7044'31—dc22                      2009044962

A British Cataloging-in-Publication record for this book is available
from the British Library.

Visit our Web site: http://rutgerspress.rutgers.edu

Manufactured in the United States of America

*For my parents, Theodore and Donna,*
*who have always encouraged me to find my own voice,*
*even when it did not resonate with theirs.*

# Contents

# FOREWORD

AMID THE FRENZY of the attacks on September 11, the Bush administration pushed forward its plan to invade and occupy Iraq—a nation that had no involvement with the terrorist plot. Those developments prompted some observers to recall the memorable words of Senator Hiram Johnson, who declared: "The first casualty when war comes is truth" (Stevenson, 1948, p. 2445). With that concern in mind we turn to *Mass Deception: Moral Panic and the U.S. War on Iraq*. In this very important book, Scott Bonn offers to criminologists and sociologists, as well as students and citizens alike, an opportunity to understand in-depth the mechanics of political manipulation. The penetrating analysis herein relies on critical communication theory to decipher the Bush narrative on 9/11 and the alleged links to Saddam Hussein. Integrating concepts from sociological theory and media studies, Bonn focuses on moral panic, the power elite, and manufactured consent, thereby paying tribute to the enduring work of Stanley Cohen, C. Wright Mills, and Noam Chomsky.

In these opening comments on *Mass Deception*, I wish to reflect on a triangle of influence in which Bonn blends the thoughts of Cohen, Mills, and Chomsky while not losing sight of his own critique of mass communication. From the onset, Bonn elaborates on the meaning of moral panic, a concept used to interpret exaggerated and turbulent reactions to a putative social problem. The concept was initially developed in the 1960s by Cohen in his groundbreaking book *Folk Devils and Moral Panics*. Since then the concept has been used—and misused—by an array of researchers, journalists, and social commentators (see Garland, 2008). The third edition of the book (2002) allowed Cohen to look back on the idea of moral panic along with areas of inquiry where it has made further impact, ranging from welfare issues to asylum seekers. While recognizing its many territories of expansion, it is also crucial to attend to the depth and complexity of the concept. The 2002 version of *Folk Devils and Moral Panics* stands apart from its previous editions for its ability to delineate further the explanatory power of moral panic. Cohen considers three extensions of moral panic theory that lend themselves to the efforts of another generation of scholars, particularly those interested in social constructionism, risk, and media.

Although Bonn addresses each of those offshoots of moral panic, his work thrives in social constructionism, especially as it passes into the field of mass communication. As a former media executive, he is uniquely qualified to explore the mechanisms of persuasion that pave the way for claims-making in which government sets the agenda for what constitutes a social problem and therefore a threat to society. While much of the world remained fixated on the terrorist attacks on the World Trade Center and the Pentagon, Bonn— inspired by Cohen, Mills, and Chomsky—refused to take his eye off the center of power. His commitment to critical sociology is unmistakable in the manner by which *Mass Deception* cuts to the core of moral panic while bringing to light its lasting destructive forces, namely, war.

Bonn puts forth his view of power in the age of war by turning timely attention to C. Wright Mills. In *The Power Elite* (1956), Mills exposed an emerging network of state power that continues to be siphoned off by the corporate sector, most notably defense contractors. Mills's description of what he coined the military-industrial complex soon became standard fare in the conversation on American power. President Dwight D. Eisenhower in 1961 advised the nation to "guard against the acquisition of unwarranted influence" by the military-industrial complex (Jarecki, 2006). More recently, the documentary titled *Why We Fight*, issues a Millsian caution, as a former C.I.A. officer remarks: "When war becomes profitable, we will see more of it" (Jarecki, 2006). Despite those warnings, the sheer force of the industries driving the war agenda is still downplayed by corporate-dominated media. It should be noted that the biggest recipients of U.S. spending in the occupation of Iraq are the top American defense contractors, contributing to the largest deployment of private military companies in the history of warfare (Hartung, 2004; Singer, 2003; see Michalowski, 2009).

Linking Millsian sociology to the insights of Cohen, Bonn convincingly presents a case for the elite-engineered model of moral panic whereby a powerful group undertakes a deliberate campaign to create and sustain fear over a particular problem even though it does not constitute a bona fide social threat. Indeed, the narrative produced by the Bush White House to explain the events of September 11th and the supposed links to Saddam Hussein speaks to the power of moral panic maneuvered by elites. Taken further, it is through a thoughtful application of critical communication theory that Bonn unravels the complex process of exploiting public opinion over the invasion of Iraq.

To illuminate the relationship among various concepts discussed in *Mass Deception*, we should remain mindful that in developing the concept of moral panic, Cohen recalls being inspired by the early critiques of mass communication via Marshall McLuhan (1964). Today, the writings of McLuhan and Cohen are easily read, along with those of Noam Chomsky, in particular his *Manufactured Consent*: an analysis of media's capacity to advance the agenda for war (Herman & Chomsky, 1988; see Chomsky, 2002; Cohen, 2001). Carrying on that tradition, Bonn demonstrates the influence that Chomsky has on his own study of mass communication by revealing how elected leaders pursue war not only for their own political gain but also for those profiting from the military-industrial complex.

The timeliness of Bonn's project is evident, given the current wave of U.S. militarism sparked by 9/11. Similarly, other investigators also have delved into the latest incarnation of wartime propaganda. In 2009, *New York Times* journalist David Barstow earned the prestigious Pulitzer Prize for revealing the method by which communications experts recruited retired military officers in an attempt to assure Americans that the Bush team was on target with its war in Iraq. "Hidden behind that appearance of objectivity, though, is a Pentagon information apparatus that has used those analysts in a campaign to generate favorable news coverage of the administration's wartime performance" (Barstow, 2008a, p. A1). The deliberate manufacturing of political spin goes beyond ideological and military allegiances since most of the analysts have ties to military contractors vested in the very war policies they are asked to appraise while appearing on television (Barstow, 2008b). Perhaps not surprisingly, Barstow's revelations have been spurned by corporate media. Following the Pulitzer ceremony, his only invitation to speak publicly about the links between mass communication and the military-industrial complex took place on independent radio (www.democracynow .org, 2009).

Whereas investigative journalists deserve a wide audience for their analyses of media, government, and the military agenda, so do like-minded scholars—especially those who present their research in the context of sociological theory. In this well-planned book, Bonn offers readers a compelling critique of how the power elite in the Bush administration engineered a moral panic that drew the country into a long-term war that now has few supporters. Given the politics and profits of war, coupled with the systematic manipulation of public opinion, *Mass Deception* gives us good reason to monitor mass communication in a post-9/11 world.

Michael Welch
July 13, 2009
Author of *Crimes of Power & States of Impunity*
and *Scapegoats of September 11th*

# PREFACE

As a critical sociologist and former media executive, I have long been interested in the processes and mechanisms of persuasion that influence public attitudes on important issues in society. I am particularly interested in the social forces that facilitate the construction of so-called problems and alleged threats to the social order. I spent more than twenty years in the corporate world as an advertising and media executive before pursuing a doctorate in sociology. My transition from media executive to academician occurred shortly after the terrorist attacks of September 11, 2001. I was in graduate school when President George W. Bush began to bang the war drums toward Iraq. When it became clear that the United States was going to invade Iraq in 2003, I wondered why Americans generally believed the Bush administration's claim of a grave and gathering threat from Iraq, and why the U.S. public generally supported the unprovoked invasion of that country.

It is my contention that the Bush administration created a panic by deliberately deceiving Americans about Iraq's possession of weapons of mass destruction (WMD) and its links to 9/11, and that the U.S. news media, perhaps unwittingly, fueled the panic by promoting the Bush administration's false and deceptive rhetoric. I contend that President G. W. Bush knew with reasonable certainty that Iraq had no WMD but claimed otherwise to justify an invasion of that country, thus enabling him to pursue a hidden agenda that included oil, family legacy, and geopolitical domination. I further maintain that the Bush administration's actions leading up to the invasion manifested the higher immorality of the power elite and that the war and occupation of Iraq were violations of domestic and international laws.

In this book I attempt to provide insights into the social construction of social problems and the elite-engineering of moral panics. I examine the key roles of political leaders and the news media in shaping public attitudes and opinions concerning alleged threats to society. I have formulated a unique, integrated, and interdisciplinary approach, herein called critical communication theory, to help explain how and why political elites and the news media periodically create public panics that are mutually beneficial. The Iraq war, particularly the buildup to the 2003 invasion, provides the context and framework for the discussions presented throughout this book. It is my hope that the theories, concepts, and arguments advanced in this book will encourage intellectual debate among students, academics, and critical thinkers everywhere.

I owe numerous debts of gratitude concerning this book. First, I would like to thank two great friends and mentors, Amie Nielsen and Michael Welch, for their expertise, guidance, and insightful comments on earlier drafts of this book. A special thanks to Michael Welch for writing a compelling foreword to this book. Thanks to Noam Chomsky for his inspiration and his words of encouragement. Thanks to my student assistants, Tania Linares at the University of Miami, and Caitlin Colletti, Victoria Aguirre, Sunita Bhargava, and Thomas Basgil at Drew University for their dedication and excellent research assistance on this project. Thanks also to my editors, Doreen Valentine, Ray Michalowski, and Adi Hovav, for their commitment to this book and their support. Thanks to Roy Roberg for encouraging me to pursue a doctorate in sociology after spending more than twenty years in the corporate world and for inspiring a highly curious "old dog" to learn important "new tricks." Thanks to Mike Brewi for his friendship. Thanks to Sumru Tufekcioglu for her love and affection, as well as her helpful suggestions on this project. Finally, thanks to all of my students and colleagues at Drew University who inspire me daily.

*Mass Deception*

# CHAPTER 1

# George W. Bush and the Drums of War

"Beware the leader who bangs the drums of war."

—Anonymous, sometimes attributed to Julius Caesar

ON THE MORNING OF September 11, 2001, the United States was attacked by international terrorists. A series of coordinated suicide attacks were carried out that day in which hijackers simultaneously took control of four U.S. domestic commercial airliners. The hijackers crashed two planes into the World Trade Center Towers in Manhattan, New York, and they flew the third plane into the U.S. Department of Defense headquarters, the Pentagon, in Arlington County, Virginia. The fourth plane crashed into a field in rural Somerset County, Pennsylvania, following passenger resistance. The Twin Towers of the World Trade Center collapsed and the Pentagon was seriously damaged as a result of the attacks. The official count records 2,986 deaths in the attacks, including the hijackers (www.answers.com, 2006).

It has been argued that despite overwhelming evidence that the attacks had been solely orchestrated by Osama Bin Laden's al Qaeda network (including its claim of responsibility), the administration of U.S. President George W. Bush initiated a campaign to link 9/11 to Iraq, Saddam Hussein and his Baath Party (Scheer, 2003). However, in October 2001, a few weeks after 9/11, based on recommendations from the Pentagon and then Secretary of State Colin Powell, President Bush sent U.S. military forces to Afghanistan to overthrow the Taliban regime, which had harbored al Qaeda, and to capture or kill Bin Laden. Unfortunately, Bin Laden and his key lieutenants escaped capture and disappeared in December 2001 during a showdown with U.S.-led forces in Tora Bora, a cave complex situated in the White Mountains of eastern Afghanistan.

At the same time that the military assault on Afghanistan was taking place, the Bush administration was initiating an 18-month campaign to convince the U.S. public and the world that Iraq (1) was involved in the attacks

of 9/11; (2) possessed weapons of mass destruction (WMD); and (3) represented a grave and growing threat to U.S. security (Scheer, 2003). In fact,
Paul Wolfowitz, then deputy secretary of defense under Donald Rumsfeld,
began to link Iraq to 9/11 within 48 hours following the terrorist attacks
(Clarke, 2004). By the fall of 2002, President Bush was proclaiming that "the
Iraqi dictator must not be permitted to threaten America and the world with
horrible poisons and diseases and gases and atomic weapons" (Scheer, 2003,
p. 1). Although the United States was never directly threatened or provoked
by Iraq, President Bush declared war allegedly to "disarm Iraq . . . and to
defend the world from grave danger" on March 19, 2003 (Scheer, 2003, p. 1).
The Bush administration's propaganda campaign was so successful that 70% of
the U.S. public believed Iraq was directly involved in the attacks of 9/11
when the U.S.-led invasion of Iraq began (Corn, 2003).

By almost all measures the war in Iraq has been a mistake and a catastro-
phe of massive proportions. By mid-2008, five years after the invasion and
occupation began, despite the capture and execution of Saddam Hussein and
the failure to find any WMD, Iraq was embroiled in a civil war, and over
forty-one hundred U.S. soldiers and more than one million Iraqis (3.7% of
the population) had been killed (www.icasualties.org, 2008; Opinion Research
Business, 2008). In Baghdad, more than 40% of households had lost a family
member. In addition, more than four million Iraqi citizens had been displaced
by the conflict—i.e., almost 20% of the pre-war population—nearly half of
which had fled to neighboring countries such as Syria and Jordan. The ongoing financial cost of the war in Iraq to the United States was over $10 billion
per month. The actual spending on the war by July 2008 totaled more than
$550 billion and another $135 billion had been requested by President Bush
and approved by Congress for its continuation (www.nationalpriorities.org,
2008). Although the Iraqi prime minister, Nuri al-Maliki, stated in the summer of 2008 that he favored then U.S. presidential candidate Barack Obama's
timetable for troop withdrawals, in a seeming contradiction he also stated that
Iraq would not be able to independently defend itself until 2018 (Mazzetti &
Rohde, 2008). By then, even at 50% of the 2008 spending level, the war and
occupation of Iraq would cost the U.S. nearly $1.5 trillion. Not surprisingly, the
G. W. Bush administration preferred not to discuss such inconvenient truths.

Also, by the spring of 2008, President Bush was trying to convince the
U.S. public of the need to remain in Iraq indefinitely by linking al Qaeda in
Mesopotamia, a home-grown Sunni group, to the terrorist network responsible for the attacks of 9/11. The Bush administration doggedly adhered to
this mythical position despite the facts that (1) Saddam Hussein had no relationship with al Qaeda prior to 9/11, and (2) al Qaeda in Mesopotamia did
not even exist prior to the U.S.-led invasion of Iraq in 2003 (Strobel & Talev,
2006). At the same time, President Bush was attempting to convince the

public that his so-called surge strategy (i.e., increased number of troops in Baghdad) was succeeding by focusing on a declining number of suicide attacks and roadside bombings around the capital rather than on the fractured and unstable state of the Iraqi government. A statistical reduction in the number of attacks (due in large part to the emergence of the "Sunni Awakening" movement in which thousands of Sunnis were paid by the U.S. government to fight insurgents, and a cease-fire called by the influential anti-U.S. Shia cleric Muqtada al-Sadr, who controls one of Iraq's most powerful militias) is a poor and callous measure of "success," and it is very different from the emergence of civil society. Moreover, violence escalated north of Baghdad shortly after the surge began, suggesting that the insurgents were simply displaced by the increased military presence in the capital.

The troop surge did not produce the political gains in Iraq that the Bush administration had anticipated. In spring 2008, President Bush predicted that the American troop surge would create an opportunity for the various Iraqi factions to resolve their political differences. In August 2008, the Iraqi parliament adjourned for the summer without passing a crucial election law that the Bush administration had hoped would stabilize the fragile Iraqi government (Robertson & Oppel, 2008). The adjournment resulted in the postponement of provincial elections, which were seen as vital to reconciling the deep-seated tensions among Iraq's political and sectarian groups, until 2009. Despite the Bush administration's claims of progress on the political front, the decision to go on vacation rather than settle the issue underscored how little progress had been made on the most important political question to confront Iraqi leaders. The military intervention and occupation by the United States did not resolve either the sociopolitical conflict or the thirteen hundred-year history of bad blood between ethnic factions and religious sects in Iraq.

The deplorable situation in Iraq presents another cruel irony. Although it is likely that few lament the demise of Saddam Hussein, the overthrow of his government and the war have left Iraq a broken country in turmoil, and thus have made the U.S. more vulnerable—not safer—as President G. W. Bush would have liked the U.S. public to believe (Clark, 2006; Mazzetti & Rohde, 2008). The occupation of Iraq stretched the U.S. military to a point where it compromised its ability to adequately defend itself elsewhere. In addition, the U.S. occupation of Iraq became a symbol of Western colonialism and a useful recruiting tool for Islamic Jihadists. Arguably, Osama Bin Laden could not have asked for a more powerful call to arms than the U.S. invasion and occupation of a sovereign Arab nation. Moreover, the war in Iraq diverted important resources and attention from the hunt for Bin Laden, and it revealed that Saddam Hussein had replaced him as "public enemy number one" in the eyes of the Bush administration as early as 2002 (Clarke, 2004; Mazzetti & Rohde, 2008).

Seven years after 9/11, Saddam Hussein was dead and the real architect responsible for the terrorist attacks was still at large. As a result of the diversion and concentration of U.S. military and surveillance assets in Iraq, al Qaeda had successfully regrouped and relocated to Pakistan, and Taliban insurgents had reemerged as a dangerous threat to the U.S.-backed government of Afghanistan. Al Qaeda and Taliban militants had regained strength in the tribal areas of Pakistan, which they have often used as a base for raids into Afghanistan—an increasingly sore point for the U.S. and Afghan governments by mid-2008. By June 2008, the war in Afghanistan had roared back into public view as a result of an expanding threat to U.S. forces from the Taliban. Combat deaths in Afghanistan were greater in June 2008 than in any month since the U.S.-led invasion began in 2001, and the total number of Americans and allied forces who died there (twenty-three U.S. and forty-six total) exceeded the total in Iraq (thirty-one) for a second straight month (Mazzetti & Rohde, 2008). The following month, July 2008, was only slightly less deadly, with twenty U.S. deaths compared with six in Iraq. On July 22, 2008, nearly seven years after the war began on October 7, 2001, the United States lost its five hundredth soldier in the Afghanistan war (Semple & Lehren, 2008).

At the same time, listening to American politicians from both major parties discuss the ongoing debacle in Iraq, it is easy to conclude that few were in favor of the war when it began. Yet, prior to the March 19, 2003, invasion of Iraq, 64% of the U.S. public supported going to war (Gallup, 2003), as did the vast majority of the members of Congress. By January, 2006, less than three years later, 51% of the U.S. public believed the war in Iraq was a mistake, and 53% believed the Bush administration deliberately misled the American public about Iraq's possession of WMD (Moore, 2006). By December 2006, almost two-thirds (64%) of the U.S. public—that is, identical to the percentage that supported the invasion in the first place—believed that the war was a mistake (Hutcheson, 2006).

Many critics have argued that the war and occupation of Iraq were the result of deliberate distortions on the part of President Bush's administration after 9/11 regarding the actual threat to the United States posed by Saddam Hussein and his followers. Even Scott McClellan, the former White House press secretary who was long considered to be one of President G. W. Bush's most loyal assistants, now argues that the president was "not open and forthright" about the war and that the Bush administration relied on "propaganda" and "manipulating" public opinion in the run-up to the invasion of Iraq (McClellan, 2008). Predictably, the Bush administration's response to such accusations is that the president was "very clear" about the reason(s) for going to war (Woodward, 2008). Arguably, he was neither clear nor honest in that regard.

What has been lacking up until now, however, is empirical evidence that the deceptive rhetoric of the Bush administration actually manufactured or manipulated U.S. public support for invading Iraq. This absence of evidence is significant because the culpability of the Bush administration for allegedly deviant and/or criminal actions has become a subject of considerable debate among scholars, politicians, the media, and the general public. This book examines two propositions:

1. The war was legitimized by an *elite-engineered moral panic* precipitated by the G. W. Bush administration and reinforced by the news media which exploited pre-existing negative stereotypes of Arabs (Merskin, 2004) and influenced public opinion on support for the invasion of Iraq (Chomsky, 2005).
2. The Bush administration perpetrated elite deviance or "wrongdoing" (Mills, 1956; Simon, 2002), as well as state crimes and war crimes in their actions concerning Iraq (see Hogan, Long, Stretesky & Lynch, 2006; Kramer, Michalowski & Rothe, 2005; Ritter, 2006). More specifically, the moral panic engineered by the Bush administration constituted elite wrongdoing, and the invasion and occupation of Iraq were state crimes and violations of international criminal law.

## WHAT IS MORAL PANIC?

In order to provide the context for the remainder of this book, it is important to examine moral panic in some detail. Generally, moral panic has been defined as a condition or situation in which public fears and state interventions greatly exceed the objective threat posed to society by a particular group that is claimed to be responsible for the condition (S. Cohen, 1972; McCorkle & Miethe, 1998). Specifically, an elite-engineered moral panic occurs when an elite group deliberately undertakes a campaign to generate and sustain concern or fear on the part of the public over an issue that is not terribly threatening to society (Goode & Ben-Yehuda, 1994).

The moral panic concept remains popular among scholars studying social problems, crime, media, and collective behavior (Garland, 2008; Welch, 2006b). Introduced by Young (1971), the moral panic concept was developed and popularized by the criminologist Stanley Cohen (1972) when he described the public reaction to disturbances by youths called "mods and rockers" at seaside resorts in Brighton, England, during the 1960s. Cohen's work illustrated how those reactions influenced the enforcement and formation of social policy, law, and societal perceptions of threat posed by the youth groups. As originally explained by Cohen (1972, p. 9), a moral panic has occurred when:

> a condition, episode, person or group of persons emerges to become defined as a threat to societal values or interests; its nature is presented in a stylized and stereotypical fashion by the mass media; the moral barricades are

to provide tantalizing news content (Goode & Ben-Yehuda, 1994). Altheide (2002, p. 153) states this key element succinctly: "The mass media, especially organized entertainment news, and the agencies of social control are synergistically joined in an ecology of communication. Mass media . . . require . . . periodic crises to gain the attention of audiences that are increasingly fragmented . . . [while creating] legitimacy and need [i.e., dependency on the part of the public] are problems for law makers." The moral panic concept describes how political elites and the mass media are symbiotically linked; together they can manufacture public fear and launch public crises that serve their mutual interests. Therefore, situations and events that may or may not exist or pose objective threats to society (e.g., the threat from Iraq) may be transformed by the media and elites into the object of public concern and fear. Furthermore, groups and individuals can become defined as "evil" or folk devils through similar processes. A theoretical discussion on the framing of social problems by political elites and the news media is presented in chapter two.

Of particular relevance to the central topic of this book is the "elite engineered" model of moral panic. According to Goode and Ben-Yehuda (1994, p. 135), and consistent with the tenets of critical sociology (see chapter two), the "elite-engineered" model of moral panic argues that "an elite group deliberately and consciously undertakes a campaign to generate and sustain concern, fear, and panic on the part of the public over an issue that they recognize not to be terribly harmful to the society as a whole." Often times, such a campaign is intended to divert public attention away from other objective or real problems in society, whose solution might jeopardize or undermine the interests of the elite group (Goode & Ben-Yehuda, 1994). Moreover, an elite-engineered moral panic can play an important role in "enabling the ruling stratum to maintain its privileged position" (Chambliss & Mankoff, 1976, p. 15).

The elite-engineered model of moral panic is based on the assumption that political/economic elites have tremendous power over other members of society. It is the elites who define or establish and disseminate the dominant ideology in society. Specifically, the elites frame issues for public discourse, control the distribution of valuable resources, dominate the mass media, and determine the content of legislation and the direction of law enforcement (Chambliss & Mankoff, 1976). Thus, elite-engineered moral panic represents a "top-down" conceptual model. That is, public concern or fear over an issue is orchestrated from above by elites who control the governing ideology and have unfettered access to mass media outlets.

It has been argued, for example, that the U.S. war on drugs in the 1980s, which had widespread public support, resulted from a moral panic engineered by the administration of President Reagan (Hawdon, 2001; Reinarman & Levine, 1989). However, this does not mean that the drug issue did not exist objectively or that illegal drugs did not represent a serious problem in certain isolated neighborhoods in the United States. Rather, it has been argued that the punitive position adopted by President Reagan toward illegal drug users exaggerated the threat of drugs to the general population, and that the news media reinforced the punitive and exaggerated rhetoric of the president (Hawdon, 2001).

Although the moral panic approach has been applied to a variety of other social problems, this is the first known empirical application of the elite-engineered model of moral panic to (1) the G. W. Bush administration's discourse regarding Iraq following 9/11 (although Rothe & Muzzatti, 2004, analyzed the *war on terror* as a moral panic) and (2) examining the extent to which the policy rhetoric of a U.S. president helped to legitimate an international event—specifically, war. Throughout this book, the Bush administration's framing of the alleged threat posed by Iraq is examined through the lens of the elite-engineered model of moral panic. An in-depth analysis of the Iraq war is undertaken to demonstrate the role of political rhetoric in the perpetration of elite deviance (i.e., moral panic), state crime, and violations of international law.

However, it has been argued that not all moral panics are elite engineered (Goode & Ben-Yehuda, 1994). An alternative approach—the grassroots model of moral panic—states that "panics originate with the general public; the concern about a particular threat is a widespread,—if perhaps mistaken—[but nevertheless genuine] concern" (Goode & Ben-Yehuda, 1994, p. 127). Unlike the elite-engineered model of moral panic (i.e., a top-down approach in which elites orchestrate the panic from above), the grass roots model stipulates that the expression of concern in other spheres, including the media and polity, are really expressions of more widespread concern from the masses. The grassroots model of moral panic argues that political elites and the news media cannot fabricate public concern where none existed initially (Goode & Ben-Yehuda, 1994). Thus, the grassroots model of moral panic is a "bottom-up" approach. The Salem witchcraft trials of the 1600s in Massachusetts are an example of a grassroots moral panic.

In this book it is argued that the actions of the Bush administration and the U.S. news media leading up to the invasion of Iraq constitute an elite-engineered moral panic. However, it could be argued that those events are more consistent with public arenas theory. As articulated by Hilgartner and Bosk (1988), public arenas theory of social problems elaborates on the symbolic interactionist model that views such problems as products of a process of collective definition. More specifically, the theory states that many different issues compete with each other for "problem status" in institutional arenas of public discourse at any given point in time. Consistent with social constructionism, as discussed in chapter two, the theory states that a situation does not become a social problem until it is labeled as such in the arenas of public discourse and action. These arenas include governmental agencies, private foundations, and the media. Concerning the media, the theory further postulates that clear and unified presentations (or frames) of social problems are rarely disseminated to the public. Instead, competing frames are presented in the media arena, which offer different interpretations of the same social problem and vie for public acceptance. This perspective would point to the alternative and conflicting representations of the Iraqi threat (e.g., the White House versus the United Nations) depicted in the news media leading up to the U.S.-led invasion.

Offering another perspective, Welch (2006a, 2006b) argued that the United States can be viewed as a "risk society" following 9/11. Risk society is seen as a condition or manifestation of late modern society. According to risk society theory, the United States became hypersensitized to terrorist threats after the attacks of 9/11 and its members became hypervigilant. Therefore, the American public became preoccupied with national security and more likely to support officials who not only offer assurances of security but also demonstrate a willingness to "kick some ass" among its enemies (Welch, 2006a, 2006b). Indeed, many Americans wanted revenge after 9/11. Welch (2007) makes a distinction between risk society and moral panic: "Moral panic theory is retrospective, looking at tense moments that are volatile. Risk society theory implies a societal condition that is more enduring." In a post-9/11 risk society, heightened public fear of terrorism can be manipulated by the government to gain support for policy initiatives (Croft, 2006; Welch, 2006a, 2006b). From this perspective, political elites periodically tap into existing social anxiety in order to justify their actions. The social anxiety allows a government and its respective officials to enact policies that are unfair and unnecessary due to an exaggerated need for social control and maintenance of national security.

The elite-engineered model of moral panic is used throughout this book. Nevertheless, the grassroots model of moral panic, public arenas theory, and risk society theory each offer compelling perspectives on the central topic of this book, i.e., the events leading up to the invasion of Iraq, and offer contrasting insights to those of the moral panic perspective. These important theoretical interpretations are considered in chapter seven, based on the empirical evidence after arguments are presented and conclusions drawn from an elite-engineered moral panic perspective.

OVERVIEW OF THIS BOOK

The focus of this book is on the social processes, such as the framing of issues, through which presidential rhetoric influences public attitudes and opinion, as well as the role of such rhetoric in elite deviance, state crime, and war crime. Chapter two presents an integrated theoretical framework to provide a more comprehensive understanding of moral panic. An interdisciplinary and integrative theoretic approach (merging critical sociology and criminology, communication theory, and the social construction of reality) is used in an attempt to expand upon the literature (S. Cohen, 2002; Goode & Ben-Yehuda, 1994; Rothe & Muzzatti, 2004; Welch, 2000) and provide a more detailed and synthetic foundation for understanding the elite-engineered model of moral panic. This unique, integrated theoretic approach, herein called critical communication theory, provides a more complete explanation of how and why moral panics may be socially constructed or engineered through the framing of alleged problems by political elites and the news media. A more comprehensive understanding of the processes involved in moral panic provides a firm theoretical foundation for the propositions advanced in this book. More specifically, critical communication theory guides an examination of: (1) the Bush administration's rhetoric regarding the alleged threat from Iraq; (2) how the issue was organized and framed by the media; and (3) the influence of presidential rhetoric as presented in the news frame (Tuchman, 1978) on public opinion after the attacks of 9/11.

What determines whether or not a situation qualifies as a moral panic? How can one empirically measure a moral panic? To answer these questions, chapter two also provides a discussion of the literature on moral panic and social problems, and offers specific criteria for determining whether the Bush administration engineered a moral panic regarding the alleged threat posed by Iraq. Stanley Cohen (2002), who developed and popularized the moral panic concept, identified five criteria that must be met before a condition can be considered a moral panic. The five criteria proposed by Cohen and discussed in chapter two are: concern, hostility, consensus, disproportionality, and volatility. Because these criteria are well established in the moral panic literature, they are used here to examine an argument that the Bush administration engineered a moral panic over the threat posed by Iraq.

Chapter three summarizes the findings of a research study conducted to examine the proposition that the Bush administration contrived public support for the invasion of Iraq by engineering a moral panic. It has been argued that the attacks of September 11, 2001, were historic, symbolic, and pivotal—and that they became the defining moments of the U.S. war on terror (C. Scheer, R. Scheer & Chaudry, 2003). Therefore, an examination of presidential policy rhetoric concerning Iraq before and after the terrorist attacks of September 11, 2001, enables a determination of whether the policy rhetoric changed in significant and meaningful ways following that historic event. The methodology employed was similar to the one used to examine the war on drugs in the United States from a moral panic perspective (Hawdon, 2001). Specifically, an analysis of opinion polls that measured public support for going to war in Iraq helps to determine whether there were shifts in opinion that mirrored the policy rhetoric. Together, these analyses allowed an empirical examination of the elite-engineered moral panic perspective applied to the events leading up to the Iraq war.

In chapter four it is argued that the findings of the study meet or fulfill the five criteria of a moral panic identified by Cohen (2002). It is contended that the actions of the Bush administration and the news media and their combined influences on public opinion leading up to the invasion of Iraq constitute an elite-engineered moral panic as conceptually defined (Garland, 2008; Goode & Ben-Yehuda, 1994). It is argued that the media's complicity in the moral panic can be explained from the perspective of the "news net," and that the public's response is consistent with the theory on "news as frame" (Tuchman, 1978). In addition, it is argued that the research findings demonstrate the agenda-setting influence of the president and, consistent with the communication and moral panic literature, reveal that public opinion concerning an issue often mirrors the president's framing of that issue (Hawdon, 2001; Johnson, Wanta & Boudreau, 2004; Reinarman & Levine, 1989).

Significantly, however, not all Americans were swept up in the moral panic over Iraq. Also, public support for the war began to diminish when the quick victory promised by the Bush administration failed to occur. Chapter four offers insights into why a sizable minority of the public never accepted the Bush administration's argument for war and why public support for the war eroded greatly over time.

Evidence is presented in chapter four that events leading up to the invasion of Iraq, as well as facts made public since the invasion, provide additional support for Cohen's five criteria of moral panic. In this chapter the so-called intelligence and alleged proof that the Bush administration used to build its case for war are examined. Over the past few years, the various intelligence sources and reports used by the Bush administration to bolster its argument for the invasion of Iraq have largely been debunked. In 2006, for example, the Senate Intelligence Committee reported that the Bush administration had used faulty intelligence assessments to justify invading Iraq, and furthermore, the administration knew the intelligence was faulty, based on repeated warnings from both the Central Intelligence Agency and the Pentagon, but chose to use it anyway (Strobel & Talev, 2006).

Can the actions of the Bush administration concerning Iraq be considered elite deviance, state crimes, or war crimes? First, does the Bush administration's engineering of a moral panic over Iraq constitute elite deviance? In order to determine whether the Bush administration perpetrated elite wrongdoing, in chapter five it is proposed to examine the Bush administration's rhetoric and policies concerning Iraq (in particular, the engineering of a moral panic) from the perspectives of Millsian sociology (Mills, 1956; Simon, 1995). In his seminal work, Mills (1956) explained that the "power elite" are a small group of wealthy and influential individuals who control America's dominant institutions (i.e., economic, political, and military), and are the creators of the dominant ideology. Frequently, the power elite frame policy discussions in ways that promote their own interests and perpetuate their power. Mills argued that elite acts that cause social harm, regardless of their criminality in a legal sense, are part of the "higher immorality" of the "power elite."

Second, does the war in Iraq, which, as argued here, resulted from a Bush administration-engineered moral panic, also constitute state crime? Chapter five presents a theoretical and legal foundation to examine whether or not the March 2003 invasion of Iraq, a sovereign nation that neither threatened nor provoked the United States, constitutes state crime. In order to answer this question, the scholarly literature on state crime is explored. For example, Chambliss (1988, p. 327) argued that state crime "consists of acts committed by state or government officials in the pursuit of their job as government officials." Third, can the actions of the Bush administration concerning Iraq be considered war crimes? To answer this question, this book proposes to examine whether the invasion and occupation of Iraq constitute war crimes in violation of international law, as defined by the Geneva Conventions of 1929 and 1949, and the Nuremberg Charter of 1950. Chapter five concludes with a discussion on the International Criminal Court in The Hague, Netherlands, which prosecutes war criminals.

In chapter six the theoretical framework presented in chapter five is used to examine whether the Bush administration committed elite deviance, state crime, or war crime in their actions concerning Iraq. The rhetoric and actions of the Bush administration concerning Iraq are critically analyzed from the sociological perspectives of elite wrongdoing (Mills, 1956; Simon, 2002). Mills argued that bound by mutual interests, the power elite, who control the dominant institutions in the United States, periodically commit acts of elite wrongdoing (e.g., lying to the public) and enact policies (including the declaration of war) that are designed to perpetuate their power and maintain their dominance over society. Evidence is provided that a moral panic engineered by the Bush administration using false and deceptive political rhetoric regarding the alleged Iraq threat, which was then used to justify the invasion, can be understood as a manifestation of the "higher immorality of the power elite" (Mills, 1956).

In chapter six it is argued that the 2003 invasion of Iraq constitutes state crime as defined by scholars, particularly Kramer et al. (2005). Also, evidence is provided that the invasion and occupation of Iraq are war crimes in violation of international criminal law. Under the Nuremberg Charter, for example, the supreme international crime is that of initiating a war of aggression, e.g., the unauthorized invasion of Iraq, because it is the crime from which all war crimes follow. Also, the possibility of prosecuting key members of the

military actions of the Bush administration against Iraq to a critical examination from the perspective of international criminal law, this book expands the literature on war crimes as well.

Finally, it is important to consider the topics and events discussed in this book, including the research findings presented in chapter three, within their appropriate social and historical contexts. In order to do so, certain key events and dates must be kept in mind throughout these discussions. To aid the reader in this regard, the following provides a chronological listing of events that are central to the propositions advanced in this book.

CHRONOLOGY OF KEY EVENTS

| | |
|---|---|
| January 21, 2001 | George W. Bush is inaugurated as the forty-third president of the United States. |
| September 11, 2001 | The United States is attacked by international terrorists. |
| October 7, 2001 | The United States invades Afghanistan. |
| January 29, 2002 | President Bush introduces the term "axis of evil" in his State of the Union address. |
| February 5, 2003 | Secretary of State Colin Powell addresses the United Nations and declares that "Iraq fails to disarm." |
| March 19, 2003 | The United States invades Iraq. |
| May 1, 2003 | President Bush declares "mission accomplished" in Iraq. |
| November 2, 2004 | President Bush is reelected to a second term. |
| January 20, 2009 | G. W. Bush leaves the White House and the Iraq war approaches its seventh year. |

CHAPTER 2

# Why Do Many in Society Drink the Kool-Aid Served in a Moral Panic?

IN MUCH OF THE moral panic literature, considerable attention is given to analyzing whether a particular condition conforms to its
conceptual tenets, i.e., establishing that a situation is a moral panic (e.g., Best,
1994; Hawdon, 2001; McCorkle & Miethe, 1998; Reinarman & Levine,
1989; Rothe & Muzzatti, 2004). However, little attention is paid to explaining
why moral panics occur in society in the first place. Stated differently, moral
panics are often treated in the literature as existing *sui generis*. What is lacking
is a broader approach for understanding the processes and mechanisms through
which moral panics are able to occur.

In this chapter, a novel, integrated theoretical approach to explaining
elite-engineered moral panic is introduced and approaches to analyzing moral
panic are discussed. More specifically, there are three goals for this chapter:

1. To introduce critical communication theory—an integrated theoretical framework involving critical sociology, communication theory,
   and social constructionism—to help explain (a) *how* and *why* moral panics are engineered by political elites and the news media and (b) how
   such moral panics influence public opinion.
2. To discuss research methodologies and findings that support and provide insights into the moral panic concept.
3. To discuss the measurement criteria established by Cohen (2002) that
   are used to examine the first of two theoretical propositions advanced
   in this book.

Organizationally, this chapter begins by introducing and then discussing the
integrated theoretical perspective on elite-engineered moral panic. The chapter proceeds with a discussion of contemporary sociology and communication
research that is directly related to the first theoretical proposition advanced
herein. The chapter concludes with a discussion of the conceptual framework
and specific empirical criteria used to analyze elite-engineered moral panic in
this book.

## CRITICAL COMMUNICATION THEORY:
## AN INTEGRATED THEORETICAL PERSPECTIVE

Arguably, moral panic is a concept rather than a theory (S. Cohen, 2002; Garland, 2008). It is contended here that a broader theoretical framework is needed to understand the moral panic concept, and that such a framework requires an integrated approach that draws upon several literatures. Although Cohen (2002), who explained and popularized the moral panic concept, has recently addressed the various contributions of critical sociology, social constructionism, media and cultural studies, and social anxiety (risk society theory) to the development and evolution of the moral panic concept, an integrated theoretic approach that provides the basis for understanding how they occur is lacking.

It is a goal of this book to build upon the work of Cohen (2002) and others (e.g., Goode & Ben-Yehuda, 1994; Rothe & Muzzatti, 2004; Welch, 2000, 2006a) in order to extend the understanding of moral panic. Specifically, an integrated theoretical approach involving critical sociology (and criminology), communication theory, and social constructionism is proposed to help explain how and why moral panics can be engineered by societal elites, fueled by the media, and how and why these panics can impact public opinion. This integrated theoretical perspective, herein called critical communication theory, seeks to provide a more detailed and comprehensive explanation of elite-engineered moral panics and the processes involved in their social construction than is offered in prior moral panic literature. Critical communication theory provides a comprehensive, interdisciplinary base for explaining why moral panics occur. Stated differently, this integrated theoretical approach can help explain how and why many members of society drink the tainted Kool-Aid served by the elites in a moral panic—that is, accept as real and valid the elite framing of alleged social problems, such as the framing of the alleged Iraq threat by the Bush administration and the news media.

Critical communication theory is an interdisciplinary and integrated theoretical approach to explaining the elite-engineered model of moral panic. An examination of the various theoretical traditions that together comprise critical communication theory is fundamental to understanding the contributions of each one. Those theoretical perspectives are discussed below. First, the central tenets and key concepts of critical sociology (and critical criminology) that offer important insights into the social construction and elite engineering of moral panics are discussed. Second, the guiding perspectives, processes, and mechanisms of communication theory that help to explain the shaping of public opinion (e.g., consensus in a moral panic) are discussed. After that, the foundation of the moral panic concept and its key assumptions are connected to the social constructionist perspective on social problems. Finally, the concept of "evil" is analyzed from a social constructionist perspective, including a discussion of its considerable importance to the moral panic concept.

### Critical Sociology (The Frankfurt School)

Critical sociological theory provides insights into the role of media and political rhetoric in influencing public opinion. The Frankfurt School of critical theory can be traced back to the Institute of Social Research in Frankfurt, Germany, founded in 1923. Heavily influenced by Karl Marx, these theorists were dissatisfied with the state of Marxian theory, particularly its tendency toward economic determinism (Habermas, 1975). They sought to extend and update the Marxian tradition by examining the domination and oppression of the masses by societal elites in advanced capitalist societies.

The Frankfurt writers viewed oppression in modern society as being more subtle and more deceptive than traditional Marxians had described it. They also argued that the locus of domination in the modern world had shifted from the economy to the cultural realm (Adorno, 1997). Frankfurt theorists saw mass culture in general, and media technology in particular, as modern agents of oppression (Habermas, 1975). The Frankfurt theorists wrote extensively on the falseness of the *culture industry*, i.e., rationalized and bureaucratized structures such as the mass media. These writers argued that modern societal elites who control the culture industry use it to disseminate false ideologies designed to confuse and oppress the masses (Horkheimer, 1987). Moreover, these writers asserted that rhetoric and "legitimations" (systems of ideas) are manufactured by the polity to justify its own existence (Habermas, 1975).

Lowenthal (1989) argued that public agitation instilled through the mass media creates an undesirable dependency on "so-called leadership," i.e., political elites who exploit public concern in order to justify their policies and legitimize their authority. Lowenthal (1989, p. 234) further argued that a key task of critical theorists must be to unmask the "aggressive and destructive impulses hidden behind [the] rhetoric" in mass communication. In their "critique of domination," critical theorists argued that the political elites produce ideologies that are often false and obfuscating, but which support the existence of the polity (Agger, 1978). The culture industry, especially the mass media, provide the political elites with an ubiquitous forum in which to disseminate their ideology in the guise of news and thereby influence attitudes, set agendas, and legitimize their policies. Distorted mass communication results in the creation of a false consciousness among the masses that serves the interests of those in power (Agger, 1978). From a critical perspective, the mass media can be viewed as oppressive instruments of modern capitalist ideology and the political system (Chomsky, 2002; Kellner, 1990).

The Frankfurt writers offer useful insights into the explanation of why issues underlying moral panics are generally accepted as real threats by the

the mechanisms of formal social control, while "fostering the development of negative ideologies concerning subordinate groups" (Barkan & Cohn, 2005). Significantly, however, conflict theory does not specifically discuss mass communication as a form of oppression in the modern world, nor does it seek to explain why the masses passively accept the political rhetoric of powerful elites as reality. Because these issues are central to the Frankfurt tradition of critical sociology, and by extension, critical criminology, it provides a stronger theoretical basis for understanding moral panic.

In summary, the Frankfurt School of critical sociology, although not typically used as a theoretical foundation for examining the social construction of reality and moral panic, offers very useful insights into the role of mass media and elites in shaping the dominant ideology in society. In fact, Cohen (2002) has recently stated that the moral panic concept was informed in part by critical sociology. The Frankfurt tradition provides a basis for explaining both how and why moral panics are successfully orchestrated by modern societal elites, who either control or have unfettered access to the mass media (Kellner, 1990), and why the general population accepts the premises and arguments underlying them as real and valid. Moreover, critical criminology helps to explain how folk devils are created by those in power and directs attention away from the activities of those in power. These insights are valuable as they apply to the dissemination of punitive ideology and rhetoric regarding Saddam Hussein and Iraq by the Bush administration and its influence on public opinion following the attacks of 9/11.

*Communication Theory*

The media play key roles in moral panics, although how and why they do so are not often considered. Communication scholars have useful insights into such processes. Over the past eighty years, communication researchers have examined media effects on society (Lowery & DeFleur, 1995). More specifically, they have analyzed certain processes (e.g., agenda setting) and mechanisms (e.g., framing and priming) whereby the mass media help to shape public perceptions, attitudes, and opinions. The following discussion of agenda setting, framing, priming, and political rhetoric may complement the central tenets of critical theory and help to expand our understanding of media effects on public opinion, the social construction of reality, and elite engineering of moral panic. Significantly, much of the contemporary communication research that now offers insights into the creation of moral panics was unavailable when the moral panic concept was first introduced in the early 1970s (S. Cohen, 2002).

AGENDA-SETTING. It has been argued that the press may not be successful in telling people what to think, but it is stunningly successful in telling people what to think about (B. Cohen, 1963). This premise is central to the hypothesis developed by McCombs and Shaw (1972) that the press has a significant *agenda-setting* function. By studying news media content during the 1968 presidential campaign and comparing it to voters' perceptions of the key political issues, McCombs and Shaw identified a strong positive correlation between the emphasis placed on campaign issues by the media and the perceived importance of those topics to voters. The core mechanism operating in what is now referred to as the first-level agenda-setting process involves the *transfer of salience* (i.e., issue importance) from the press to the public (Kiousis, 2003). Thus agenda-setting theory postulates that the news media set the agenda for public discourse (or the public agenda) by specifying which issues are important to consider or think about, based on their coverage of particular issues and neglect of others.

Communication researchers have more recently shifted their focus from first-level agenda setting to second-level agenda setting. The second level of agenda setting "investigates the transmission of attributes of actors [or issues] in the news from media coverage of these attributes to the public's recall of the same attributes" (Wanta, Golan & Lee, 2004, p. 365). Specifically, second-level agenda-setting theorists postulate that the attributes (positive or negative) of issues or individuals emphasized in the news media become the central attributes in public perceptions of those issues or individuals. This involves a much more subtle analysis than first-level agenda-setting research, which focuses generally on the salience of issues and its transfer from press to public (Wanta et al., 2004).

Closely related to second-level agenda setting are the concepts of *framing* and *priming*. Framing refers to the way an issue is presented to the public (or "angle" it is given) by the news media. Framing involves calling attention to certain aspects of an issue while ignoring or obscuring other elements. In short, framing gives meaning to an issue. In her seminal work, Tuchman (1978) proposed that the news media rely on "news frames" to determine what events to cover and how to cover them. Just as the photographer's choice of lens affects a photograph, the journalist's choice of news frame affects a story. Tuchman (1978) theorized that journalists select news frames for a story based in part on routine procedures and the organizational constraints of their particular medium. In addition, the choice of frame is influenced by prior news frames (e.g., existing templates), the power and authority of news sources, history, and, central to this book, ideology. Thus, news frames are contested or negotiated phenomena rather than objective events (Entman, 1993; Tuchman, 1978). Most significantly, an audience can react very differently to an issue or story depending on how it is framed by the news media.

In contrast, priming is a psychological process whereby the news media emphasis on a particular issue not only increases the salience of the issue on the public agenda, but also activates in people's memories previously acquired information about that issue (Lowery & DeFleur, 1995). The priming mechanism explains how the news frame used in a particular story can trigger an individual's pre-existing attitudes, beliefs, and prejudices regarding that issue. Priming is thus an individual-level factor that can have great variability within a society, given past events and news coverage. An example of priming would be the triggering of individual responses such as fear, anger, or outrage by Americans to televised images of the 2005 subway terrorist attacks in London, based on the U.S. news media's prior framing of the events of 9/11 as the evil acts of madmen.

Significantly, Cohen (2002) argued that the news media do play an important agenda-setting role in moral panic "dramas." Welch (2000, pp. 172–173) goes further, arguing that "with its technological prowess, the media can project images that amplify and exaggerate a perceived threat, and at key historical moments these messages can contribute to a growing sense that public disorder is imminent." Second-level agenda-setting, therefore, provides theoretical insights into the processes by which specific attributes and dispositions are attached to issues by the news media, which may facilitate a moral panic. As such, second-level agenda-setting theory informs the analyses presented here by offering an explanation of how and why the news media can influence public perceptions about major issues such as the threat of Iraq to the United States. While this issue is not explicitly examined in this book, it provides a plausible explanation for how and why rhetoric may impact public opinion.

POLITICAL RHETORIC. It has been demonstrated that politicians participate in the agenda-setting process in society (Beckett, 1994; Hawdon, 2001). A key way that they do so is through political rhetoric that is disseminated in the news media. *Webster's College Dictionary* (1997, p. 1114) defines rhetoric as "the art of *effectively* using language to communicate, including the use of *figures of speech*" (emphases added). Political rhetoric involves the effective use of language, including figures of speech, by politicians for mass dissemination (Johnson, Wanta & Boudreau, 2004). Significantly, it has been argued that symbolic political language or rhetoric that is dutifully reported by the news media is at the heart of setting the agenda for public discourse (Edelman, 1988).

In contemporary communication studies on political rhetoric, researchers often explore the processes through which political elites attempt to influence public opinion to their advantage. In order to explain the public's attitude change on a policy issue under discussion by political elites, communication researchers frequently analyze how the issue is framed by politicians and how the frame interacts with an individual's memory to prime certain considerations and preferences (Merskin, 2004). While priming at the individual level is not the focus of this discussion, it is nevertheless important for understanding the broader agenda-setting processes.

It has been argued that "political elites attempt to mobilize public opinion to their advantage by framing the issue in terms that prime considerations that will move public opinion in the direction they desire" (Koch, 1998, pp. 209–210). By defining and overly simplifying a complex issue through framing, political elites manipulate the set of considerations that citizens will use in formulating their preferences and attitudes regarding that issue. The set of considerations established by the frame are usually those that will move public opinion in the direction desired by societal elites. At the individual level, the frame then interacts with an individual's memory so as to prime or make some considerations more accessible than others and, therefore, more likely to be used in formulating a policy preference.

By successfully framing a policy issue according to their interests, political elites participate in the social construction of reality by restricting the perspectives available for public understanding of an issue. This, in turn, primes the particular aspects of an issue in an individual's memory that are most likely to guide opinion formation in the direction desired by political elites. As summarized by Koch (1998, p. 211), "Through rhetoric, political elites attempt to draw attention to particular features of a policy proposal—while drawing attention away from others—thereby increasing the importance and accessibility of those considerations for citizens."

The consequences of elite framing of issues are powerful. Such framing can facilitate an elite-engineered moral panic. Once the elites frame an issue, all other interpretations of reality are critiqued through the lens of elite formulations (Garland, 2008). Moreover, "even public opinion does not exist as an entity separate from and independent of dominant, elite interests" (Goode & Ben-Yehuda, 1994, p. 137). Rather, public opinion is shaped or engineered by multiple elite interests, mechanisms, and processes (Chomsky, 2002; Welch, 2006a). As it relates to the creation of a moral panic, political elites may engineer public opinion by framing and presenting issues in such a way as to raise concerns or invoke fear (Altheide, 2002; Chomsky, 2002; Hawdon, 2001; Welch, 2006a). This insight is useful herein because it helps to explain how existing beliefs (e.g., public concern about national security) were exploited by the Bush administration in order to create a panic over an alleged threat from Iraq.

Although widespread public concern or fear is an essential element in all moral panics, the fear must be articulated and given direction—that is, the foundation of a moral panic must first be socially constructed (S. Cohen, 2002). Because of their elite status and power, presidents can provide the necessary outlet for public concern that moral panics require (Goode & Ben-Yehuda, 1994). Johnson et al. (2004) argued that through their rhetoric, presidents can create issues and instill fear, offer policy solutions, and influence the public's perception of issues, as well as the public's relationship to those issues. Kieve (1994, p. 16) explained that "presidents are image makers. As such, they seek the opportunity to define [or frame] situations and *construct the reality* they want the public to accept" (emphasis added) and, thereby, influence the public agenda. It has also been argued that a president's ability to prime public support for an issue is directly related to how much emphasis he/she places on the issue (Johnson et al., 2004). That is, the greater the emphasis placed on an issue by the president, the greater the likelihood that the public will come to support his/her position on that issue. In this way, presidential rhetoric can help to shape the direction of public opinion (see Hawdon, 2001). This is an important insight as it relates to the Bush administration's decision to go to war in Iraq in 2003 and is discussed in greater detail in chapter six.

In summary, communication theory provides insights into how the social construction of reality and public opinion are established, and how public opinion (i.e., concern) may facilitate a moral panic. Communication researchers have identified key processes (e.g., agenda setting) and mechanisms (e.g., framing and priming) through which the news media help to shape public perceptions, attitudes, and opinions. These insights guide this discussion, particularly as they apply to the news media's dissemination of presidential rhetoric and framing of the alleged threat posed by Saddam Hussein and Iraq, and its influence on public opinion post-9/11.

*Social Constructionism*

A number of social theorists believe that the severity of a condition or behavior may be exaggerated by politicians, law enforcement agencies, and the media in order to justify policy proposals or to enhance the legitimacy of the affected organizations (e.g., Altheide, 2002; Barak, 1988; Chomsky, 2002). The elite-engineered model of moral panic describes how political elites and the mass media are symbiotically linked, and how together they can manufacture public fear and launch public crises that serve their mutual interests. Cohen (2002, p. xxii) states that the moral panic concept originally was "informed by the sixties fusion of labeling theory, cultural politics and critical sociology." Not yet available in the 1960s was the literature on social constructionism that Cohen (2002, p. xxii) now cites as central to understanding the "construction of new social problem categories."

The social constructionist perspective is rooted in philosophical idealism, particularly the writings of Immanuel Kant. A brief discussion of the idealist tradition is warranted here. As articulated by Kant (1781), transcendental idealism is the view that matter does not exist in its own right. Kant's doctrine maintains that the human experience of things consists of how they appear to us, implying a fundamentally subjective orientation, rather than simply comprehending things as they are, in and of themselves, or recording outside data in an accurate manner. Kant argued that matter is a product of the mind. Because all objects are constructed of matter, all objects are thus mental creations. According to philosophical idealism, the world is the sum of all objects. Therefore, reality itself is a mental construction and subject to interpretation. This perspective is in direct opposition to philosophical realism, whose adherents believe in a reality that is completely ontologically independent of our conceptual schemes, linguistic practices, and beliefs. For example, the positivist science of August Comte (1798–1857), one of the founders of sociology, is a realist perspective because it assumes that the laws of the natural sciences can be applied to society and the human condition. Kant (1781) would disagree with Comte and argue that the human experience is too subjective to quantify using the laws of formal logic or the natural sciences.

Following in the idealist tradition, social constructionism has emerged over the past forty years as a sociological theory of knowledge that considers how social phenomena develop in particular social contexts. According to Berger and Luckmann (1966), all knowledge, including the most basic, taken-for-granted commonsense knowledge of everyday life, is actually constructed and reinforced through social interaction. Social constructionists see reality as a dynamic and constantly contested process—that is, reality is reproduced by people acting on their knowledge and their socially constructed interpretations of it.

As a logical extension, social constructionism postulates that social problems do not exist objectively like a mountain or a river. Rather, they are constructed by the human mind, socially created or constituted by the definitional process (Berger & Luckmann, 1966). Therefore, the objective existence of a harmful condition such as a disease does not, in and of itself, constitute a social problem. From the social constructionist perspective, an objective condition does not constitute a social problem unless it is defined as such by the members of a society in a particular context. Moreover, an objective condition does not even have to exist to be defined as a problem. That is, if something is thought to exist and it elicits fear then it is real, despite the fact that it does not exist objectively. The witch hunts in colonial New England are an example of a nonobjective, socially constructed crisis. From a constructionist perspective, what makes a condition a social problem is the degree of *felt concern* by a society about that condition, regardless of whether it actually exists or whether it is objectively harmful. This understanding is central to the moral panic concept. Thus, as it has evolved over the past forty years, the social constructionist perspective provides an important contemporary theoretical perspective on the creation of moral panics (S. Cohen, 2002).

An additional element within the social constructionist tradition, not typically addressed by those examining moral panic, offers insights into how certain groups become socially defined as folk devils (for exceptions, see Cohen, 2002). This involves an examination of the concept of *evil* as a social construction. An analysis of the social construction of evil expands our understanding of moral panic by providing an explanation of the processes and mechanisms by which those in power and authority in society can demonize a particular group and establish that evil identity in the public consciousness.

The definition of "evil" is a social construction (Bromley, Shupe & Ventimiglia, 1979). The word evil itself has a long linguistic history. The *Oxford English Dictionary* (1971) attributes the original derivation of the word "evil" to the Goths of the fourth century AD who defined it as "exceeding due measure" or "overstepping proper limits." *Webster's College Dictionary* (1997, p. 453) defines evil as "morally wrong or bad; immoral; wicked; harmful or injurious; due to actual or imputed bad conduct or character; evil quality, intention or conduct." As argued by Coyle (2004, p. 15), it is clear that the definitions of evil "are all socially constructed and socially defined. Behaving evilly, producing evil and being evil are radically social processes [which are defined] in a social context."

The definitions of evil are also tautological—that is, the definitions involve circular reasoning. One may be labeled as evil because one does evil things, and if one does evil things, then one is evil. This tautology is problematic because a circular argument cannot be tested or falsified. As a result, the tautological definition of evil can be exploited by those who apply the label of "evil" to an individual or group. If the labelers' arguments cannot be falsified, then their claims are not subject to meaningful debate or critique by skeptics. The Bush administration, for example, used this strategy in their labeling of Saddam Hussein and Iraq by arguing that the proof of their evilness was evident in their deeds (Kellner, 2005; Merskin, 2004).

Bromley and colleagues (1979) argued that societal elites and the news media often use "atrocity tales" to amplify and support their arguments in the social construction of evil. What exactly are atrocity tales? Bromley et al. (1979, p. 43) stated:

> An atrocity may be defined as an event which is viewed as a flagrant violation of a fundamental cultural value. Accordingly, an *atrocity tale* is a presentation of that event (real or imaginary) in such a way as to (a) evoke moral outrage by specifying and detailing the value violations, (b) authorize, implicitly or explicitly, punitive sanctions, and (c) mobilize control efforts against the alleged perpetrators.

The intent of atrocity tales is not to present the complexity of an event dispassionately. Rather, the intent is to provide so-called evidence in support of a claim that the targeted group is in fact evil and thus deserving of punishment. The use of atrocity tales in the social construction of evil provides insights into the labeling of folk devils in a moral panic. Similar to the claims used by elites to label folk devils in a moral panic, it is not important whether the allegations made in atrocity tales are actually true or false (Bromley et al., 1979). Rather, they are designed to illicit an emotional response. For example, the U.S. military effectively integrated atrocity tales into propaganda films used to incite outrage among new recruits toward Nazi Germany during World War II (Lowery & DeFleur, 1995).

Once a disvalued individual or group is socially defined as evil, those in power have the moral authority and even obligation to eliminate the evildoer(s) (S. Cohen, 1972). This premise is central to the moral panic concept. As discussed above, the identification and labeling of folk devils is an essential step in the creation of a moral panic. Moreover, the folk devil does not necessarily exist objectively; rather, the folk devil is labeled as such by political elites and the news media (S. Cohen, 1972). The label then becomes a self-fulfilling prophecy as public fear and media coverage both prompt and justify punitive actions by legal authorities toward the folk devils. As discussed throughout this book, the Bush administration's use of the term "axis of evil" in reference to Iraq, Iran, and North Korea provides such an example.

In summary, critical communication theory is a unique, interdisciplinary, and integrative approach (merging critical sociology and criminology, communication theory, and the social construction of reality) introduced here to provide a more detailed and synthetic foundation for understanding the elite-engineered model of moral panic and thus expand upon the moral panic literature (S. Cohen, 2002; Garland, 2008; Goode & Ben-Yehuda, 1994; Welch, 2000). Each one of the various theoretical traditions that comprise critical communication theory offers important insights into moral panic. The Frankfurt School of critical sociology provides a basis for explaining how and why moral panics are successfully engineered by societal elites and the news media, and why the public generally accepts the elite arguments (ideology) as real and valid. Communication theory provides information on how the social construction of reality and public opinion are established, and how public opinion (i.e., concern) may facilitate a moral panic. Critical criminology helps to explain how disvalued groups become defined as folk devils in an elite-engineered moral panic. Together, these approaches provide a more complete explanation of how and why moral panics can be socially constructed or engineered by societal elites and the news media. Finally, this integrated, multitheory perspective does not apply to the grassroots model of moral panic, a bottom–up approach, in which the concern over a situation or condition originates with the public.

## How Can Moral Panic Be Empirically Measured?

As previously stated, the first theoretical proposition advanced in this book is: The war in Iraq was legitimized by an elite-engineered moral panic, precipitated by the Bush administration and reinforced by the news media, which exploited pre-existing, negative stereotypes of Arabs and increased public support, as measured by opinion polls, for the invasion in 2003. This proposition raises an important question. Specifically, what determines whether or not a situation or condition qualifies to be a moral panic? Although Cohen (1972), Goode and Ben-Yehuda (1994), and Garland (2008), among others, have addressed this issue, an examination of the scholarly literature below provides important insights into how other sociologists and communication researchers have approached questions related directly to those considered in this book.

### Research on Political Rhetoric, Media Effects, and Moral Panic

A number of empirical studies have analyzed news media content and political rhetoric to gain insights into the social construction of reality, media effects on public opinion, and the elite engineering of moral panic. As a body of research, those studies suggest that political elites (especially presidents) and the news media both play prominent roles in the social construction of issues and, as a result, in the generation and shaping of public concern and policy preferences concerning those issues (Beckett, 1994; Gonzenbach, 1996; Hall, Critcher, Jefferson, Clarke & Roberts, 1978; Hawdon, 2001; Johnson et al., 2004; Reinarman & Levine, 1989; Rothe & Muzzatti, 2004; Welch, 2000). The studies that are most relevant to the propositions advanced in this book are examined in the following section. Considered first are empirical studies that focus on official rhetoric and the news media, followed by studies focused on agenda setting, public opinion and moral panic, and other relevant topics.

OFFICIAL RHETORIC AND THE NEWS MEDIA. The literature suggests that the relationship between political elites and the news media is reciprocal or mutually beneficial (Altheide, 2002; Goode & Ben-Yehuda, 1994; Kellner, 1990; Lang & Lang, 1983). For example, Welch, Fenwick, and Roberts (1997) explored the news media's heavy reliance on politicians and police in formulating the primary definitions of crime (i.e., as authors of the official rhetoric). More specifically, they examined the processes by which the official rhetoric of crime is shaped into news by analyzing the content of articles in major U.S. newspapers. Welch et al. (1997) examined the nature of quotes offered by two groups of experts—state managers (police and politicians) and intellectuals (professors)—in order to determine the underlying ideology, and from whose perspective the news media image of crime is constructed and shaped. Their rationale for grouping law enforcement officials and politicians together was based on their similar roles as "state managers."

Welch et al. (1997) examined a sample of 105 feature articles published in the *New York Times, Washington Post, Los Angeles Times,* and the *Chicago Tribune* between 1992 and 1995. The unit of analysis in the study was the specific quote offered by a crime expert, which yielded 267 total quotes from 179 experts. Of the 179 experts quoted, 63% (n=112) were state managers and 37% (n=67) were intellectuals. The group of state managers accounted for 60% (n=159) of the 267 total quotes. More importantly, however, the authors determined that when a state manager and a professor were both quoted in an article, the state manager generally provided the primary and "official" definitions of crime. Even when a professor was the only expert quoted, the insights were typically presented as secondary "unofficial" interpretations of crime, indicating that the definitional context had already been established. Almost half (46%) of all expert quotes were from state managers who presented "alarmist reactions to crime" and declared that "crime and public fear are problems." Quotes from state managers were found to be more ideological than those from professors in that they distorted (or neglected) the causal connection between social conditions and crime.

Welch and colleagues (1997) concluded that the relationship between state managers and the news media is mutually rewarding in that state officials help journalists define crime news at the same time they promote their own institutional agendas. Frequently, this relationship results in media images of crime that promote public fear which, in turn, benefits both the state managers and the news media. The findings of Welch and his colleagues support the existence of a symbiotic relationship between policy makers and the news media, which is a key tenet of the moral panic perspective and is consistent with the theory on "news frames" (Tuchman, 1978).

NEWS MEDIA AND AGENDA SETTING. Over the past thirty years, studies have demonstrated the agenda-setting effects of the news media on the public (Kiousis, 2003; McCombs & Shaw, 1972). For example, in a recent test of first-level and second-level agenda-setting theories, Wanta and colleagues (2004) examined the influence of international news on public perceptions of foreign nations. The authors sought to expand agenda-setting research by focusing on perceptions of foreign nations rather than individuals in the news, as most prior studies had focused on the latter. The authors had two propositions. The first concerned the *volume* of news coverage, and the second concerned the *tone* of the coverage. The first proposition was that the more overall media coverage a nation receives (i.e., number of stories), the more individuals will think it is of vital importance to U.S. interests (first-level agenda setting).

Nevada in 1989 introduced the Gang Abolishment Act which promised a complete ban on gang membership. After strong criticism from ACLU officials, who claimed the bill had disturbing racial overtones, a less overtly biased version called the "Gang Enhancement Statute" was passed in 1991. By 1992, law enforcement officials and politicians claimed victory by stating they had control over the Las Vegas gang problem.

Despite public fear, an analysis of official crime reports indicated there never was a real gang problem in Las Vegas (McCorkle & Miethe, 1998). The percentage of violent index crimes linked to gangs was a low and stable 3% for all reported violent crimes committed in the county from 1989 to 1993. Less than 4% of charges filed for illegal drug sales during the same period involved known gang members. McCorkle and Miethe (1998) concluded that the gang phenomenon in Las Vegas was actually a moral panic precipitated by the Las Vegas police, supported by state and local politicians, and fueled by the news media. This study informs the arguments presented in this book by providing empirical support by means of a case history for the moral panic perspective.

It has been empirically demonstrated that presidential policy rhetoric played a major role in the creation of a moral panic over illegal drugs in the 1980s (Beckett, 1994; Hawdon, 2001). According to Simon and Feeley (1995, p. 167), both Presidents Ronald Reagan and George Bush (Sr.) saw:

> illegal drug use as signifying a deep moral decline in certain portions of American society, and mounted the equivalent of war on it, and spectacular media coverage of the violence associated with drugs helped build a public conception of drugs as a catalyst for violence . . . this in turn has contributed to a continuous expansion of penalties for drug possession and . . . extraordinarily harsh sentences for drug use.

The following two studies (Beckett, 1994; Hawdon, 2001), which analyzed political rhetoric and public opinion concerning drugs, helped to frame the research design used in this book. Hawdon (2001) examined the processes by which the U.S. president participates in the social construction of reality and second-level agenda-setting through mass communication. More specifically, he analyzed the role presidential policy rhetoric assumed in creating, sustaining, and terminating a *moral panic* over illegal drugs in the United States in the 1980s. Hawdon (2001) predicted that moral panics begin when *communitarian/proactive* and *punitive* statements are used in combination by a president. He further predicted that moral panics subside when *individualistic/reactive* and *rehabilitative* rhetorical statements are issued concurrently by a president.

To test his propositions, Hawdon (2001) conducted a content analysis of 167 drug-related speeches and public addresses by Presidents Reagan and Bush for the years 1981 through 1992. The content of the presidential messages was coded for communitarian rhetoric (e.g., "we must pull together"), punitive arguments (e.g., "users must be punished"), reactive (e.g., "individual users are victims") or rehabilitative rhetoric (e.g., "we must educate or cure"). The public's perception of the problem was measured by the percentage of Americans who listed the drug issue as an urgent concern in the Gallup poll that immediately followed a presidential speech.

The results were largely consistent with Hawdon's (2001) predictions. He found that proactive-punitive arguments decreased over time while reactive-rehabilitative arguments increased over time. Furthermore, public opinion tended to mirror the rhetorical content of the presidential messages, such that increased punitive and communitarian rhetoric predicted increased public concern over drugs, thus supporting the second-level agenda-setting theory. President Reagan used proactive policy statements aggressively to help define the urban, drug-dealing "folk devils." Similarly, he often evoked a war metaphor (e.g., "drugs are as much a threat to the United States as enemy planes and missiles"). By using emotional appeals to the collective identity (e.g., "our children" and "the American family"), the threat was exaggerated to include the entire society. Hawdon stated that by 1987 the news media had popularized the punitive position. Once that was accomplished, public opinion and political rhetoric reinforced each other.

Hawdon notes that the consensual validation of reality that moral panics require had been established, despite the actual decline in drug use in the United States throughout the period. His analysis revealed that rehabilitative arguments were increasingly added to the proactive/punitive policy statements during the middle stage of the moral panic. One week after the Anti-Drug Abuse Act (1986) was signed, and only one month after his television appearance urging aggressive action (punitive), President Reagan modified his rhetoric to include a call for drug education (rehabilitative). Hawdon argues that moral panics are created by aggressively punishing the enemy but they are sustained by aggressively helping the victims. He further states that the implementation of a proactive policy such as the Anti-Drug Abuse Act typically marks the zenith of a moral panic.

Consistent with his expectations, Hawdon (2001) discovered that reactive and rehabilitative rhetoric dominated presidential speeches in the final stage of the panic. Although the drug issue was central in the 1988 presidential election, by 1990 public concern about drugs had dwindled. During President George H. W. Bush's first year in office, 1989, more than 30% of Americans considered drug abuse to be the most important problem facing the nation; however, by mid-1990, this figure had dropped to 8%. Hawdon argues that "rehabilitative policy cannot by itself sustain a moral panic; folk devils cannot be defined as victims. The public had grown weary; users were now the victims. The moral panic was over" (2001, p. 432). In summary, and consistent with critical theory, this empirical study demonstrates that the president may disseminate distorted sets of ideas (ideology) through the mass media and engineer a moral panic in order to legitimize policy initiatives. Moreover, this study guides an examination of the war in Iraq by demonstrating that *punitive* and *communitarian* rhetoric used by a president increase public concern about an issue and can precipitate a moral panic, while *reactive* and *rehabilitative* rhetoric by a president tend to decrease public concern about that issue and dissipate the moral panic.

In a related study, Beckett (1994) examined the constructionist versus the objectivist explanations of social problems by analyzing shifts over time in the levels of public concern about crime and illegal drugs. The author focused on the processes through which some members of the public came to define crime and drugs as the most important problems facing the nation. More specifically, she sought to determine how the issues of "street crime" and drug use came to assume such central places in the public agenda in the 1970s and 1980s.

Beckett (1994) argued that two primary and conflicting explanations of the politicization of street crime can be identified in the literature. Each approach specifies a different relationship between reported rates of crime/drug use, state and media initiative, and public concern about crime and drugs. The first approach—the objectivist model—postulates that "the increased incidence of 'street crime' and drug use has led to increased public concern about those issues. [According to this view,] the Nixon, Reagan, and Bush [senior] administrations' 'get tough' approach to crime [was] a response to public concern, itself a consequence of the increased incidence of crime" (Beckett, 1994, p. 428). She further argued that objectivist perspectives on crime and illegal drug issues tend to merge or integrate objectivism with the pluralist contention that political elites primarily react to, rather than shape, public opinion. Beckett (1994) derived two propositions from this model: the objectivist thesis anticipates a positive relationship between the reported incidence of crime/drug use and subsequent levels of public concern regarding these issues, while the pluralist thesis predicts that shifts in the level of public concern *precede* corresponding shifts in the level of state anti-crime and anti-drug activity.

The second approach—the constructionist model—as previously discussed, postulates that reality does not exist objectively. Rather, reality must be comprehended through "frames" that select, order, and interpret that reality (Lowery & DeFleur, 1995). Beckett (1994, p. 428) argues that "constructionists emphasize the subjective, social and political dimension of social problems." She further states that the constructionist perspective informs the elite theorists' agenda-setting argument that shifts in the level of state initiative precede shifts in the level of public concern about a social problem. Beckett (1994) derived two propositions based on the constructionist model that compete with those derived from the objectivist model. First, the constructionist thesis suggests that state initiative and media coverage shape public opinion. Second, the agenda-setting thesis predicts that state initiative drives public concern about street crime and drugs.

The outcome of interest in Beckett's (1994) analyses, i.e., public concern, was derived from the Gallup poll and the *New York Times*/CBS public opinion polls. The percentage of respondents identifying "crime," "juvenile delinquency," or "breaking the law and order" in the crime case, and "drugs" or "drug use" in the drug case as the "most important problem facing the nation" served as the measure of public concern. In the drug case (1985–1992), there were twenty-five polls taken in which this question was asked (N=25). In the crime case (1964–1974), 29 such polls were conducted (N=29).

Beckett (1994) used a number of independent predictors of public concern in her analyses. First, information regarding the reported (official) crime rate was taken from the FBI's Uniform Crime Report (1964–1974). The rate of "violent crimes" (per hundred thousand population) was used as the measure of "street crime." Second, data regarding the incidence of drug use were taken from the National Institute on Drug Abuse (NIDA) survey, the National Household Survey on Drug Abuse (NHSDA). The percentage of survey respondents age twelve and older reporting drug use in the past month was used as an indicator of the incidence of drug use. Third, the level of media initiative (i.e., number of news stories) was derived from the Television News Index and Abstracts for the drug case and the *New York Times* Index for the crime case. Only stories in which "federal state actors" were *not* quoted or cited as sources were included in this measure. Finally, the number of speeches, statements, and other crime- or drug-related activities undertaken by "federal state actors" (i.e., politicians and law enforcement officials) and reported in the mass media (the *New York Times* for the crime case and network television newscasts for the drug case) was utilized as an indicator of state initiative.

Beckett (1994) tested her various propositions using statistical regression analyses. This involved trend analysis of repeated surveys (i.e., public opinion polls), controlling for time-lagged effects. More specifically, Beckett's predictors were measured in terms of their average rate in the three- to five-month period preceding a public opinion poll. She also analyzed models using lags of six to ten months and nine to twelve months "in order to assess the extent to which the explanatory variables [i.e., predictors] were associated with delayed shifts in the level of public concern" (1994, p. 431).

Beckett's findings provide "significant support" for the constructionist thesis, but not for the objectivist thesis. In the crime case, both state and media initiatives were significant predictors of public concern, while in the drug case only state initiative was a significant predictor of public concern. The reported (official) incidence of crime/drug use was not a significant predictor of subsequent public concern about those issues. Also, the analyses

Maxwell et al. (2000) conducted a content analysis of domestic violence news articles published in the *Philadelphia Inquirer, Philadelphia Daily News* and the *New York Times*, between 1990 and 1997. In total, 10,568 articles were analyzed. The timeframe was selected to establish trends leading up to the Simpson case and to examine effects during and after the criminal trial. As predicted, the overall level of domestic violence coverage (*volume*) increased significantly during the Simpson trial, including articles not related to the case. Neither the *Philadelphia Inquirer* nor the *Philadelphia Daily News* maintained their heightened volume of domestic violence coverage after the Simpson criminal trial ended, although the *New York Times* maintained a level of domestic violence coverage consistently higher than in the pre-Simpson period. The authors also predicted that the Simpson case would change the nature (*tone*) of domestic violence news coverage—that is, articles would become more issue, and less incident, focused. This argument was not supported by the findings. Although articles published after the Simpson case focused more attention on the abuser's behavior, Maxwell et al. (2000, p. 270) found that victims were still presented in stereotypical terms and that "the onus of responsibility remains with the victim who is expected to end the violence through her own actions." Thus, Maxwell and colleagues concluded that the Simpson case had no meaningful or lasting effect on the nature or tone of domestic violence news coverage or the way victims are portrayed. This study guides an examination of the events leading up to the invasion of Iraq by demonstrating the importance of analyzing the volume and tone of rhetorical content in the news media.

In summary, the literature supports the existence of a symbiotic relationship between state managers (i.e., policy makers) and the news media (Altheide, 2002; Welch et al., 1997). It has also been demonstrated that the news media (Kiousis, 2003; Wanta et al., 2004) and state managers (Beckett, 1994) both help to set the public agenda and influence public opinion on key issues. Moreover, empirical research supports the moral panic perspective (McCorkle & Miethe, 1998; Welch, 2000; Welch, Price & Yankey, 2002) and demonstrates that the president of the United States participates in the social construction of reality, the agenda-setting process, and the elite engineering of moral panics (Hawdon, 2001; Johnson et al., 2004; Reinarman & Levine, 1989; Rothe & Muzzatti, 2004). Together, these studies guide an examination of the war in Iraq by suggesting that state elites and the news media play prominent roles in the construction of social issues/problems and, as a result, in the generation and shaping of public concern (including elite-engineered moral panic) as well as policy preferences regarding those issues/problems.

*The Empirical Criteria of Elite-Engineered Moral Panic*

As introduced in chapter one, the elite-engineered model of moral panic premises that "an elite group deliberately and consciously undertakes a campaign to generate and sustain concern, fear and panic on the part of the public over an issue that they recognize not to be terribly harmful to the society as a whole" (Goode & Ben-Yehuda, 1994, p. 135). Often times, such a campaign is intended to divert public attention away from other objective or real problems in society, whose solution might jeopardize or undermine the elite group's interests (Goode & Ben-Yehuda, 1994). The elite-engineered model of moral panic assumes that political/economic elites have tremendous power over other members of society. Societal elites frame issues for public discourse, control the distribution of valuable resources, dominate the mass media, and determine the content of legislation and the direction of law enforcement (Chambliss & Mankoff, 1976). Through the lens of elite-engineered moral panic, public concern or fear over an issue is viewed as orchestrated from above by elites who control the governing ideology, have unfettered access to mass media outlets, and promote fear or concern among the masses. Thus, elite-engineered moral panic represents a "top-down" conceptual model. Stated differently, an elite-engineered moral panic is the public response to an exaggeration or distortion by societal elites and the media of the threat posed by some disvalued group or condition. In summary, elite-engineered moral panic is the conceptual framework used herein to analyze the Iraq war.

As articulated by Cohen (2002), in order to be a moral panic, a situation or condition must include an exaggeration of certain events according to empirical criteria such as the number of individuals involved, the level and extent of violence, and the amount of damage caused. As discussed in chapter one, however, this is not something that happens spontaneously, but rather, is a result of the complex dynamics and interplay among several social actors. In his seminal work, Cohen (1972) explained that at least five sets of social actors are involved in a moral panic, including: folk devils, law enforcers, the media, politicians, and the public. The public is likely the most important in a moral panic because the success of politicians, law enforcers, and the media in precipitating and sustaining a moral panic is ultimately contingent upon how successfully these sets of actors fuel public concern and outrage toward the folk devils (Rothe & Muzzatti, 2004). Given the significance of these actors in a moral panic drama, an analysis of the buildup to the Iraq war in chapter four includes an examination of the roles played by all five of them.

Beyond the actors in a moral panic, what are its defining elements? Significantly, Stan Cohen has done more than just explain and popularize the moral panic concept. Cohen (2002, p. xxii) has also identified five criteria by which a social issue or condition can be considered and analyzed as a moral panic:

1. *Concern* (rather than fear) about the potential or imagined threat;
2. *Hostility*—moral outrage toward the actors (folk devils) who embody the problem and agencies (naïve social workers, spin-doctored politicians)

who are "ultimately" responsible (and may become folk devils
themselves);
3. *Consensus*—a widespread agreement (not necessarily total) that the
threat exists, is serious and that "something should be done." The
majority of elite and influential groups, especially the mass media,
should share this consensus;
4. *Disproportionality*—an exaggeration of the number or strength of the
cases, in terms of the damage caused, moral offensiveness, potential
risk if ignored. Public concern is not directly proportionate to objective harm;
5. *Volatility*—the panic erupts and dissipates suddenly and without
warning.

Moral panic theorists distinguish between public *concern* and *fear*. From a
moral panic perspective, the public reaction to a possible or alleged threat
need not take the form of fear in order to qualify (Goode & Ben-Yehuda,
1994). Rather, genuine felt concern about the situation is sufficient to constitute the public reaction criterion of moral panic. Felt concern demonstrates
that the social condition is perceived to be a problem. The hostility criterion
of moral panic involves an outraged, punitive response by society toward
those allegedly responsible for the threat. According to moral panic theorists,
hostility toward the folk devils that embody the threat is fueled by moral
entrepreneurs (or crusaders), political elites, and the news media. The consensus criterion is established when a substantial portion of society believes
that the threat exists. Unanimity of opinion, however, is not required in order
for a condition to constitute a moral panic. Consensus, therefore, can exist in
a matter of degrees, so long as it reflects a widespread agreement that the
threat is real, serious, and caused by the folk devils and their troublesome
behavior. Disproportionality involves an exaggeration by elites and the news
media regarding the actual threat or risk posed by the alleged folk devils. As a
result, public concern is disproportionate to the objective threat posed to
society by folk devils. Finally, the level of attention given to the so-called
problem by elites and the news media fluctuates over time, as does the degree
of public concern. Thus, there is an ebb and flow in both attention and concern about the folk devils that is positively related, i.e., more attention leads
to more concern.
Goode and Ben-Yehuda (1994, p. 41) succinctly summarized the inter-
connectedness of the five criteria when they stated that a moral panic "locates
a 'folk devil,' is shared, is out of synch with the measurable seriousness of the
condition that generates it, and varies in intensity over time." However, in
some cases, particularly when an allegedly threatening condition has not yet
manifested, the objective (i.e., quantifiable) level or degree of the threat is

difficult to measure (Goode & Ben-Yehuda, 1994; Rothe & Muzzatti, 2004). In such instances, Cohen (2002, p. vii) argued that the disproportionality criterion is fulfilled and "the attribution of the moral panic label . . . [is appropriate when] the 'thing's' extent and significance has been exaggerated (1) in itself (compared with other more reliable, valid and objective sources) and/or (2) compared with other, more serious problems." For example, disproportionality can be demonstrated in a comparison of the alleged "grave and gathering threat" posed by Iraq after 9/11, according to the Bush administration, and the actual atrocities, including the support of genocide, perpetrated by the Sudanese government on the people in Darfur (East Africa).

Cohen's five criteria have been put to empirical examination. For example, Welch et al. (2002) utilized the five criteria of moral panic when they examined the phenomenon of wilding. The term "wilding" was sensationalized by the news media following the brutal rape and murder of a young, professional, white female jogger by a group of young minority males in Manhattan's Central Park on April 19, 1989. The authors contend that the term "wilding" became a generalized reference to sexual violence committed by a group of youths, usually of racial minority status. The moral panic perspective suggests that news media framing of "folk devils" often perpetuates negative stereotypes of a minority group and reinforces social inequalities (Goode & Ben-Yehuda, 1994). By employing the five key indicators of a moral panic, Welch and colleagues sought to determine whether the wilding phenomenon met the criteria of a moral panic.

Welch et al. (2002) asserted that the news media instilled fear into the public over the "Central Park jogger" incident, and exploited social anxiety, while directing attention to race/ethnicity and social class. To test this proposition, the authors conducted a content analysis of articles published between 1989 and 1997 in *New York Newsday, New York Post,* the *New York Times,* and *New York Daily News,* commencing with the Central Park incident and concluding seven years after the trial of the offenders. A total of 156 articles were included in the analysis, all of which contained the word "wilding." Welch and colleagues determined that the race of wilding suspects appeared in 8% of the articles, the race of the victim in 5% of the articles, and the race of both in 7% of the articles. The authors argued that race was central to the definition of wilding, as when identified, victims were almost always white females, while suspects were almost always males of racial/ethnic minority status.

Welch et al. (2002) stated that shared public *concern* is the primary factor leading to a moral panic. In order to explain the high level of public distress caused by the "Central Park jogger" incident, the authors argued that heavy news coverage of the crime confirmed that a threat was present in society. Likewise, public *consensus,* although not necessarily universal, must be present in a moral panic to demonstrate a shared sense of danger (Welch et al., 2002).

period overlap the presidency of William J. Clinton). Phase II includes articles that were published during the eighteen-month period beginning September 12, 2001, and ending March 18, 2003—the day before the launch of the war in Iraq. By organizing the study in this way, i.e., in two eighteen-month phases, it was possible to compare the volume and tone of presidential policy rhetoric regarding Saddam Hussein and Iraq *before* the attacks of 9/11 to the volume and tone of presidential rhetoric regarding the same *after* the attacks.

Using a coding scheme adapted from Hawdon (2001), newspaper articles containing presidential (or key nonadministration) rhetoric on Iraq were coded for their content (tone), based on a range of indicators of *communitarian* and *punitive* statements (including key words such as "evil" and "threat"), as well as any *reactive* or *rehabilitative* statements. These are described in detail below. The focus was on the rhetoric that President Bush's administration and key nonadministration sources used prior to launching a preemptive strike in Iraq. Articles offering an alternative view or counterclaim concerning Iraq and/or Hussein (e.g., "Iraq does not possess weapons of mass destruction") were also coded, as well as any that contained either indefinite or positive presidential rhetoric regarding Hussein/Iraq (importantly, no positive rhetoric was found).

Prior to beginning the data coding, an instrument was developed to guide the coding of rhetoric. Two researchers trained in the coding guide coded all news articles used in this study for tone. During the course of the coding process, the two researchers met to discuss validity and reliability issues. A random sample comprising 12.4% (n=134) of the newspaper articles included in the content analysis were coded by both researchers in order to ensure intercoder reliability of at least 90%. On the basis of these articles, the actual intercoder reliability score was 91.8%. Also, a random sample of official statements regarding Iraq issued by the White House were selected over thirty-six months (March 1, 2000–March 18, 2003) and compared to quotes by the administration that appeared in news articles published on the same dates that the official statements were released. This was done to ensure criterion validity—that is, to make sure that the news source was selecting quotes that accurately represented the tone/content of official rhetoric, rather than "cherry picking" quotes that misrepresented presidential rhetoric regarding Iraq. Official White House transcripts were obtained from the Federal News Service (FNS) using the LexisNexis electronic database. Criterion validity was confirmed because 100% of the administrative quotes used in the news articles represented the tone/content of White House statements.

Two types of data were used in this study: newspaper articles to assess volume and tone, and a public opinion poll to assess the public's attitude toward invading Iraq. News articles containing administration and nonadministration rhetoric on Iraq published in the *New York Times* over thirty-six months (March 1, 2000–March 18, 2003) were analyzed. This newspaper was selected based on its relative importance as a news source and its large national circulation. Moreover, the *New York Times* is frequently used in newspaper content analyses (see Beckett, 1994; Maxwell et al., 2000; Welch, Fenwick & Roberts, 1997; Welch, Price & Yankey, 2002). The *New York Times* has a total readership of 4,974,000 on weekdays and 5,111,000 on Sunday (Mediamark Research Inc., 2005). Significantly, 51% of the weekday audience (2,533,989) and 56% of the Sunday audience (2,857,477) reside *outside* the New York marketing area (Mediamark Research Inc., 2005). In addition, the *New York Times* Web site (www.nytimes.com) receives 11,405,000 unique visits per month nationally (Nielsen, 2005).

General news articles from the *New York Times* were obtained from the LexisNexis electronic database using two general sets of key search terms. These include: (1) President Bill Clinton *or* President George W. Bush *and* Iraq *or* Saddam Hussein; and (2) Iraq *or* Saddam Hussein *and* evil *or* threat *or* weapons of mass destruction *or* terrorism *or* sanctions. The list of search terms resulted from a pretest of LexisNexis in which articles containing relevant quotes frequently included these key words. Only articles that include an *actual quote* from Presidents Clinton or Bush *or* key members of their respective administrations (e.g., press secretary, secretary of defense, secretary of state, or vice president) *or* influential nonadministration sources regarding the regime of Saddam Hussein or Iraq were included in the analysis. In addition to the president, statements by key members of his administration/cabinet were included as they are highly influential officials, and they are frequently quoted as purveyors of presidential policy rhetoric. Key nonadministration sources such as Kofi Annan, secretary general of the United Nations, as well as its chief weapons inspector, Hans Blix, were included because they were frequently quoted in the press and potentially influenced public opinion regarding Iraq.

The coding of only direct quotes by the actual sources provided a control for editorial bias in the content analysis. Specifically, this coding strategy ensured that official policy rhetoric was used in the analysis rather than editorial opinion regarding the official rhetoric from the news source. As discussed in chapter two, the dominant news frame on an issue such as Iraq in the general media is routinely provided by political elites, particularly presidents (Tuchman, 1978). As argued by Kieve (1994) and demonstrated by Hawdon (2001), presidents are powerful agenda setters and image makers, and public opinion concerning an issue tends to mirror their rhetorical framing of that issue. Therefore, the use of official quotes is consistent with theory and prior research, and it captures the official framing of the Iraq issue by the president and his administration, as well as influential nonadministration sources.

The *New York Times* provided data for both *volume* (number of articles) and *tone* (nature or type) of rhetoric regarding Iraq/Saddam Hussein by presidential administration and key nonadministration sources. Concerning the latter, similar to Hawdon (2001), important variables in the analyses were measures of both communitarian (e.g., "we must pull together") and punitive (e.g., "Saddam Hussein is evil") official rhetoric (tone). Also included was any reactive ("protecting the rights of individual Iraqis") or rehabilitative (e.g., "the people of Iraq are our allies") policy rhetoric that was used. In addition, any articles containing counterclaims suggesting that Iraq was not a threat to the United States were coded. More specifically, any counterclaims issued by the president's administration and/or key sources outside of the administration, such as United Nations officials or members of Congress, were included. This was done in an attempt to determine whether there were any dissenting opinions either within or outside the administration that may have influenced public opinion regarding the threat of Iraq. Finally, articles containing indefinite statements regarding Iraq or Saddam Hussein by the president or senior administration officials as well as key nonadministration sources (e.g., "we're watching the situation in Iraq") were coded for analysis because Wanta, Golan, and Lee (2004) showed that even "neutral" statements about nations in the news can influence public opinion.

Multiple measures of key constructs were included to increase the internal validity of the measurement tool. For example, in addition to coding for the presence of punitive statements generally ("yes" or "no"), the two researchers also coded for the presence ("yes" or "no") of certain key words such as "evil," "terrorism," and the phrase "weapons of mass destruction," all of which were used repeatedly, are punitive in tone, and therefore should independently measure the *punitive* construct. These "stylized" words and phrases may have special meanings that potentially increased public concern about Iraq even beyond general punitive rhetoric (S. Cohen, 1972).

In addition to the *New York Times* articles, public opinion concerning Iraq was also examined. The measure of public opinion was derived from twenty-four Gallup polls conducted between February, 2001, and March, 2003, in which the percentage of the U.S. public that approved of invading Iraq was measured. The dates, sample sizes, and results of all of the Gallup polls are located in the Appendix of this book (table A.1). The same question was asked repeatedly, using identical wording over time and with the same response categories. Together, these polls provided a continuous measure of public support for an invasion of Iraq over time. Gallup is an independent research organization with a long history of conducting national public opinion polls of U.S. adults (age eighteen and older). The interviews are conducted over the telephone, and a sample consisting of approximately a thousand respondent households are selected for each poll by computerized random digit dialing (RDD). Gallup claims accuracy of within plus or minus 3% (Gallup, 2006). The sampling methodology (both in terms of using

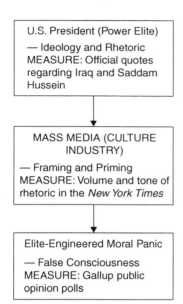

Figure 1. Conceptual Model of Elite-Engineered Moral Panic (Top-Down Approach)

RDD and the selection of respondents) was the same for all polls used in this study.

Based on critical communication theory, Figure 1 illustrates how key concepts and elements of the integrated and interdisciplinary theoretical approach to elite-engineered moral panic were operationalized in this study.

A number of variables were examined in this study. Each variable was assigned to one of the following categories: volume, tone, time, and public opinion. A complete list of the variables employed in the study is located in the Appendix (table A.2).

1. *Volume*: Number of articles containing administration policy rhetoric by source (i.e., articles with quotes from the president or key members of the administration or those with quotes from important non-administration sources).

2. *Tone*: Indicators of (a) communitarian and (b) punitive administration policy rhetoric—also, any (c) reactive or (d) rehabilitative policy rhetoric or (e) alternative views (counter claims) or (f) indefinite rhetoric regarding Iraq. Indicators of communitarian rhetoric include phrases such as "American values," "joining forces," "call to freedom," and "will of the people." Indicators of punitive rhetoric include phrases such as "imminent threat," "Iraqi dictator," "madman," "evil-doers," "disarm Iraq," and "weapons of mass destruction." Reactive rhetoric includes phrases such as "the individual rights of Iraqis must be protected." Rehabilitative rhetoric includes phrases such as

"the Iraqi people are our allies." Counterclaims are any quotes issued by the administration and/or other key sources such as U.N. weapons inspectors suggesting that Iraq was *not* a threat to the United States. Indefinite rhetoric is any benign or ambiguous language such as "we are monitoring the events in Iraq" or any business/economic references to issues such as oil prices. Additionally, the key words or phrases "evil/evildoer," "threat," "weapons of mass destruction," and "terrorism," are included and coded separately as measures of punitive tone, and the word "sanctions" is included as a measure of indefinite tone.

The analyses of public opinion (i.e., support for invading Iraq) controlled for time-lagged effects. Importantly, time-lag measures enabled an assessment of the extent to which the volume and tone of rhetoric are associated with subsequent shifts in the level of public support for the invasion of Iraq (Beckett, 1994). Specifically, the predictors were time-lagged measures (two weeks, one month, three months, and five months) of rhetoric by type (tone) and by source derived from the *New York Times* data. Time-lagged measures were created for each type (tone) of rhetoric, key word, and source of rhetoric based on their volumes (i.e., number of articles containing such quotes) in the specified time intervals preceding each Gallup poll. These specific time lags were selected based in part on the work of Beckett (1994), although shorter lags were added in this study because some of the Gallup polls were conducted only one or two weeks apart, especially in the final three months preceding the invasion of Iraq.

3. *Time period*: Post-versus pre-9/11, and concurrent measures for the post-9/11 timeframe. Post-versus pre-9/11 is the eighteen months of phase II (9/12/01–3/18/03) relative to the eighteen months of phase I (3/1/00–9/11/01). Concurrent measures for post-9/11 are in one-month and three-month time intervals in order to allow more refined analyses.

4. *Public opinion*: Public approval for invading Iraq. In each of the repeated Gallup polls, respondents were asked: "Would you favor or oppose invading Iraq with U.S. ground troops in an attempt to remove Saddam Hussein from power?" Given the small sample size (N=24) and limited variance between observations, the variable was dichotomized for the purposes of statistical analysis (1=same or higher level of support for invasion than the previous poll, 0=lower level of support than previous poll).

Two sets of statistical analyses were conducted to test the proposition that the Bush administration engineered a moral panic over Iraq. The first set of analyses involving newspaper content examined the relationship between volume, tone, and time. Independent sample *t*-tests of the mean proportion of articles containing rhetoric by source during phases I and II were conducted to determine whether the sheer number of news articles containing rhetoric regarding Iraq significantly increased post-versus pre-9/11. Chi-square statistics and logistic regression analyses were used to examine any changes in the tone and volume of rhetoric concerning Iraq post- versus pre-9/11. The role of volume/tone of rhetoric for public opinion was also examined. In the second set of analyses, logistic regression analyses were used to examine the relationship between public approval/support for going to war and time, volume, and tone. Given the small sample size (N=24) of the dependent variable in the public opinion analyses, alpha equal to .10 was set to determine statistical significance, while alpha equal to .05 was used for the news content analyses.

### News Content Analysis

Over five thousand of the *New York Times* articles published between March 1, 2000, and March 18, 2003, dealt with issues related to Iraq/Saddam Hussein. A total of 1,083 articles contained direct quotes regarding Iraq from the administration or other key sources and were included in the analyses (N=1,083). The following summarizes the descriptive statistics, including frequencies and percentages, for the variables examined in the content analysis. It is important to note that each article in the analysis could contain multiple sources of rhetoric (e.g., President Bush and Vice President Dick Cheney) and multiple types/tones of rhetoric (e.g., punitive and communitarian). Consequently, the total percentages of articles containing each type of rhetoric (or source of rhetoric) exceeded 100%.

Not surprisingly, only 4.7% (n=51) of the articles in the analysis were published during the Clinton administration, while 95.3% (n=1,032) were published during the Bush administration. Also, 89.1% (n=965) of the articles were published after the terrorist attacks of 9/11 and only 10.9% (n=118) were published prior to those events. Furthermore, 77.6% (n=840) of the articles contain direct quotes regarding Iraq by members of either the Bush or Clinton administrations, while 22.4% (n=243) contain rhetoric from nonadministration sources.

The single most frequent individual source of rhetoric was President George W. Bush, as more than one-third (38.6%) of the articles contain a quote from him regarding Iraq/Saddam Hussein. The second most frequent source of rhetoric was an unnamed "senior official" in the president's administration, as about one-quarter (23.9%) contain such a quote. Secretary of State Colin Powell was the third most frequent source of rhetoric with 14.1% (n=153) of articles containing a quote from him, followed by Secretary of

Defense Donald Rumsfeld with 7.1% (n=77), and then Press Secretary Ari Fleischer with 5.9% (n=64). Other specific individuals, administration and nonadministration, were quoted at lower frequencies.

The most frequent type of rhetoric was indefinite as 72.4% (n=784) of the articles contained this type of tone. Punitive rhetoric was the second most frequent type with 44.3% (n=480). This was followed in descending order by articles whose quotes involved rhetoric that was communitarian 7.3% (n=79), reactive 6.6% (n=71), and rehabilitative 2.5% (n=27). Counterclaims were made in quotes in 4.0% (n=43) of the articles. Punitive and communitarian rhetoric were found in combination in 6.1% (n=66) of the articles, while punitive and indefinite rhetoric were together in almost one-fifth (18.3%) of articles. The most frequently used or quoted key word was "evil" (or "evil-doer"), as it was found in 15.4% (n=167) of all articles in the analysis. This was followed by the specific items "weapons of mass destruction" (13.4%), "threat" (11.1%), "terrorism" (10.7%), and "sanctions" (3.6%).

Table 1 provides the results of independent sample *t*-tests conducted to compare post-9/11 versus pre-9/11 mean levels (volume) of quotes/rhetoric regarding Iraq by key sources (e.g., President George W. Bush, Secretary of Defense Donald Rumsfeld, and National Security Advisor Condoleezza Rice) in the sample of news articles (N=1,083). These analyses provided a test of the prediction that the volume of news articles containing quotes from President Bush and/or key members of his administration regarding Iraq/Saddam Hussein increased after 9/11. The means examined in each of these tests were the proportions of news articles that contained rhetoric regarding Iraq/Saddam Hussein by a particular source during the eighteen months following 9/11 versus the eighteen months preceding 9/11. The *t*-test statistics indicate whether the proportion of news articles containing rhetoric/quotes from specified sources differed significantly post- versus pre-9/11. Positive and statistically significant *t* statistics in these tests indicate that the mean level or volume of rhetoric regarding Iraq increased after 9/11 versus before that date.

The results of the *t*-tests supported the predictions for the analyses. Specifically, the independent sample *t*-tests indicated significant increases in post- versus pre-9/11 Iraq policy rhetoric volume for George W. Bush, Donald Rumsfeld, Condoleezza Rice, Ari Fleischer, and all administration sources (aggregated). The results were consistent with the expectations, as these sources significantly increased their rhetoric after 9/11. Interestingly, however, the results were not significant for Dick Cheney, Colin Powell, or an unnamed "senior official" of the administration. Also of note, only one nonadministration source had an increased volume of rhetoric concerning Iraq after 9/11, i.e., Democrat policy makers (aggregated).

TABLE I
*Comparison of Means Post- versus Pre-9/11 for Volume of Rhetoric by Source*

| Variable | Mean Pre-9/11 | Mean Post-9/11 | t | Mean Difference | S.E. | df |
|---|---|---|---|---|---|---|
| Bush (yes=1) | .17 | .41 | 6.370*** | .243 | .038 | 170 |
| Cheney (yes=1) | .01 | .03 | 1.761 | .017 | .010 | 214 |
| Rumsfeld (yes=1) | .03 | .08 | 2.224* | .042 | .019 | 184 |
| Rice (yes=1) | .01 | .04 | 3.017** | .032 | .011 | 274 |
| Powell (yes=1) | .16 | .14 | −.652 | −.022 | .034 | 1081[a] |
| Wolfowitz (yes=1) | .03 | .03 | −.295 | −.005 | .017 | 1081[a] |
| Fleischer (yes=1) | .01 | .07 | 4.887*** | .057 | .012 | 378 |
| Senior Official (yes=1) | .19 | .24 | 1.268 | .050 | .039 | 152 |
| Source of Rhetoric (Admin.=1) | .64 | .79 | 3.199** | .148 | .046 | 138 |
| Blix (yes=1) | .05 | .08 | 1.491 | .033 | .022 | 166 |
| Annan (yes=1) | .07 | .04 | −1.313 | −.032 | .024 | 133 |
| Republican policy maker (yes=1) | .06 | .06 | −.103 | −.002 | .023 | 1081[a] |
| Democratic policy maker (yes=1) | .05 | .11 | 2.689** | .061 | .023 | 181 |

NOTE: N=1083. Mean is the proportion of articles containing rhetoric by source.
[a] Equal variances assumed.
*$p < .05$   **$p < .01$   ***$p < .001$

Based on the first theoretical proposition, it was expected that (1) administrative rhetoric concerning Iraq would become increasingly communitarian and punitive in tone after 9/11, and (2) rhetoric from key nonadministration sources would become increasingly indefinite in tone (including counterclaims to the threat regarding Iraq presented by the administration) following 9/11. In the analyses conducted to test these predictions, volume and tone of rhetoric were regressed on time, while controlling for the source of rhetoric, specifically administration (coded 1) versus nonadministration (coded 0) sources. Accordingly, the dependent variable in each analysis was either a type of rhetoric (coded 1=present, 0=absent), such as punitive, or a key word, such as "evil."

Two statistical models were created for each dependent variable. This was done in order to determine the likelihood of each type of rhetoric post- versus pre-9/11 overall, as well as in shorter time intervals for the post-9/11 period, in order to examine differences in rhetoric/key word across more refined periods, while controlling for the source of rhetoric. As such, in the first model, time was a dichotomous measure coded 1=post-9/11 and 0=pre-9/11, while in the second model, time was represented as a series of dummy variables. Specifically, in the second model time was dummy coded for pre-9/11 (yes=1), and into one-month or three-month intervals for the post-9/11 period (as appropriate based on volume of rhetoric); the comparison (excluded) category was the time period most closely following September 11, 2001. Because the independent variables were all dichotomous in these models, the logistic regression coefficient and odds ratio are presented for each dependent variable in the tables, but the results are discussed in terms of odds ratios, which are more intuitive. The odds ratio is an estimate of the odds of the response occurring as a result of the independent variable. Although fifteen separate analyses were conducted and the results supported expectations, the findings for only four that capture the highlights or essence of these analyses are presented here. They are presented in tables 2 through 5 and discussed below.

Table 2 presents the logistic regression results for *punitive* rhetoric. In model 1, source of rhetoric is positive and significant, while controlling for time, as expected. The odds ratio shows that punitive rhetoric is 7.6 times as likely (or 760% greater likelihood) from administration versus nonadministration sources, controlling for time. In model 1, post-9/11 is also positive and significant, net of the effects of source of rhetoric, as expected. The odds ratio indicates that punitive rhetoric is 6.5 times as likely post-9/11 than pre-9/11, controlling for the source of rhetoric. In model 2, the post-9/11 period is dummy coded into one-month intervals, and September 12 through October 31, 2001, is the excluded time category. In this model, source of rhetoric is again positive and significant, while controlling for time. The odds ratio reveals that punitive rhetoric is 7.6 times as likely from administration versus nonadministration sources. Also, while pre-9/11 is not significant, fifteen of the seventeen one-month intervals after 9/11 are positive and significant (January 2002–March 2003). These results indicate that punitive rhetoric was significantly more likely to have been used in each of these months relative to the immediate post-9/11 period (9/12/01–10/31/01). Of particular interest is the month of February 2002, because it immediately followed President Bush's January 29, 2002, State of the Union address in which he first proclaimed that Iraq was part of an "axis of evil." The odds ratio indicates that punitive rhetoric is 96.7 times as likely during that month than it was right after 9/11.

Table 3 presents the logistic regression results for *punitive* and *communitarian* rhetoric used in combination. In model 1, source of rhetoric is positive and significant, while controlling for time, as expected. The odds ratio indicates that punitive and communitarian rhetoric used together is 18.8 times as likely from administration than from non-administration sources. The post-9/11

Table 2

*Logistic Regression Coefficients and Odds Ratios for "Punitive" Rhetoric*

| Variable | Model 1 | | Model 2[a] | |
|---|---|---|---|---|
| | b | Odds Ratio | b | Odds Ratio |
| Rhetoric Source (Admin.=1) | 2.030*** (.207) | 7.610 | 2.032*** (.213) | 7.631 |
| Post-9/11 (yes=1) | 1.873*** (.299) | 6.505 | – | – |
| Pre-9/11 (yes=1) | – | – | 1.219 (1.069) | 3.385 |
| Nov 01 | – | – | 2.258 (1.257) | 9.563 |
| Dec 01 | – | – | 1.487 (1.298) | 4.425 |
| Jan 02 | – | – | 4.193** (1.298) | 66.206 |
| Feb 02 | – | – | 4.572*** (1.103) | 96.726 |
| Mar 02 | – | – | 4.027** (1.118) | 56.107 |
| Apr 02 | – | – | 3.394** (1.107) | 29.787 |
| May 02 | – | – | 2.989** (1.139) | 19.866 |
| Jun 02 | – | – | 3.787** (1.232) | 44.137 |
| Jul 02 | – | – | 2.956** (1.115) | 19.216 |
| Aug 02 | – | – | 2.401* (1.078) | 11.032 |
| Sep 02 | – | – | 3.562** (1.047) | 35.241 |
| Oct 02 | – | – | 3.102** (1.050) | 22.252 |
| Nov 02 | – | – | 2.577* (1.063) | 13.156 |
| Dec 02 | – | – | 2.426* (1.059) | 11.310 |
| Jan 03 | – | – | 3.339** (1.049) | 28.812 |
| Feb 02 | – | – | 2.791** (1.047) | 16.304 |

*(continued)*

TABLE 2 *Logistic Regression Coefficients and Odds Ratios for "Punitive" Rhetoric (continued)*

| | Model 1 | | Model 2[a] | |
|---|---|---|---|---|
| Variable | b | Odds Ratio | b | Odds Ratio |
| Mar 03 | – | – | 3.331** (1.055) | 27.962 |
| Constant | −3.617*** (.347) | | −4.839** (1.049) | |
| Wald $\chi^2$ | 195.129*** | | 278.388*** | |
| (df) | (3) | | (20) | |
| log-likelihood | 1292.228 | | 1208.969 | |

NOTE: N=1083. Standard errors in parentheses.
[a] The excluded category (reference) in model 2 is September 12–October 31, 2001.
*p < .05   **p < .01   ***p < .001

period is positive and significant, as expected. Punitive/communitarian rhetoric is 7.1 times as likely post-9/11 than pre-9/11. In model 2, the post-9/11 period is dummy coded into three-month intervals, and September 12 through December 31, 2001 is the excluded time category. Source of rhetoric is positive and significant; punitive/communitarian rhetoric is 18.7 times as likely from administration than from non-administration sources, net of the effects of time. The pre-9/11 period is negative and significant, as expected. The odds ratio indicates that punitive/communitarian rhetoric is .10 times as likely pre-9/11 relative to the period immediately following September 11, 2001. However, none of the three-month post-9/11 time intervals are significant in model 2. These results indicate that punitive/communitarian rhetoric was less likely to be used pre-9/11 than post-9/11, and it was more likely to be used by administration than non-administration sources, as expected.

Table 4 presents the logistic regression results for *indefinite* rhetoric and *counterclaims* used together. Only one model is presented because no counterclaims were found prior to August 2002, precluding a post- versus pre-9/11/01 comparison. The post-9/11 period is dummy coded into three-month intervals beginning October 2002, and July 1 through September 30, 2002, is the excluded time category. As the table reveals, source of rhetoric is negative and significant, controlling for the effects of time, as expected. The odds ratio indicates that the combination of indefinite rhetoric and counterclaims are .18 times as likely from administration than from nonadministration sources. Both of the three-month post-9/11 time intervals are positive and significant (October–December 2002 and January–March 2003), net of the effects of the source. The odds ratios indicate that indefinite rhetoric and counterclaims were

TABLE 3

*Logistic Regression Coefficients and Odds Ratios for Combination*
*"Punitive/Communitarian" Rhetoric*

| Variable | Model 1 | | Model 2[a] | |
|---|---|---|---|---|
| | b | Odds Ratio | b | Odds Ratio |
| Rhetoric Source (Admin.=1) | 2.936** (1.011) | 18.841 | 2.931** (1.012) | 18.741 |
| Post-9/11 (yes=1) | 1.955* (1.015) | 7.067 | – | – |
| Pre-9/11 (yes=1) | – | – | −2.317* (1.138) | .099 |
| Jan 02–Mar 02 | – | – | −.358 (.662) | .699 |
| Apr 02–Jun 02 | – | – | −1.887 (1.141) | .152 |
| Jul 02–Sep 02 | – | – | −.063 (.587) | .939 |
| Oct 02–Dec 02 | – | – | −.668 (.609) | .513 |
| Jan 03–Mar 03 | – | – | −.269 (.575) | .764 |
| Constant | −7.283*** (1.406) | | −4.961*** (1.129) | |
| Wald $\chi^2$ | 34.016*** | | 40.993*** | |
| (df) | (3) | | (8) | |
| log-likelihood | 463.191 | | 456.214 | |

NOTE: N=1083. Standard errors in parentheses.
[a]The reference category in model 2 is September 12–December 31, 2001.
*p < .05   **p < .01   ***p < .001

significantly more likely to have been used in combination in these intervals (3.0 and 3.5 times as likely, respectively) relative to the July–September 2002 period. These findings indicate that indefinite rhetoric/counterclaims were increasingly used in combination in the months immediately preceding the invasion of Iraq, unlike indefinite rhetoric alone. Importantly, these indefinite rhetoric/counterclaims were *less* likely to be disseminated by administration than nonadministration sources, as expected.

Table 5 presents the logistic regression results for the key word "evil." In model 1, source of the word "evil" is positive and significant, net of the effects of time, as expected. The odds ratio shows that the word "evil" (or "evildoer") is 7.4 times as likely from administration versus nonadministration

TABLE 4

*Logistic Regression Coefficients and Odds Ratios for Combination "Indefinite/Counterclaims" Rhetoric*

|                              | Model[a]            |            |
| ---------------------------- | ------------------- | ---------- |
| Variable                     | b                   | Odds Ratio |
| Rhetoric Source (Admin.=1)   | $-1.699$*** (.380)  | .183       |
| Oct 02–Dec 02                | 1.100* (.520)       | 3.003      |
| Jan 03–Mar 03                | 1.264* (.498)       | 3.541      |
| Constant                     | $-3.317$*** (.447)  |            |
| Wald $\chi^2$ (df) log-likelihood | 30.464*** (4) 250.957 |       |

NOTE: N=1083. Standard errors in parentheses.
[a] The reference category is July 1–September 30, 2002.
No counterclaims were found prior to August 2002.
*p < .05    **p < .01    ***p < .001

sources. Also, time is positive and significant, controlling for the source, as expected. The odds ratio indicates that the word "evil" is 21.2 times as likely post-9/11 than pre-9/11. In model 2, the post-9/11 period is dummy coded into three-month intervals, and September 12 through December 31, 2001, is the excluded category. Source of the word "evil" is again positive and significant and it is 5.6 times as likely to be used by administration than nonadministration sources. The pre-9/11 time period is negative and significant, as expected. The odds ratio indicates that the word "evil" is .096 times as likely pre-9/11 than the period immediately following September 11, 2001. Also, two of the three-month post-9/11 time intervals (i.e., January–March 2002 and April–June 2002) are positive and significant, controlling for the source. These results indicate that the word "evil" was more likely to have been used in each of these intervals relative to the immediate post-9/11 period. Of particular interest is the January–March 2002 interval. The odds ratio indicates that the word "evil" is 21.1 times as likely during that particular time period than right after 9/11. As noted above, President Bush introduced the phrase "axis of evil" in reference to Iraq during his State of the Union address on January 29, 2002, which falls within that interval.

TABLE 5

*Logistic Regression Coefficients and Odds Ratios for Key Word "Evil"*

| Variable | Model 1 | | Model 2[a] | |
|---|---|---|---|---|
| | b | Odds Ratio | b | Odds Ratio |
| Rhetoric Source (Admin.=1) | 1.997*** (.395) | 7.364 | 1.727*** (.411) | 5.621 |
| Post-9/11 (yes=1) | 3.056** (1.010) | 21.237 | – | – |
| Pre-9/11 (yes=1) | – | – | −2.347* (1.137) | .096 |
| Jan 02–Mar 02 | – | – | 3.048*** (.581) | 21.079 |
| Apr 02–Jun 02 | – | – | 1.338* (.606) | 3.810 |
| Jul 02–Sep 02 | – | – | .448 (.568) | 1.565 |
| Oct 02–Dec 02 | – | – | .203 (.568) | 1.225 |
| Jan 03–Mar 03 | – | – | −.058 (.566) | .943 |
| Constant | −6.388*** (1.071) | | −3.792*** (.658) | |
| Wald $\chi^2$ | 78.178*** | | 219.481*** | |
| (df) | (3) | | (8) | |
| log-likelihood | 853.046 | | 711.743 | |

NOTE: N=1083. Standard errors in parentheses.
[a] The reference category in model 2 is September 12–December 31, 2001.
*p < .05   **p < .01   ***p < .001

In summary, a series of independent sample *t*-tests revealed that the volume of the *New York Times* articles containing quotes by President Bush and key members of his administration regarding Iraq/Saddam Hussein increased significantly post-9/11 versus pre-9/11, as predicted. However, with the exception of Democratic policy makers, whose volume of quotes significantly increased post- relative to pre-9/11, changes in the volume of quotes from nonadministration sources were not significant. It was anticipated that certain key nonadministrative sources of rhetoric concerning Iraq, such as U.N. Chief Weapons Inspector Hans Blix, would have increased significantly after 9/11. This was not the case.

Chi-square statistics (not shown here) revealed significant differences in the use of rhetoric tone and certain key words by administration versus nonadministration sources. Overall, administration sources were more likely to use punitive rhetoric (including certain key words such as "evil") and communitarian rhetoric, while nonadministration sources were more likely to use indefinite rhetoric and counterclaims. Logistic regression analyses revealed that punitive and communitarian rhetoric regarding Iraq/Saddam Hussein, both independently and in combination, were more likely post-9/11 than pre-9/11, and these types of rhetoric were more likely from administration than nonadministration sources. The key word "evil" was more likely to be used in reference to Iraq post-9/11 than pre-9/11, and it was more likely to be used by administration than nonadministration sources. Also, the word "terrorism" was not used in reference to Iraq until *after* the events of 9/11. This finding is important as it demonstrates that "terrorism" was more likely to be used by Bush administration sources in the months immediately preceding the invasion of Iraq than in the period immediately following 9/11.

Together, these findings reveal that following the events of 9/11, the Bush administration, with the support of the news media, pushed the alleged threat from Iraq into the public agenda. As argued by Kieve (1994) and demonstrated by Johnson et al. (2004), presidents are powerful agenda setters and image makers, and public opinion concerning an issue tends to reflect their rhetorical framing of that issue. The use of punitive rhetoric, particularly words such as "evil" and "terrorism," defined Saddam Hussein and his followers as folk devils, as is consistent with moral panic processes. Moreover, the above findings are consistent with Hawdon's (2001) analysis of the war on drugs, which revealed that elite-engineered moral panics can begin when punitive and communitarian rhetoric are used in combination by the president.

Although not shown here, the results of the content analysis also revealed that reactive and rehabilitative rhetoric were used in combination only by administration sources and *only* after July 2002. These types of rhetoric were more likely to be used together during the months *immediately preceding* the invasion of Iraq (January–March 2003), relative to July through September 2002. These findings are contrary to those of Hawdon (2001), who determined that increased reactive and rehabilitative rhetoric by the president occurred *after* the zenith of a moral panic and predicted decreased public concern about the drug issue. However, it has been documented that all moral panics operate somewhat differently (Goode & Ben-Yehuda, 1994; Welch, 2000). While they tend to follow similar patterns, all moral panics have some unique characteristics. Perhaps presidential rhetoric functions somewhat differently regarding an alleged domestic threat, such as illegal drugs, than it does in the engineering of a moral panic to justify the invasion of another country, which has obvious, dire potential for casualties and high financial costs. Intuitively, the rationale must be more profound in the latter case, as well as more multifaceted, in order to appeal to a wide and heterogeneous audience (Chomsky, 2002).

As communication theory states, priming (i.e., individual-level responses to the news framing of an issue) can have great variability within a society given past experiences and prior news framing of related events. It is probable that some individuals responded more favorably to presidential appeals based on reactive (e.g., "the Iraqi people need our help") or rehabilitative (e.g., "the Iraqis embrace freedom") rhetoric than to punitive (e.g., "Iraq is part of an axis of evil") or communitarian (e.g., "Iraq threatens every American") rhetoric. Therefore, the increased use of reactive and rehabilitative rhetoric together by the Bush administration during the final months preceding the invasion of Iraq was likely an attempt by the administration to appeal to those individuals not influenced by the primary (dominant) news frame which emphasized punitive and communitarian rhetoric (Chomsky, 2005; Tuchman, 1978). Also, President Bush appeared to use the media to speak directly to the Iraqi people while using reactive and rehabilitative rhetoric in the weeks just prior to the invasion, e.g., "A free Iraqi people will set the course of history, and free people will keep the peace of the world" (Kellner, 2005).

Furthermore, the analyses of the *New York Times*'s content revealed that indefinite rhetoric was significantly less likely post-9/11 than pre-9/11, as expected. No counterclaims were found prior to August 2002. However, counterclaims used independently and in combination with indefinite rhetoric were more likely in the months immediately preceding the invasion of Iraq. As expected, counterclaims (independently and in combination with indefinite rhetoric) were *less* likely to be disseminated by administration than nonadministration sources. Thus, influential nonadministration sources who were opposed to invading Iraq raised their voices—that is, the volume of such rhetoric increased markedly in the news media—in the final months prior to the invasion.

### Public Opinion Analysis

In order to more fully examine the first theoretical proposition, analyses of public opinion were conducted to explore the relationship between public approval/support for going to war in Iraq and (1) time, (2) volume of rhetoric, and (3) tone of rhetoric. The theoretical proposition would predict that (a) changes in the public's approval of invading Iraq are related to changes in volume and tone of administrative rhetoric; and (b) changes in the public's approval of invading Iraq are not affected by changes in volume and tone of nonadministrative rhetoric. Public approval/support for going to war in Iraq was regressed on source and tone of rhetoric, controlling for time-lagged effects. Although twenty-five separate analyses were conducted and the findings supported research expectations, the results of only five analyses that demonstrate the most important findings are presented here. Tables 6 through 10 provide the results of these analyses.

The data for the dependent variable came from twenty-four Gallup polls conducted between February 2001 and March 2003. The predictors are time-lagged measures of rhetoric by type (tone) and by source derived from the *New York Times* data. The independent variables are continuous measures of the number of articles that contain a type of rhetoric such as punitive, a key word such as "evil," or a source of rhetoric such as President Bush. These measures were aggregated for two-week, one-month, three-month, and five-month time lags preceding each Gallup poll. These four time-lagged variables were entered into separate logistic regression models, so that for each type of independent measure (e.g., punitive rhetoric) four models are presented. This allowed a determination of the change in the likelihood of public support of the invasion of Iraq in each of the time lags. Because all of the independent variables are continuous in these models, the logistic regression coefficient and odds ratio are presented for each dependent variable in the tables, but the findings are discussed in terms of log odds. The logistic regression coefficient is an estimate of the change in the log odds of the response (public support of invasion) increasing, given a one-unit increase in the independent variable (volume of quotes).

Table 6 presents the logistic regression results for "support invasion" and the time-lagged measures of *punitive* rhetoric. Punitive rhetoric is associated with public support for the invasion of Iraq, as expected. In model 1, punitive rhetoric in two-week lags is positive and significant. That is, a one-unit increase in punitive rhetoric in the two weeks preceding the Gallup polls increases the log odds by .11 that public support of invasion is higher in subsequent polls. Stated differently, for each additional article with punitive rhetoric in the stated time period, the likelihood of greater support for invasion was also higher. In model 2, punitive rhetoric in one-month lags is positive and significant; a one-unit increase in punitive rhetoric increases the log odds of support of invasion by .05. In model 3, punitive rhetoric in three-month lags is also positive and significant, with a one-unit increase in punitive rhetoric increasing the log odds of support of invasion by .03. In model 4, punitive rhetoric in five-month lags is not significant.

Table 6 also shows logistic regression results for "support invasion" and *communitarian* rhetoric. Models 5 through 8 provide the results for communitarian rhetoric in each of the time lags. Communitarian rhetoric is somewhat related to invasion support. In model 5, communitarian rhetoric in two-week lags is not significant, nor is communitarian rhetoric in one-month lags significant in model 6. However, in model 7, communitarian rhetoric in *three-month lags* is positive and significant, such that a one-unit increase in communitarian rhetoric in that period preceding the Gallup polls increases the log odds of increased public support of invasion by .10. In model 8, communitarian rhetoric in five-month lags is not significant.

TABLE 6

Logistic Regression Results for "Favor Invasion of Iraq"[a]: Number of Articles with Punitive and Communitarian Rhetoric

| Variable | Model 1 | Model 2 | Model 3 | Model 4 | Model 5 | Model 6 | Model 7 | Model 8 |
|---|---|---|---|---|---|---|---|---|
| *Punitive* | | | | | | | | |
| 2-wk. Lag | .108* | — | — | — | — | — | — | — |
| Odds Ratio | 1.114 | | | | | | | |
| | (.058) | | | | | | | |
| 1-mo. Lag | — | .048* | — | — | — | — | — | — |
| Odds Ratio | | 1.049 | | | | | | |
| | | (.028) | | | | | | |
| 3-mo. Lag | — | — | .027** | — | — | — | — | — |
| Odds Ratio | | | 1.027 | | | | | |
| | | | (.014) | | | | | |
| 5-mo. Lag | — | — | — | 0.013 | — | — | — | — |
| Odds Ratio | | | | 1.013 | | | | |
| | | | | (.008) | | | | |
| *Communitarian* | | | | | | | | |
| 2-wk. Lag | — | — | — | — | 0.708 | — | — | — |
| Odds Ratio | | | | | 2.029 | | | |
| | | | | | (.522) | | | |
| 1-mo. Lag | — | — | — | — | — | 0.197 | — | — |
| Odds Ratio | | | | | | 1.218 | | |
| | | | | | | (.146) | | |

(continued)

TABLE 6
*Logistic Regression Results for "Favor Invasion of Iraq"[a]: Number of Articles with Punitive and Communitarian Rhetoric (continued)*

| Variable | Model 1 | Model 2 | Model 3 | Model 4 | Model 5 | Model 6 | Model 7 | Model 8 |
|---|---|---|---|---|---|---|---|---|
| 3-mo. Lag Odds Ratio | — | — | — | — | — | — | .103* 1.108 (.059) | — |
| 5-mo. Lag Odds Ratio | — | — | — | — | — | — | — | .055 1.057 (.036) |
| Constant | -.566 (.993) | -.382 (.990) | -1.052 (1.217) | -.534 (1.207) | -.163 (.846) | .200 (.845) | -.169 (.904) | -.025 (.945) |
| Wald $\chi^2$ (df) | 5.297** (2) | 4.063** (2) | 4.834** (2) | 2.750* (2) | 6.344** (2) | 2.796* (2) | 3.642* (2) | 2.524 (2) |
| log-likelihood | 19.267 | 20.5 | 19.729 | 21.814 | 18.219 | 21.767 | 20.921 | 22.039 |

NOTE: N=24. Standard errors in parentheses.

[a] Same or higher than previous poll=1.

*p < .10   **p < .05

Table 7 presents the logistic regression results for "support invasion" and the key word "evil." The word "evil" is associated with support for the invasion of Iraq. In model 1, the coefficient for "evil" in two-week lags is positive and significant, as expected. A one-unit increase in the word "evil" in the two weeks preceding the Gallup polls increases the log odds of support for invasion by .48. In model 2, "evil" in one-month lags is positive and significant, such that a one-unit increase in "evil" increases the log odds of supporting the invasion by .23. In model 3, "evil" in three-month lags is also positive and significant. A one-unit increase in "evil" increases the log odds of support for invading Iraq by .32. In model 4, "evil" in five-month lags is not significant.

Table 7 also shows logistic regression results for "support invasion" and the key word "terrorism" or "terror." Models 5 through 8 provide the results for "terrorism" with each of the time lags. The word "terrorism" is unrelated to invasion support. None of the coefficients in any of the four models are statistically significant.

Table 8 presents the logistic regression results for "support invasion" and articles with quotes from President George W. Bush. President Bush is strongly associated with support for the invasion of Iraq, as expected. In model 1, the coefficient for President Bush quotes in two-week lags is positive and significant, as expected. A one-unit increase in the number of articles with quotes by President Bush in the two weeks preceding the Gallup polls increases the log odds by .32 of public support for the invasion of Iraq remaining stable or increasing. In model 2, President Bush quotes in one-month lags is positive and significant, with a one-unit increase in articles with such quotes increasing the log odds of support of invasion by .18. In model 3, President Bush quotes in three-month lags is also positive and significant. A one-unit increase in articles with quotes by President Bush increases the log odds of support by .04. In model 4, however, President Bush quotes in five-month lags is not significant.

Table 8 also shows the logistic regression results for "support invasion" and the number of articles with quotes from Vice President Dick Cheney. Models 5 through 8 provide the results for Dick Cheney quotes in each of the time lags. Cheney is largely unrelated to support for invasion. Interestingly, however, in model 8 the variable is significant and positive; a one-unit increase in articles with quotes by Dick Cheney in the five months preceding the Gallup polls increases the log odds of support for invading Iraq by .21. For some reason, unlike President Bush, Cheney's quotes seem to have influenced the public over time, rather than in the short-term. Perhaps this is due to the fact that Cheney served a support role in the propaganda campaign against Iraq and, therefore, his effects on public opinion were cumulative over time.

TABLE 7

Logistic Regression Results for "Favor Invasion of Iraq"[a]: Number of Articles with "Evil" and "Terrorism"

| Variable | Model 1 | Model 2 | Model 3 | Model 4 | Model 5 | Model 6 | Model 7 | Model 8 |
|---|---|---|---|---|---|---|---|---|
| *"Evil"* | | | | | | | | |
| 2-wk. Lag | .477* | — | — | — | — | — | — | — |
| Odds Ratio | 1.612 | | | | | | | |
| | (.287) | | | | | | | |
| 1-mo. Lag | — | .227* | — | — | — | — | — | — |
| Odds Ratio | | 1.254 | | | | | | |
| | | (.133) | | | | | | |
| 3-mo. Lag | — | — | .318** | — | — | — | — | — |
| Odds Ratio | | | 1.375 | | | | | |
| | | | (.160) | | | | | |
| 5-mo. Lag | — | — | — | .026 | — | — | — | — |
| Odds Ratio | | | | 1.027 | | | | |
| | | | | (.036) | | | | |
| *"Terrorism"* | | | | | | | | |
| 2-wk. Lag | — | — | — | — | .429 | — | — | — |
| Odds Ratio | | | | | 1.535 | | | |
| | | | | | (.278) | | | |
| 1-mo. Lag | — | — | — | — | — | .072 | — | — |
| Odds Ratio | | | | | | 1.074 | | |
| | | | | | | (.074) | | |

|  |  |  |  |  |  |  |  |  |
|---|---|---|---|---|---|---|---|---|
| 3-mo. Lag Odds Ratio | — | — | — | — | — | — | .058<br>1.059<br>(.043) | — |
| 5-mo. Lag Odds Ratio | — | — | — | — | — | — | — | .036<br>1.037<br>(.030) |
| Constant | −.205<br>(.839) | −.746<br>(1.220) | −6.640*<br>(3.919) | .178<br>(1.597) | .105<br>(.774) | .671<br>(.788) | .163<br>(.935) | .143<br>(1.041) |
| Wald $\chi^2$ (df) | 5.381**<br>(2) | 3.653*<br>(2) | 10.366**<br>(2) | .555<br>(2) | 4.313**<br>(2) | 1.068<br>(2) | 1.939<br>(2) | 1.549<br>(2) |
| log-likelihood | 19.183 | 20.910 | 14.198 | 24.008 | 20.251 | 23.496 | 22.625 | 23.014 |

NOTE: N=24. Standard errors in parentheses.

[a]Same or higher than previous poll=1.

*p < .10  **p < .05

TABLE 8

*Logistic Regression Results for "Favor Invasion of Iraq"[a]: Number of Articles with Quotes from Bush and Cheney*

| Variable | Model 1 | Model 2 | Model 3 | Model 4 | Model 5 | Model 6 | Model 7 | Model 8 |
|---|---|---|---|---|---|---|---|---|
| *Bush* | | | | | | | | |
| 2-wk. Lag | .317** | – | – | – | – | – | – | – |
| Odds Ratio | 1.373 | | | | | | | |
| | (.143) | | | | | | | |
| 1-mo. Lag | – | .178** | – | – | – | – | – | – |
| Odds Ratio | | 1.195 | | | | | | |
| | | (.088) | | | | | | |
| 3-mo. Lag | – | – | .036** | – | – | – | – | – |
| Odds Ratio | | | 1.036 | | | | | |
| | | | (.018) | | | | | |
| 5-mo. Lag | – | – | – | .013 | – | – | – | – |
| Odds Ratio | | | | 1.013 | | | | |
| | | | | (.009) | | | | |
| *Cheney* | | | | | | | | |
| 2-wk. Lag | – | – | – | – | .842 | – | – | – |
| Odds Ratio | | | | | 2.321 | | | |
| | | | | | (.990) | | | |
| 1-mo. Lag | – | – | – | – | – | .239 | – | – |
| Odds Ratio | | | | | | 1.269 | | |
| | | | | | | (.271) | | |

| | | | | | | | | |
|---|---|---|---|---|---|---|---|---|
| 3-mo. Lag Odds Ratio | — | — | — | — | — | — | .673 1.960 (.664) | — |
| 5-mo. Lag Odds Ratio | — | — | — | — | — | — | — | .210* 1.234 (0.113) |
| Constant | -2.642 (1.634) | -3.194 (2.155) | -1.278 (1.297) | -.329 (1.164) | .890 (.571) | .944 (.595) | -.628 (1.379) | -.415 (.969) |
| Wald $\chi^2$ (df) | 10.189** (2) | 9.499** (2) | 5.183** (2) | 2.313 (2) | 2.348 (2) | 1.280 (2) | 6.203** (2) | 4.006** (2) |
| log-likelihood | 14.374 | 15.064 | 19.380 | 22.251 | 22.216 | 23.283 | 18.361 | 20.557 |

NOTE: N=24. Standard errors in parentheses.
[a]Same or higher than previous poll=1.
*p < .10  **p < .05

Face validity and the moral panic literature (e.g., Hawdon, 2001; Johnson et al., 2004; Reinarman & Levine, 1989) both suggest that the relationship between news articles with President Bush quotes and changes in levels of support for invading Iraq are particularly important given the primacy of presidential rhetoric in influencing public opinion. In order to determine the robustness of the results for quotes by President Bush and "public support for invasion," additional models were analyzed in which quotes from other sources of rhetoric, types of rhetoric (tone), and key words were included as additional independent variables. For example, the various types of rhetoric considered in the study (e.g., punitive) were each examined in separate models along with President Bush. Other conceptually important combinations of independent variables (e.g., President Bush and the word "evil") were also included in the analyses. Four models for each set of independent variables were conducted in order to determine the change in the likelihood of public support for invading Iraq increasing in each of the four time-lagged periods preceding the Gallup polls. Tables 9 and 10 provide the highlights of the analyses involving more than one independent variable, although the excluded analyses yielded the expected results.

Given the power of the U.S. president as an agenda setter in society, it was expected that nonadministration sources would have negligible influence on public opinion, net of the effects of presidential rhetoric. Table 9 shows the logistic regression results for "support invasion" and the number of articles with quotes from President Bush and quotes from nonadministration sources. Controlling for nonadministration sources, President Bush is strongly associated with support for the invasion. In model 1, as expected, quotes from President Bush in two-week time lags is positive and significant, controlling for quotes from nonadministration sources. A one-unit increase in articles with quotes from President Bush in the two weeks before the polls increases the log odds of public support for the invasion of Iraq by .28. However, as anticipated, the number of articles with quotes from nonadministration sources is not significant in model 1. In model 2, the number of articles with quotes from President Bush in one-month time lags is positive and significant. A one-unit increase in the number of articles with quotes by President Bush increases the log odds of support of invasion by .20. Once again, quotes from nonadministration sources is not significant in model 2. None of the coefficient estimates in either models 3 or 4 (number of articles with quotes from President Bush and quotes from nonadministration sources in three-month and five month time lags, respectively) is statistically significant.

Table 10 presents logistic regression results for "support invasion" and quotes from President Bush and the key word "evil." In three of these models, either President Bush or the word "evil" is associated with support for the invasion of Iraq. In model 1, number of quotes from President Bush in two-week

TABLE 9

*Multivariate Logistic Regression Results for "Favor Invasion of Iraq"[a]: Number of Articles with Quotes from Bush and Nonadministration Sources*

| Variable | Model 1 | Model 2 | Model 3 | Model 4 |
|---|---|---|---|---|
| *Bush* | | | | |
| 2-wk. Lag | .276* | – | – | – |
| Odds Ratio | 1.318 | | | |
| | (.147) | | | |
| 1-mo. Lag | – | .201* | – | – |
| Odds Ratio | | 1.215 | | |
| | | (.106) | | |
| 3-mo. Lag | – | – | .057 | – |
| Odds Ratio | | | 1.059 | |
| | | | (.039) | |
| 5-mo. Lag | – | – | – | .018 |
| Odds Ratio | | | | 1.019 |
| | | | | (.018) |
| *Nonadmin.* | | | | |
| 2-wk. Lag | .116 | – | – | – |
| Odds Ratio | 1.123 | | | |
| | (.134) | | | |
| 1 mo. Lag | – | .025 | – | – |
| Odds Ratio | | 1.026 | | |
| | | (.071) | | |
| 3-mo. Lag | – | – | −.027 | – |
| Odds Ratio | | | .973 | |
| | | | (.040) | |
| 5-mo. Lag | – | – | – | −.008 |
| Odds Ratio | | | | .992 |
| | | | | (.024) |
| Constant | −3.186 | −3.176 | −1.567 | −.445 |
| | (1.959) | (2.152) | (1.452) | (1.229) |
| Wald $\chi^2$ | 10.976** | 9.574** | 5.665 | 2.420 |
| (df) | (3) | (3) | (3) | (3) |
| log-likelihood | 13.587 | 14.986 | 18.899 | 22.111 |

NOTE: N=24. Standard errors in parentheses.
[a] Same or higher than previous poll=1.
*p < .10  **p < .05

time lags preceding the Gallup polls is positive and significant, controlling for the word "evil," as expected. A one-unit increase in articles with quotes by President Bush increases the log odds of public support for the invasion by .31. However, the word "evil" is not significant in model 1, net of the effects of Bush quotes. In model 2, quotes from President Bush in one-month time lags is positive and significant, such that a one-unit increase in articles with

TABLE 10

*Multivariate Logistic Regression Results for "Favor Invasion of Iraq"[a]: Number of Articles with Quotes from Bush and "Evil"*

| Variable | Model 1 | Model 2 | Model 3 | Model 4 |
|---|---|---|---|---|
| *Bush* | | | | |
| 2-wk. Lag | .310* | – | – | – |
| Odds Ratio | 1.363 | | | |
| | (.163) | | | |
| 1-mo. Lag | – | .156* | – | – |
| Odds Ratio | | 1.169 | | |
| | | (.090) | | |
| 3-mo. Lag | – | – | .000 | – |
| Odds Ratio | | | 1.000 | |
| | | | (.021) | |
| 5 mo. Lag | – | – | – | .016 |
| Odds Ratio | | | | 1.016 |
| | | | | (.011) |
| *"Evil"* | | | | |
| 2-wk. Lag | .424 | – | – | – |
| Odds Ratio | 1.528 | | | |
| | (.297) | | | |
| 1-mo. Lag | – | .121 | – | – |
| Odds Ratio | | 1.128 | | |
| | | (.167) | | |
| 3-mo. Lag | – | – | .317* | – |
| Odds Ratio | | | 1.374 | |
| | | | (.191) | |
| 5-mo. Lag | – | – | – | −.014 |
| Odds Ratio | | | | .986 |
| | | | | (.041) |
| Constant | −4.006* | −3.902 | −6.634* | −.005 |
| | (2.197) | (2.570) | (4.007) | (1.497) |
| Wald $\chi^2$ | 13.152** | 10.034** | 10.366** | 2.430 |
| (df) | (3) | (3) | (3) | (3) |
| log-likelihood | 11.412 | 14.530 | 14.198 | 22.134 |

NOTE: $N=24$. Standard errors in parentheses.
[a] Same or higher than previous poll$=1$.
*$p < .10$   **$p < .05$

quotes by the president in the month prior to the polls increases the log odds of supporting the invasion by .16. The word "evil" is not significant in model 2. In model 3, quotes from president Bush in three-month lags is not significant. However, the key word "evil" is positive and significant in model 3, controlling for quotes from President Bush. A one-unit increase in articles containing the word "evil" in the three months preceding the polls increases the log odds of support for the invasion by .32. Neither of the coefficient estimates in model 4 (five-month lag) is statistically significant.

In summary, a series of logistic regression analyses were conducted to examine the relationships between public support for invading Iraq and time, volume, and tone. The analyses for whether "support of invasion" of Iraq changed on volume and tone of rhetoric took into account the amount of rhetoric in specified time intervals prior to when the Gallup polls were conducted. The results revealed that punitive rhetoric increased the likelihood that public support for the invasion remained stable or increased (in three out of four time lags), as expected. Communitarian rhetoric increased the probability of supporting the invasion, as expected. These findings are highly consistent with moral panic processes which state that moral panics can begin when punitive and communitarian rhetoric are used together by the president (Hawdon, 2001). Also, greater numbers of articles with the key word "evil" increased the odds of support for the invasion in three out of four time lags, while the word "threat" was positive and significant in one time lag. Interestingly, the word "terrorism" or "terror" had no influence on support for invading Iraq.

As expected, source of rhetoric was very important for public support of invading Iraq. Aggregated administration sources (not shown here) and President Bush each independently increased the odds of support for invasion in three out of four time lags preceding Gallup polls, as anticipated. Quotes from Vice President Dick Cheney were positive and significant in one time lag, while articles with quotes from Defense Secretary Donald Rumsfeld and National Security Advisor Condoleezza Rice (not shown here) were positive and significant in two time lags each. As expected, nonadministration sources had negligible impacts on public opinion. For example, the volume of articles with quotes from Democratic policy makers (not shown here) was unrelated to support for invasion, despite the fact that the volume of rhetoric from this group significantly increased post- versus pre-9/11. Similarly, although frequently quoted in the news media, articles with statements from U.N. Chief Weapons Inspector Hans Blix (not shown here) were not related to support for the invasion of Iraq.

When other sources or tones of rhetoric were added as independent variables in models along with President G. W. Bush, the number of articles with quotes from Bush continued to have important impact on public support for invasion. That is, a greater number of articles with Bush quotes increased the probability of support in two out of four time-lagged models, controlling for each type (tone) of rhetoric in the study, including counterclaims, while the tones of rhetoric were not related to support in any of the models analyzed (results not shown here). In models containing President Bush and nonadministration sources (aggregated), a greater number of articles with quotes from the president increased the odds of support for invasion in two out of four time-lagged models, taking into account the other source of rhetoric, while nonadministration sources were not related to support. Interestingly, the key word "evil" was related to support for invasion in three-month time lags preceding the Gallup polls, even after taking into account (controlling for) quotes from President Bush.

In conclusion, the findings regarding presidential rhetoric and public opinion supported a priori research expectations as well as the moral panic literature (Hawdon, 2001; Reinarman & Levine, 1989; Rothe & Muzzatti, 2004) which demonstrates that the president of the United States participates in the social construction of reality and the elite engineering of moral panics. Furthermore, the findings support the primacy of the U.S. president as a source of ideology (rhetoric) and as an agenda setter (Hawdon, 2001; Johnson et al., 2004; Kieve, 1994) because other sources and tones of rhetoric were *not* associated with support for invading Iraq once the impact of quotes from President Bush was taken into account. Importantly, these findings support the argument of Goode and Ben-Yehuda (1994), who stated that due to their elite status and power, presidents can provide the necessary outlet for public concern that moral panics require. Moreover, consistent with communication literature, these findings demonstrate that public opinion concerning an issue often mirrors the president's framing of that issue in the news media (Beckett, 1994; Johnson et al., 2004). Finally, the results of this study demonstrate the rhetorical power of the word "evil" (Bromley, Shupe & Ventimiglia, 1979; Rothe & Muzzatti, 2004) and, in particular, its considerable impact on public opinion (Entman, 2003; Merskin, 2004).

## STUDY LIMITATIONS

As in any research, this study is not without limitations. Three specific limitations of the study warrant discussion. The first limitation is the small sample of Gallup polls (N=24) used in the analyses of public opinion (i.e., support for invading Iraq). There were actually twenty-five Gallup polls conducted between February 2001 and March 2003 in which the percentage of the U.S. public that approved of invading Iraq was measured using the same question wording and response categories, but one poll (November 26, 2001) was eliminated as an extreme outlier that skewed the data (see table A.1 in the Appendix for a discussion of this issue). The small sample of Gallup polls used in the logistic regression analyses reduced the statistical power of the significance tests (J. Cohen, 1992), which limited the analyses to including only two independent variables per model. This is because at least eight to ten cases are required for each predictor in such analyses (Pagano & Gauvreau, 2000).

Due to the above limitation, it was not possible to examine the effects of multiple sources and tones of rhetoric on support for invading Iraq. For example, it would have been theoretically interesting to have analyzed a model including both administration and nonadministration sources as well as including both punitive rhetoric and counterclaims as separate predictors. Would administration sources and punitive rhetoric still be positively and significantly associated with support for invading Iraq in such a model? Also, it would have been useful to include the number of articles with quotes from President Bush and all of the tones of rhetoric as separate predictors in a single model. Had a larger number of Gallup polls been available, more elaborate multiple logistic regression models could have been analyzed.

However, it should be noted that Gallup is the only polling organization known to have conducted repeated surveys measuring public support for invading Iraq in which the same question was asked each time, using identical wording and with the same response categories. Although limited to twenty-four observations, these polls provide a valuable measure of public support for invading Iraq over time. Also, as previously noted, because some of the Gallup polls were conducted so closely together, a number of the time-lagged variables (predictors) contain overlapping or nonindependent observations, particularly in the three- and five-month time lags. Nevertheless, the assumption of independence of error terms in logistic regression analyses was not violated.

A second limitation of this study is having only one data source of political rhetoric, i.e., the *New York Times*. It would have been valuable both methodologically and theoretically to examine any significant differences in the volume and tone of rhetoric, and sources quoted, across news media outlets (Maxwell et al., 2000; Welch et al., 2002). Also, it is unknown whether the influences of political rhetoric on public opinion (i.e., support for invading Iraq) that were observed based on the *New York Times* articles would be replicated using other news media sources, including other media technologies or delivery systems such as television. As previously noted, the *New York Times* was selected based on its relative importance as a news source and its large national circulation. Also, it is frequently used in news content analyses (see Beckett, 1994; Maxwell et al., 2000; Welch et al., 1997; Welch et al., 2002). Despite the limitation of having only one source of rhetoric, editorial bias was drastically minimized, if not eliminated, because only articles that included an actual quote from either administration sources or influential nonadministration sources regarding Saddam Hussein/Iraq were included in the analyses. Moreover, criterion validity was confirmed because 100% of administrative quotes that appeared in a random subsample of the *New York Times* articles represented the rhetorical content and tone of White House statements obtained from the Federal News Service (FNS) for the same dates as the news articles; thus, providing great confidence in the results.

A third limitation of this study is the lack of *individual-level* measures of media usage. Unfortunately, such measures were unavailable from Gallup, so this research constitutes a macro-level study only. However, there are theoretical reasons to believe that increased media usage at the individual level would be associated with increased concern regarding the alleged threat posed by Iraq. In particular, a "cultivation hypothesis" of media effects was introduced by Gerbner and Gross (1976). Its basic premise is that dominant messages of television become accepted views of reality among heavy viewers. Heavy viewers are exposed to such large doses of violence and crime-related imagery that they come to view the world as more violent and more dominated by criminality than it really is. Thus, the cultivation hypothesis predicts that heavy television viewing fosters a "mean world view" manifested in elevated fear of crime and increased estimates of one's risk of victimization (Gerbner & Gross, 1976). Therefore, responses to violent imagery vary at the individual level in society based on the volume of media one consumes. Similarly, research has demonstrated that greater television viewing and newspaper readership at the individual level are associated with increased concern about drugs (Nielsen & Bonn, 2008).

A number of scholars have expanded upon cultivation theory to examine in more detail the relationship between TV viewing and fear of crime. Issues related to media and crime are relevant to this research study because social constructionism and media effects theories have influenced both fear of crime and moral panic research (see Beckett, 1994; Chiricos, Eschholz & Gertz, 1997; Hawdon, 2001). Such studies generally support the conclusion that increased exposure to televised images of crime at the individual level predicts greater fear of crime (e.g., Chiricos, Eschholz & Gertz, 1997; Chiricos, Padgett & Gertz, 2000), although more recent research suggests that neighborhood context, program type, and audience traits may mediate the TV-fear relationship (Eschholz, Chiricos & Gertz, 2003).

In addition to increasing public fears, the media's heavy emphasis on violence and their news framing of it has other powerful influences on public attitudes, including support for presidential policy (Beckett, 1994; Hawdon, 2001). In the current context, the sight of the World Trade Center collapsing on 9/11 was a powerful television image that most likely heightened public concern regarding the alleged Iraq threat and increased public support for its invasion. As discussed, the Bush administration manipulated public anxiety by deliberately linking Iraq to 9/11 in its rhetoric, following the terrorist attacks (Kellner, 2005; Scheer, 2003). That rhetoric primed retaliatory sentiments among a U.S. public hungry for revenge after 9/11 when it was combined with visual images of the Twin Towers collapsing on television news programs (Entman, 2003; Kellner, 2005). This issue is discussed in further detail in chapters four, six, and seven.

From the macro-level perspectives of social constructionism and moral panic, presidential rhetoric and the mass media play key roles in creating meaning and concern in society about social problems, including national security threats (Mueller, 2006). These conclusions are further supported by macro-level concepts in communication theory, including agenda setting and framing. For example, agenda-setting theory presupposes greater media consumption at the individual level and, consequently, greater exposure to presidential rhetoric. Such macro-level perspectives, in conjunction with the more micro-level approaches of priming and the cultivation hypothesis, lead one to expect that greater media exposure at the individual level should be associated with increased concern over the alleged threat posed by Iraq and, therefore, support for invasion.

## CONCLUSION

In this chapter the results of analyses of news media content and public opinion concerning Iraq prior to the March 2003 U.S.-led invasion were presented and discussed. These analyses provided a quantitative assessment of the elite-engineered model of moral panic as it applies to the events leading up to the Iraq war. An examination of presidential policy rhetoric regarding Iraq disseminated by the news media before and after the terrorist attacks of 9/11 revealed that the rhetoric changed in significant and meaningful ways following that historic event. The Bush administration's rhetoric concerning Iraq after the 9/11 attacks became increasingly punitive and communitarian in tone, as expected. An analysis of Gallup polls that measured the public's willingness to go to war in Iraq determined that there were shifts in public opinion that directly mirrored presidential policy rhetoric. Together, the findings supported the central research expectations and predictions for the study. Chapter four presents an argument that these research findings fulfill Stanley Cohen's five criteria of moral panic and thus support the proposition that the Bush administration engineered a moral panic over Iraq with the assistance of the news media. The news media's complicity in the panic is also discussed in chapter four.

CHAPTER 4

# How the Bush Administration Sold
# the Iraq War to the U.S. Public

EARLY IN SEPTEMBER 2002, White House Chief of Staff
Andy Card was asked why President G. W. Bush had waited until after Labor
Day to begin an intensive effort to persuade the American public of the need
to invade Iraq. Card responded, "From a marketing point of view, you don't
introduce new products in August" (Elliott, 2002, p. 4). Amazingly, Card's
statement compared the justification for war to an advertising campaign for a
consumer product such as Coca-Cola.

In this chapter the results of the research study discussed in chapter three
are examined within the context of moral panic theory and literature. It is
contended that the research results support the first theoretical proposition
advanced in this book. An argument is presented that the war in Iraq was
legitimized by a moral panic engineered by the Bush administration and reinforced by the news media, which influenced public support for the invasion
of Iraq (Chomsky, 2005). More specifically, it is demonstrated that the findings of the research study fulfill the five requirements of moral panic outlined
by Cohen (2002). Evidence is also provided that the sequence of events leading up to the invasion, as well as facts made public since then, further under-
score Cohen's five criteria.

### APPLYING THE FIVE CRITERIA OF MORAL PANIC
### TO THE IRAQ WAR

Before discussing each of the five criteria used to determine if a moral
panic has occurred, a brief recap of the elite-engineered model of moral panic
is in order. According to Goode and Ben-Yehuda (1994, p. 135), and consistent with the tenets of critical sociology, the "elite-engineered" model of
moral panic premises that "an elite group deliberately and consciously undertakes a campaign to generate and sustain concern, fear, and panic on the part
of the public over an issue that they recognize not to be terribly harmful to
the society as a whole." Oftentimes, such a campaign is intended to divert
public attention away from other objective or real problems in society, whose

solution might jeopardize or undermine the elite group's interests (Garland, 2008; Goode & Ben-Yehuda, 1994;). In chapter seven it is argued that the campaign used by the Bush administration to sell the Iraq war to the U.S. public served just such a purpose.

The elite-engineered model of moral panic assumes that political/economic elites have tremendous power over other members of society. As previously discussed, political elites, particularly presidents, are agenda setters and image makers. It is the elites who frame issues for public discourse, control the distribution of valuable resources, dominate the mass media, and determine the content of legislation and the direction of law enforcement (Chambliss & Mankoff, 1976). Thus, the elite-engineered moral panic represents a "top-down" model. That is, public concern or fear over an issue is orchestrated from above by elites who control the governing ideology, have unfettered access to mass media outlets, and promote fear or concern among the masses.

It has been argued that the moral panic concept is scientifically defensible and empirically measurable. In particular, Goode and Ben-Yehuda (1994, p. 41) make this case:

> The moral panic is a phenomenon—given its broad and sprawling nature— that can be located and measured in a fairly unbiased fashion. It does not matter whether we sympathize with the concern or not. What is important is that the concern locates a "folk devil," is shared, is out of sync with the measurable seriousness of the condition that generates it, and varies in intensity over time. . . . The point that the moral panic concept is scientifically defensible, and not an invidious, ideologically motivated term of debunking, needs to be stressed in the strongest possible fashion.

As discussed in chapter two, Stanley Cohen (1972) originally identified at least five sets of actors in a moral panic drama: (1) folk devils; (2) politicians; (3) law or rule enforcers; (4) the media; and (5) the public. It is argued here that Saddam Hussein and his political regime were framed as folk devils by the Bush administration after 9/11. It is further contended that the media established the Bush administration's "folk devil" message as the dominant news frame on Iraq; thus, the news media were complicit with the Bush administration in manipulating public hostility toward Iraq.

Importantly, Cohen (2002) identified five empirically measurable criteria by which a social issue or condition may be defined as a moral panic: (1) concern; (2) consensus; (3) hostility; (4) disproportionality; and (5) volatility. It has been argued that each of the five criteria must be met in order for a condition to qualify as a moral panic (Goode & Ben-Yehuda, 1994; Welch, 2007). Below, the findings of the research study are examined within the framework of Cohen's five criteria. Each criterion is addressed separately first and then conclusions are drawn collectively.

## Concern

Cohen (2002) identified concern as the first criterion of a moral panic. This refers to a heightened level of concern (or fear) about a potential or imagined threat in society. Goode and Ben-Yehuda (1994) distinguish between concern and fear when they argue that the concern felt by the public in a moral panic need not manifest itself as fear, although it can. Either way, the concern or fear is seen by those who feel it "to be a reasonable response to what is regarded as a very real and palpable threat" (Goode & Ben-Yehuda, 1994, p. 33). It has been argued that the concern criterion of a moral panic can be measured or manifested in the form of media attention or proposed legislation (Goode & Ben-Yehuda, 1994; Welch, Price & Yankey, 2002). According to both of these metrics, the events leading up to the invasion of Iraq arguably fulfill this first criterion of a moral panic.

Regarding news coverage, the content analysis of articles published between March 1, 2000, and March 18, 2003, in the *New York Times* revealed that more than five thousand articles dealt with issues related to Iraq/Saddam Hussein. That is, nearly five news articles per day for three years were directly relevant to the study. A total of 1,083 articles during the study period contained direct quotes (policy rhetoric) regarding Iraq from either the president's administration or other key sources. This means that an average of at least one article per day for three years leading up to the invasion contained presidential policy rhetoric regarding Iraq. During the six months that immediately preceded the March 2003 invasion an average of 105 articles per month in the *New York Times* contained direct quotes regarding Iraq. This represents an average of 3.5 articles per day during the six months prior to the invasion or a 350% increase from the thirty-six-month average. This finding reveals that the volume of Bush administration policy rhetoric increased significantly as the invasion of Iraq approached. It must be remembered that these numbers, as high as they are, represent only one news source. It is contented that dramatically increased rhetoric by the Bush administration regarding Iraq after 9/11 met the essential concern criterion and thus laid the foundation for an elite-engineered moral panic (Cohen, 2002; Goode & Ben-Yehuda, 1994).

Furthermore, as revealed in the content analysis, the Bush administration's policy rhetoric regarding Iraq as quoted in the *New York Times* became more punitive and communitarian after 9/11. Hawdon (2001) demonstrated that moral panics begin when punitive and communitarian forms of rhetoric are used in combination by the president regarding an alleged threat. The Bush administration employed words and phrases such as "weapons of mass destruction," "threat," "terrorism," and "evildoers" with respect to Iraq in order to frame what was alleged to be a serious problem facing the United States. In particular, the concern criterion is manifested in statements by President Bush prior to the invasion that "the Iraqi dictator must not be permitted to threaten

America and the world with horrible poisons and diseases and gases and atomic weapons" (Scheer, 2003, p. 1). The message from the Bush administration to the public was that Iraq represented a serious and imminent threat to all Americans, and action had to be taken to eliminate that threat (Fish, 2001). To do otherwise tempted disaster in the form of a "mushroom cloud," i.e., a nuclear attack on the United States (Scheer, 2003). Consider the following statement: "We have made it clear that Iraq does possess chemical and biological weapons. And what we are doing is to—what we are working to do right now with the international community, speaking with one voice, is to disarm Saddam Hussein of those weapons of mass destruction. We know that he possesses chemical and biological weapons. And we know that he seeks to acquire nuclear weapons" (White House Press Secretary Scott McClellan: November 13, 2002).

The news framing of the presidential rhetoric regarding the alleged threat confirmed for the public that Iraq did indeed pose a serious and growing threat to U.S. security. Public concern over Iraq was both fueled and validated by the Bush administration and the news media. This argument is supported by the findings of the study, which reveal that an increase in articles containing direct quotes by President Bush and/or key members of his administration in various time periods preceding Gallup polls increased the likelihood of public support for the invasion of Iraq remaining stable or increasing. Increased quotes by President Bush, in particular, increased the odds of support for invasion in three out of four time lags preceding Gallup polls, as anticipated. Quotes from Vice President Dick Cheney were positive and significant in one time lag, while articles with quotes from Defense Secretary Donald Rumsfeld and National Security Advisor Condoleezza Rice were positive and significant in two time lags each. Public attitudes and opinions thus mirrored the rhetoric of the Bush administration regarding Iraq. Therefore, based on the research findings, the concern criterion of a moral panic was established in this case study.

Before moving on to the second criterion of moral panic, the news media's complicity in the moral panic warrants consideration. As discussed in chapter two, the media are perhaps the most influential facilitator in the creation of a moral panic (Goode & Ben-Yehuda, 1994). News media coverage of events involving the folk devils is generally distorted or exaggerated. Such exaggerations make the folk devils appear to be much more threatening to society than they really are. As a result, public concern or anxiety is heightened through journalistic hyperbole.

The news content analysis demonstrates that the media adopted the punitive, pro-war framing of the Iraq issue presented by the Bush administration. However, this raises an important question: Why did the U.S. news media generally present the Bush administration's arguments for war in a passive and uncritical fashion? Beyond the insights of critical sociology in this regard (discussed in chapter two), the concept of the "news net" helps to answer this question. Tuchman's (1978) concept of the news net contends that professional training and professional associations routinize (provide schema or templates for) journalists' thinking and actions. The bureaucratic and organizational constraints of a particular medium such as television also help to establish routine activities for the professional journalists who work in that medium. As a result of the news net, journalists are primarily attuned to the ideologies and actions of societal elites because those sources provide the credibility of structural roles (e.g., the U.S. president) and confer the status of political authority to the journalists' mediating role between news sources and audience members (Tuchman, 1978). From this perspective, the U.S. news media followed routine procedures after 9/11 and relied on authoritative Bush administration sources to dutifully report the alleged threat to U.S. national security from Iraq (Edelman, 1988). The news net perspective would argue that U.S. journalists are generally uncritical due to the occupational norms, roles, and bureaucratic practices of the news business, and they would be unlikely, therefore, to question the sincerity or credibility of the Bush administration's pro-war argument. Stated differently, the news net concept would contend that U.S. news media practitioners were simply following normal journalistic routines after 9/11, which made them passive and unwitting participants in the Bush administration's moral panic over Iraq, rather than active co-conspirators in the enterprise.

*Consensus*

The second criterion of a moral panic identified by Cohen (2002) is consensus. It has been argued that there must be substantial or widespread agreement or consensus in society, although not necessarily universal, that the threat is real and serious, and caused by the alleged offenders and their behavior (Goode & Ben-Yehuda, 1994). As explained by Goode and Ben-Yehuda (1994, p. 34): "Moral panics come in different sizes—some gripping the vast majority of the members of a society at a given time, others creating concern only among certain of its groups or categories. At no exact point are we able to say that a panic exists; however, if the number is insubstantial, clearly, one does not exist." In other words, a certain minimal measure of consensus must be present in a moral panic to demonstrate a shared sense of danger (Welch et al., 2002).

The Gallup polls used in this study, which measured the percentage of the U.S. public that approved of invading Iraq over time, help to establish the consensus criterion of moral panic. In these twenty-four polls, public support for invading Iraq ranged from a low of 52.5% in February, 2001, to a high of 64.1% in March, 2003 (four days before the start of the invasion). Although public support for war fluctuated over the course of the twenty-four polls (it

actually decreased in eleven of the polls relative to the one immediately preceding them), it peaked just prior to the invasion of Iraq and climbed fairly
steadily in the last few months leading up to it (see table A.1 in the Appendix).
Importantly, the February 19, 2001, Gallup poll provides a pre-9/11 benchmark level of support for invasion. It indicates that slightly more than half of
the U.S. public supported the invasion of Iraq seven months *before* the events
of 9/11. This relatively high level of support indicates that some public concern and consensus regarding the alleged threat of Iraq *predated* the terrorist
attacks of 9/11. Nonetheless, public support for the invasion increased significantly after 9/11. It could perhaps be argued that public concern regarding
Iraq (support for invasion) *prior* to 9/11 is consistent with the grass roots
model of moral panic. The merits of this interpretation of the findings are
considered in chapter seven.

Also relevant here is the theory on "news frames," which was briefly discussed in chapter two. News frames organize reality for both newsmakers
(i.e., journalists) and the audiences that consume news stories (Tuchman,
1978). News frames are contested phenomena rather than objective events.
They involve calling attention to certain aspects of an issue while ignoring or
even obscuring other elements. As previously discussed, the news media rely
heavily on state managers, particularly presidents, to define a problem and to
establish the dominant frame for an issue (Hawdon, 2001; Johnson, Wanta &
Boudreau, 2004; Reinarman & Levine, 1989; Welch, Fenwick & Roberts,
1997). Professional journalists' choice of news frame for a story is also influenced by prior news frames.

The news frame of Saddam Hussein/Iraq as evil was first established by
the administration of President George H. W. Bush, and it then became the
dominant frame in the U.S. news media for the 1990–1991 Persian Gulf war
(Bennett & Paletz, 1994). Because this news frame predated 9/11, it was readily available for recycling and dissemination after the terrorist attacks. From
the perspective of news as frame (Tuchman, 1978), the U.S. news media followed normal journalistic routines after 9/11 and relied on authoritative
G. W. Bush administration sources to define the Iraq issue. The punitive,
pro-war argument of the Bush administration became the dominant news
frame on Iraq, and as a result, that frame defined reality for the majority of the
U.S. public. As argued by Kellner (2005, p. xvi), the "U.S. corporate media
enabled the Bush administration's policy [on Iraq]." Although there were
occasional counterclaims in the news media that disputed the pro-war argument, as demonstrated by the content analysis in this study, the overwhelming news coverage leading up to the invasion of Iraq reflected the "Iraq as
evil" news frame presented by the Bush administration.

Pre-existing news frames can help to explain public support for invading
Iraq, which was manifested even before the attacks of 9/11. The relatively

high pre-9/11 level of public support for invading Iraq was shaped in part by
pervasive, stereotypical framing in the media throughout the 1980s and 1990s
of *all* Arabs (Muslims) as ruthless terrorists, as well as such depictions of the
regime of Saddam Hussein, specifically, during the Persian Gulf war (Bennett &
Paletz, 1994; Merskin, 2004). The framing of Hussein and his followers as
rogue terrorists primed hostile sentiments among Americans even before 9/11.
Additionally, pre-9/11 support for the invasion could be an artifact of the
"unfinished business" of the Persian Gulf war with Iraq—that is, Saddam
Hussein and his followers remained in control after the war ended in 1991.
President George H. W. Bush was widely criticized after the Gulf war for not
removing Saddam Hussein from power (Scheer, 2003). These factors influenced the agenda of President G. W. Bush and provided important antecedents
to the moral panic over Iraq. The significance of these factors is discussed in
chapter seven.

Although public support for invasion increased by only twelve percentage
points over the course of the twenty-four polls, this represents a 23% increase
in concern from February, 2001, to March, 2003. Furthermore, changes in
presidential rhetoric regarding the alleged Iraq threat prior to each of the
twenty-four polls significantly changed the likelihood of support for invasion.
This indicates that public support for war was driven or manufactured by the
policy rhetoric of the Bush administration. Thus, similar to the concern criterion discussed above, consensus is demonstrated in the relationship between
the volume of presidential rhetoric and public opinion. Specifically, increased
numbers of articles with punitive and communitarian rhetoric by the Bush
administration increased the likelihood of support for invading Iraq. As previously noted, by March 15, 2003, just four days prior to the first strikes in the
invasion of Iraq, public support for it had climbed to 64.1%. In fact, public
support increased steadily in the final months before the war. Therefore, the
findings of this study, particularly the results of the news content and public
opinion analyses, establish the consensus criterion of a moral panic.

Before moving on to the third criterion of moral panic, the sizable
minority of the U.S. public that never accepted the Bush administration's
argument for war warrants discussion. There were numerous dissenters
among the U.S. public prior to the war as evidenced by the fact that approximately one-third of Americans did not support the invasion of Iraq (Gallup,
2003). Arguably, those individuals either rejected or were underexposed to
the pro-war argument of the Bush administration that became the dominant
news frame on Iraq. Communication research would suggest that Americans
who did not support the invasion were very likely influenced by counterclaims (i.e., alternative news frames to the pro-war argument) in the general
news media (see Wanta, Golan & Lee, 2004). As previously discussed, alternate news frames on Iraq occasionally appeared in the U.S. news media prior

to the invasion, including claims by the United Nation's chief weapons inspector, Hans Blix, that Iraq did not possess WMD as argued by the Bush administration.

However, such alternate framing of the Iraq issue in the general media was overwhelmed by the dominant, pro-war news frame. As discussed in chapter three, counterclaims were *not* associated with support for invading Iraq in this study once the impact of quotes from President Bush was taken into account. Also, the anti-war news frame was primarily concentrated in the leftist intellectual press, including such publications as *The Nation* and *Mother Jones*. Individuals who rejected the dominant news frame on Iraq in the general press and who were ideologically attuned to the leftist intellectual press were disproportionately exposed to the anti-war argument. From the perspective of news as frame, this group was most likely to oppose the invasion of Iraq (Tuchman, 1978). Also, as discussed in chapter three, it can be theoretically argued (see Nielsen & Bonn, 2008) that increased general media usage at the individual or micro level would predict increased support for the invasion of Iraq, due to greater exposure to the dominant pro-war news frame. Theoretically, therefore, the lightest individual users or consumers of general media (those underexposed to the dominant news frame) should be concentrated among the one-third of Americans who did not support the invasion of Iraq (Chiricos, Eschholz & Gertz 1997). Of course, it must also be stated that there are individuals in society who oppose war under any circumstances for either religious or ideological reasons and would have thus rejected the dominant news frame on Iraq regardless of their level of exposure to it. The lack of unanimity in public attitudes and opinion on the Iraq war is further discussed in chapter six.

*Hostility*

The third criterion of a moral panic identified by Cohen (2002) is hostility or moral outrage toward the social actors or folk devils who embody the problem. As discussed by Goode and Ben-Yehuda (1994, pp. 33–34), folk devils are: "collectively designated as the enemy . . . of respectable society; their behavior is seen as harmful or threatening to the values . . . possibly the very existence of the society . . . and a division is made between 'us' . . . and 'them.' . . . This dichotomization includes *stereotyping*: generating 'folk devils' or villains and folk heroes in this morality play of evil versus good." Cohen (2002) explained that in order to qualify as a moral panic, not only must the condition or behavior be seen as threatening, but a clearly identifiable group must be blamed for the alleged threat to society. This group is first labeled as folk devils through the combined efforts of law enforcement agents, politicians, and the news media, and then it is targeted for punishment or elimination by the same elite institutions.

mass shooters

Following the attacks of 9/11, the administration of George W. Bush framed the political regime of Saddam Hussein as folk devils who posed a serious and growing threat to the national security of the United States (Clarke, 2004; Scheer, 2003). The findings of this study indicate that punitive rhetoric toward Hussein and Iraq was significantly more likely to be used after 9/11, and it was much more likely to be used by Bush administration sources than by nonadministration sources. This was true for President Bush as well as key members of his cabinet such as Defense Secretary Donald Rumsfeld. Consistent with Hawdon (2001), these findings demonstrate that punitive rhetoric used by the U.S. president can define the folk devils in an elite-engineered moral panic.

Immediately after the attacks of 9/11, President Bush began to invoke the word "evil" in his rhetoric toward certain Arab (Muslim) groups, including the political regime of Saddam Hussein in Iraq (Entman, 2003; Rothe & Muzzatti, 2004). The findings of this study reveal that the word "evil" was significantly more likely to be used in reference to Iraq/Saddam Hussein after 9/11 than before the terrorist attacks, and it was much more likely to be used by administration sources, particularly President G. W. Bush, than by nonadministration sources. In addition, the Bush administration used racial stereotypes of Arabs generally as rogue terrorists to demonize Saddam Hussein and his followers (Merskin, 2004). President Bush increasingly used the terms "tyrant" and "madman" after 9/11 in his references to Saddam Hussein. He frequently promised to bring "Saddam Hussein to justice" if he did not "disarm." Furthermore, President Bush used atrocity tales to bolster his case for invading Iraq. In the months leading up to the invasion, for example, Bush frequently referred to atrocities allegedly perpetrated by Saddam Hussein against the Kurds in Iraq, e.g., "Saddam Hussein gassed his own people" (Merskin, 2004). Finally, Bush framed Iraq as part of an "axis of evil" that also included Iran and North Korea (Clark, 2006).

Consistent with the moral panic concept, President Bush reduced the world to a dichotomy after 9/11—that is, a world consisting of "good versus evil" (Rothe & Muzzatti, 2004). The significant danger inherent in this approach, as previously discussed, is that the "evil" label involves a tautological argument that is not subject to debate and cannot be tested or falsified by dissenters. This is because the evil argument relies on circular reasoning to support its claims. For example, when questioned about Iraq leading up to the war, the Bush administration would present the allegedly evil actions of Saddam Hussein and his followers as evidence of their evilness. Clearly, such an argument cannot be empirically tested or falsified.

Furthermore, the U.S. public was highly susceptible to the Bush administration's framing of Iraq as evil after 9/11. As previously discussed, the American public became preoccupied with national security after 9/11 and it was predisposed to support officials who not only offered assurances of security but also demonstrated a willingness to punish its enemies (Welch, 2006a, 2006b). Significantly, many Americans wanted revenge after the terrorist attacks of 9/11 and Iraq represented a familiar enemy to the U.S. public and a convenient, useful target for the Bush administration. The Bush administration's hidden agenda (i.e., actual reasons for invading Iraq) is discussed in chapter seven.

The news content analysis in this study revealed that the Bush administration relied on powerful emotional appeals to the collective anxiety of the U.S. public following 9/11 in their arguments for invading Iraq. For example, President Bush's repeated references to "mushroom clouds" (i.e., nuclear attack) and a "smoking gun" concerning Iraq's alleged involvement in 9/11 established powerful mental images in the public consciousness that primed and fueled anger toward Iraq. As noted by Entman (2003, p. 416), "Reminding the public of the 'evil' helped to maintain their support; merely mentioning the word could cue a whole series of conscious and unconscious thoughts and feelings about September 11." Thus, the use of punitive rhetoric, particularly such words as "evil," "threat," "mad terrorists," and "weapons of mass destruction," combined with atrocity tales and racial stereotypes, defined Saddam Hussein and his followers as folk devils. Such rhetorical framing of the Iraqis by the Bush administration fulfills the hostility criterion of a moral panic (Goode & Ben-Yehuda, 1994; Welch et al., 2002).

*Disproportionality*

The fourth criterion of a moral panic identified by Cohen (2002) is disproportionality. Disproportionality refers to an exaggeration of the objective threat posed to society by the folk devils. This criterion requires evidence that the alleged threat is greater than the actual possibility of harm (Welch et al., 2002). Goode and Ben-Yehuda (1994, p. 36) argued that the disproportionality criterion is met when: "The degree of public concern over the behavior itself, the problem it poses, or condition it creates is far greater than is true for comparable, even more damaging, actions. . . . Clearly, in locating the moral panic, some measure of objective harm must be taken." In other words, the threat or danger alleged to be caused by the behavior in question is incommensurate with and, in fact, is "above and beyond that which a realistic appraisal could sustain" (Davis & Stasz, 1990, p. 129). However, in some cases, particularly when an allegedly threatening condition has not yet manifested, the objective (i.e., quantifiable) level or degree of the threat is difficult to measure (Goode & Ben-Yehuda, 1994). Such is the case regarding Iraq's alleged possession of WMD and the threat it posed to the United States after 9/11. In such instances, Cohen (2002, p. vii) argued that the disproportionality criterion is fulfilled and "the attribution of the moral panic label . . . [is

appropriate when] the 'thing's' extent and significance has been exaggerated
(a) in itself (compared with other more reliable, valid and objective sources)
and/or (b) compared with other, more serious problems."

Arguably, the financial cost of the Iraq war demonstrates disproportionality when compared to federal spending on other objective, life-threatening
conditions facing the United States. By July 2008, more than $540 billion had
already been spent on the war in Iraq and another $135 billion had been
requested by President Bush and approved by Congress for fiscal year
2008–2009 (www.nationalpriorities.org, 2008). The total was increasing at a
rate of more than $340 million per day, more than $10 billion per month and
approximately $130 billion annually. Significantly, these numbers do not
reflect military spending on anything but the Iraq war, so the costs of the war
in Afghanistan, for example, are not included. The massive federal expenditures on the war and occupation of Iraq were occurring despite the fact that
Saddam Hussein never attacked or even threatened to attack the United States
prior to the Bush administration's so-called "preemptive strike" on Iraq in
2003. The United Nations' inspection team had found no WMD in Iraq prior
to the U.S.-led invasion, and its chief weapons inspector, Hans Blix, had
expressed skepticism that they even existed. Thus, nearly three-quarters of a
trillion dollars had been spent by 2008 on a war that was launched on the basis
of presidential rhetoric and propaganda rather than empirical evidence of an
actual threat posed by Iraq.

As the Bush administration launched its unnecessary war of choice on
Iraq, it simultaneously failed to act preemptively and proportionately to
address life-threatening diseases and other social and environmental conditions that represented far greater hazards to U.S. citizens in 2003 than did
Iraq. In comparison to spending on the Iraq war, for example, only $2.5 bil-
lion is spent by the federal government each year on research on heart disease,
the leading cause of death in the United States. Heart disease claims seven
hundred thousand lives annually and costs the United States an estimated
$400 billion in medical expenses and lost productivity (www.infoplease
.com, 2007). Moreover, heart disease affects more than sixty-two million
Americans. Similarly, about $3 billion is spent annually on HIV/AIDS research.
Approximately forty-two thousand people are diagnosed and eighteen thousand people die each year from AIDS in the United States, and nearly one
million Americans have died from AIDS since 1981 (www.avert.org, 2007).
In fact, the annual budget of the National Institute of Health (NIH) for
research on *all* diseases is $30 billion—approximately the same as the cost of
the war and occupation of Iraq every three months (www.americanheart.org,
2007). In addition, cigarette smoking, the leading preventable cause of cancer,
results in an estimated 438,000 deaths (about one of every five) in the United
States each year, including thirty-eight thousand deaths from secondhand

smoke exposure (www.cdc.gov, 2007). Despite the well documented, serious health risks to the public, the sale of cigarettes has not been banned by the federal government, which receives close to $10 billion annually in tax revenue from the sale of cigarettes (www.tobaccofreekids.org, 2007).

The Bush administration also ignored the growing threats posed by global warming. Leading scientists worldwide have argued that global warming has eclipsed other threats to the planet, such as terrorism (Satter, 2007). Stephen Hawking, the renowned cosmologist and mathematician, argues that "terror only kills hundreds or thousands of people. . . . Global warming could kill millions. We should have a war on global warming rather than the war on terror" (Satter, 2007, p. 17A). Despite such warnings, the G. W. Bush administration only grudgingly conceded that global warming even exists and never acknowledged that it is a man-made problem or that it poses a real threat to the United States and the world. Not surprisingly, the Bush administration chose not to join the international community in their efforts to address the problem. In fact, President Bush consistently resisted taking any action to reduce global warming pollution. Instead, the president called for voluntary corporate initiatives to reduce pollution, and "refused to require cuts in heat-trapping carbon dioxide pollution, significantly raise fuel economy requirements, or hold companies accountable for improving their energy efficiency." (www.nrdc.org, 2007).

A former senior official of the Environmental Protection Agency under the Bush administration, Jason Burnett, charged that Vice President Dick Cheney's office was involved in removing statements on health risks posed by global warming from a draft of his testimony to the U.S. Senate in 2007 (Revkin, 2008). The Bush administration apparently did more than just ignore the dangers of global warming. Astonishingly, it concealed evidence of the health risks from the American public. This is an example of the Bush administration deceiving the U.S. public about an objective threat—hiding the truth about global warming—in order to promote its agenda and manipulate public support for an unnecessary war in Iraq. The immorality of such behavior by the Bush administration is discussed in chapter six.

A serious problem that erupted during the Bush administration was the housing and mortgage crisis that affected millions of U.S. families. The United States was facing a serious credit and mortgage crisis by mid-2008. Global recession, a staggering federal budget deficit, the declining value of the U.S. dollar, soaring energy prices, and plunging real estate values put millions of Americans at risk of losing their homes (D. Baker, 2008). Widespread defaults and foreclosures were occurring as millions of Americans owed more on their mortgages than their homes were worth. To put it in perspective, the more than $8 trillion U.S. housing market was deflating at an annual rate of −25% by July 2008, and 11% of home mortgages faced foreclosure (D. Baker,

2008). At the same time, nearly 15% of the U.S. population was living below the federal poverty level in 2008. In fact, the number of people living in poverty in the United States increased by nearly six million during the G. W. Bush presidential administration. Those living in poverty cannot afford to purchase housing even when economic conditions are good, let alone when the economy is in decline. Throughout the two terms of the Bush administration, the poorest families in the United States found it nearly impossible to locate affordable rental housing, as well. Spending on the Iraq war by 2008 could have provided mortgage relief and affordable rental housing opportunities for literally millions of suffering American families (D. Baker, 2008).

Finally, the U.S. public faced a serious health care crisis during the Bush administration. Nearly fifty million Americans (or approximately 17% of the population) were without any form of health insurance by 2007 (www.nchc .org, 2007). The problem worsened throughout the Bush administration as the number of uninsured in the United States increased by nearly eight million between 2000 and 2007 (www.nchc.org, 2007). Latinos, the largest racial or ethnic minority group in the United States, representing 16% of the population, were particularly affected by the U.S. health care crisis. Approximately 25% of all Latino American citizens have no medical insurance. The number of uninsured Latinos in the United States is even higher if one adds undocumented workers to the total. If the $540 billion spent on the Iraq war as of July 2008 was allocated instead to health care in the United States, nearly 160 million Americans could have been insured—that is, more than half of the total U.S. population and more than three times the number uninsured in the United States (www.nationalpriorities.org, 2008). Even the $135 billion allocated to extend the war through fiscal year 2008–2009 would have provided health coverage for nearly forty million Americans, or 80% of the uninsured.

The Bush administration's excessive spending on the Iraq war compared to its spending on far more serious and life-threatening problems facing the United States demonstrates the disproportionality criterion of moral panic. In addition, the disproportionality criterion is supported by the findings of this research study. Specifically, the findings demonstrate that increased presidential rhetoric in the news and increased public support for invasion both occurred without any documented aggressive action or threat from Iraq prior to the start of the war. Although the United States was never directly threatened or provoked by Iraq, President G. W. Bush declared that an invasion was necessary in March of 2003 in order to "disarm Iraq . . . and to defend the world from grave danger" (Scheer, 2003, p. 1). Bush argued that the invasion was warranted because Saddam Hussein/Iraq threatened the United States and the world with the most horrible weapons known to mankind. As the findings of the study revealed, public support for war mirrored the Bush administration's rhetoric (particularly punitive and communitarian tones of rhetoric) in the final months before the invasion, as both increased steadily despite a lack of provocation from Iraq. In summary, disproportionality is demonstrated by increased antagonism toward Iraq among the American public and support for war, which was manufactured by inflammatory presidential rhetoric after 9/11 in the absence of an objective threat from Iraq. Disproportionality is further demonstrated by the Bush administration's massive spending on the unnecessary Iraq war relative to serious social problems and health risks facing the U.S. public.

### Volatility

The fifth and final criterion of a moral panic outlined by Cohen (2002) is volatility. Goode and Ben-Yehuda (1994, p. 38) stated that "by their very nature, moral panics are *volatile*; they erupt fairly suddenly (although they may lie dormant or latent for long periods of time, and may reappear from time to time) and, nearly as suddenly, subside." Regardless of its long-term impact, the fever pitch that characterizes a society during a moral panic is not typically sustainable over a long period of time. Moral panics are thus similar to a "fad" or "craze" and are relatively short-lived (Goode & Ben-Yehuda, 1994).

Although the suddenness of the moral panic over Iraq can be debated, volatility is demonstrated in the study by the ebb and flow of both media coverage and public concern regarding Iraq over time. Regarding news coverage, as previously noted, the content analysis of articles published between March 1, 2000, and March 18, 2003, in the *New York Times* revealed that more than a thousand articles contained direct quotes or policy rhetoric regarding Iraq from either the president's administration or other key sources during that period. This represents an average of thirty articles per month (or one per day) throughout the three-year period. However, the monthly average more than tripled to 105 articles with direct quotes concerning Iraq during the six months immediately preceding the March 2003 invasion (an average of 3.5 articles per day or a 350% increase). Therefore, consistent with the moral panic literature (Hawdon, 2001; Welch et al., 2002), news coverage increased dramatically as the moral panic approached its zenith.

The degree of public support for the war in Iraq fluctuated over time. Slightly more than half of Americans favored invading Iraq even before the terrorist attacks of 9/11. The relatively high level of pre-9/11 support for invading Iraq is consistent with the moral panic literature. As argued by Goode and Ben-Yehuda (1994, p. 39): "To describe moral panics as volatile and short-lived does not mean that they do not have *structural* or *historical* antecedents. The specific issue that generates a particular moral panic may have done so in the past, perhaps even the not-so-distant past" (emphases added). Important structural and historical antecedents of the moral panic over Iraq include popular-culture stereotypes and prior news framing of Arabs as rogue terrorists, the legacy of the Persian Gulf war and the Bush family's Middle East oil connections and businesses that facilitated and shaped two U.S. presidencies. These important topics are discussed in chapter seven.

As explained in chapter three, the twenty-four pre-war Gallup polls used in this study reveal that public support for invading Iraq ranged from a low of 52.5% in February 2001 to a high of 64.1% in March 2003. Although the actual increase in public support was modest—twelve percentage points—it represents a +23% change in public support overall. Moreover, and consistent with the moral panic concept, public support for the invasion did not steadily increase throughout the twenty-four polls. In fact, public support for the invasion actually decreased in eleven of the polls relative to the one immediately preceding it. Importantly, from a moral panic perspective, public support for war mirrored the ebb and flow of news media coverage of the issue.

As previously discussed, the Bush administration had promised a quick victory in Iraq prior to the invasion. In an infamous gaffe, President Bush declared, "Mission accomplished," while wearing an aviator's flight suit onboard an aircraft carrier on May 1, 2003, just after the fall of Baghdad. Not only was the declaration of victory grossly incorrect but violence escalated for more than four years in Iraq following the initial invasion, and the annual injury and death toll of U.S. military personnel actually peaked in 2007. Contrary to President Bush's prewar predictions, the violence, injury, and death due to the war in Iraq continued at a reduced but steady pace until he left office in January of 2009.

By late 2003, it was already apparent that there would be no quick victory in Iraq. As the U.S. death toll mounted and a civil war erupted in Iraq, the U.S. news media were obliged to present the tragic events as they unfolded there, although the Bush administration forbade the media to present visual images of returning dead American soldiers in their flag-covered coffins. Decades earlier, such visual imagery had helped to erode the American public's support for the Vietnam war, and the Bush administration apparently did not intend to let that happen to their war in Iraq. However, despite the Bush administration's attempts to control the flow of information to the public, evidence of its prewar deceptions concerning Iraq began to appear in the news media in 2004 (Kellner, 2005). Also, grotesque images of U.S. soldiers torturing Iraqi detainees at the infamous Abu Ghraib prison appeared in the news media in 2004, and those images damaged the Bush administration's credibility and moral authority on the war. Significantly, the news frames on Iraq began to change as conditions there worsened, as the U.S. death toll mounted, and in particular, as the Bush administration's prewar deceptions concerning the Iraqi threat were revealed.

The large fluctuations in public support for the war over time were driven by the ebb and flow of events that transpired in Iraq and, most importantly, by the news framing of those same events by the major media. Just prior to the "shock and awe" missile attack on Iraq, public support for the invasion peaked, with nearly two-thirds of Americans in favor of it. However, by January 2006, just less than three years later, 51% of the U.S. public believed the war in Iraq was a mistake, and 53% believed the Bush administration deliberately misled the American public about Iraq's possession of WMD (Moore, 2006). By December of 2006, almost two-thirds (62%) of the U.S. public believed that the war was a mistake (Hutcheson, 2006). Interestingly, the percentage of Americans who supported the invasion of Iraq at the start of the war was almost identical to the percentage who believed the war was a mistake four years later. Also, by September 2007, nearly half (49%) of the American public also believed that the war in Iraq had actually made the United States less safe from terrorism (Blow, 2008).

Similarly, President Bush's job approval rating fluctuated greatly over time. Riding the emotional tide of patriotism following the terrorist attacks of 9/11, his approval rating was 71% at the start of the Iraq war (Blow, 2008). By March 2008, five years after he launched the invasion of Iraq, Bush's job approval rating had plummeted to 31%. Interestingly, the forty-point drop in popularity experienced by President G. W. Bush was almost identical to the drop experienced by President Lyndon B. Johnson during the Vietnam war (Blow, 2008). In summary, the fluctuations in both presidential approval and public support for the Iraq war, which mirrored fluctuations in the volume of news coverage and the news framing of the Iraq war, demonstrate the volatility criterion of a moral panic.

## ADDITIONAL EVIDENCE OF AN
## ELITE-ENGINEERED MORAL PANIC

An examination of prewar events and the facts made public since the invasion of Iraq in 2003 help to further establish the five criteria of a moral panic. By July of 2008, more than five years after the invasion and occupation began, no weapons of mass destruction had been found, and the Senate Intelligence Committee had reported that, in all likelihood, there never were any WMD in Iraq, which is exactly what the U.N. weapons inspectors had said before the invasion (Sniffen, 2007). The same Senate panel report also stated that there never was a relationship between Iraq and Osama Bin Laden's al Qaeda network. In fact, Saddam Hussein was "distrustful" of, and felt threatened by, Osama Bin Laden. Conversely, Osama Bin Laden considered Saddam Hussein to be a corrupt Muslim whom he despised (Strobel & Talev, 2006). In an interview on CBS's *60 Minutes* in March 2004, former counterterrorism czar under the Bush administration, Richard Clarke, stated, "There's absolutely no evidence that Iraq was supporting al Qaeda, ever." In other words, Saddam Hussein and Iraq had no involvement in the attacks of 9/11, which were solely orchestrated by al Qaeda, despite the Bush administration's persistent claims to the contrary in its prewar campaign for invading Iraq.

A formal investigation by the U.S. Senate also concluded that the Bush administration had used false information to mislead the public about Iraq. In 2006, the Senate Intelligence Committee reported that the Bush administration had used faulty intelligence assessments to justify invading Iraq, and furthermore, the administration knew in 2002 that the intelligence was faulty, based on repeated warnings from the C.I.A. and Pentagon, but used it anyway in their march toward war (Strobel & Talev, 2006). Senator Jay Rockefeller, vice chairperson of the Senate Intelligence Committee, said, "The [Bush] administration ignored warnings prior to the war about the veracity of the intelligence it trumpeted publicly to support its case that Iraq was an imminent threat to the security of the United States" (Strobel & Talev, 2006, p. 16A). For example, President Bush's claim in his 2003 State of the Union address that "Iraq was trying to buy uranium in Africa for nuclear weapons," which became a key justification for the invasion two months later, turned out to be untrue (Sniffen, 2007, p. 6A).

By 2002, the Bush administration was fixated on gathering evidence that would support its policy argument for war with Iraq (Clark, 2006). However, the quality and credibility of the sources—and even the validity of the information obtained from those sources—was relatively unimportant to the Bush administration. This conclusion is supported by the famous "Downing Street memo" which contained the minutes of a secret meeting of senior British officials during July of 2002 in which they discussed U.S. foreign policy concerning Iraq. Leaked to the U.K. press in 2005, the memo quoted Sir Richard Dearlove, the head of the British Secret Intelligence Service, as saying that "[President] Bush wanted to remove Saddam through military action . . . the intelligence and facts were being fixed around the policy" [of eliminating Hussein]. In other words, British officials knew in 2002 that the Bush administration was manufacturing evidence to justify an invasion of Iraq.

The Center for Public Integrity, a research group that focuses on ethics in government and public policy, has studied transcripts and documents written by the Bush administration prior to the invasion of Iraq and has identified "at least 935 false statements" on hundreds of occasions, particularly that Iraq had massive stockpiles of WMD and terrorist links to al Qaeda (www .publicintegrity.org, 2008). Their findings reveal that even after the invasion, when a consensus emerged that the prewar intelligence assessments were incorrect, Bush administration officials doggedly argued that WMD would still be found. The Center for Public Integrity also discovered evidence that post-invasion statements by the Bush administration grossly contradicted the so-called intelligence that it trumpeted prior to the start of the war. For example, President Bush said in 2005 that "much of the intelligence turned out to be wrong" but that "it was right to remove Saddam Hussein from power" (www.publicintegrity.org, 2008). The Bush administration apparently had no problem rewriting history to fit its agenda when current events required it to do so.

A 170-page final report issued by the Senate Select Committee on Intelligence in the spring of 2008 accused President G. W. Bush, Vice President Dick Cheney, Secretary of Defense Donald Rumsfeld, and other top officials of repeatedly overstating the Iraqi threat in "the emotional aftermath of the attacks of September 11, 2001" (Mazzetti & Shane, 2008). This 2008 report effectively ended a five-year investigation into the Bush administration's pre-war claims and actions regarding Iraq. Endorsed by both Democrats and Republicans in the Senate, the report concluded that President Bush and his top aides built the public case for war against Iraq by exaggerating the available intelligence and by deliberately ignoring disagreements among spy agencies about Iraq's weapons programs and Saddam Hussein's alleged links to al Qaeda (Mazzetti & Shane, 2008).

This report supports the first proposition of this book. Specifically, it demonstrates that the war in Iraq was based on a "massive extrapolation from an unrelated, if dramatic, event [i.e., the terrorist attacks of 9/11] and on a systematic, extravagant, and fanciful exaggeration of a threat that was of very questionable magnitude" (Mueller, 2006, p. 135). Such post-invasion debunking of the Bush administration's so-called evidence against Iraq, including formal congressional charges of deception, further establishes the key criteria of a moral panic, particularly hostility and disproportionality.

In the years since the Iraq war began, former Bush administration loyalists have also spoken out against it, claiming that it was a mistake and that the objective threat to the United States was grossly exaggerated by the administration after 9/11 in order to gain popular support for the invasion. For example, Richard Perle, the former Bush administration confidante and valued advisor, who is "regarded as the intellectual godfather of the Iraq war," has stated that the invasion was a mistake and "at the end of the day, you have to hold the president responsible" (Spiegel, 2006, p. A11). For such a Bush loyalist and leading neoconservative strategist to break ranks with the administration is almost unimaginable. In addition, Richard Clarke (2004), who served as chief counterterrorism advisor under both Bill Clinton and George W. Bush (until January 2003), has charged that both before and after the attacks of 9/11, many in the Bush administration were distracted from efforts against Osama Bin Laden's al Qaeda organization by a "preoccupation" with Iraq and Saddam Hussein. He has further charged that on September 12, 2001, President Bush pulled him aside and "testily" asked him to try to find evidence that Saddam Hussein was connected to the attacks that had occurred just twenty-four hours prior. Clarke (2004) has also stated that senior Bush administration officials, particularly Paul Wolfowitz, then deputy secretary of defense under Donald Rumsfeld, began to publicly link Iraq to the attacks of 9/11 within forty-eight hours of those events.

Another former insider who has harshly criticized both President Bush and Vice President Cheney on the Iraq war is Lawrence Wilkerson, who was chief of staff to then Secretary of State Colin Powell from 2002 through 2005. Wilkerson has stated that the Bush administration fabricated evidence to make its case for invading Iraq and that the U.S. public was duped into supporting the war (www.cnn.com, 2005). Wilkerson says his involvement in Powell's infamous presentation to the United Nations General Assembly on Iraq's alleged refusal to surrender its WMD was "the lowest point" in his life (www.cnn.com, 2005, para. 1). Colin Powell's speech, delivered to the U.N. on February 5, 2003, just three weeks prior to the invasion, made the case for war by presenting U.S. intelligence that purported to prove beyond any reasonable doubt that Iraq had WMD. The evidence presented by Powell that day has since been discredited or completely debunked. Wilkerson states that the so-called evidence in Secretary Powell's presentation came from a document he described as "unsourced" and "sort of a Chinese menu from which you pick and choose," which was supplied to Powell by the White House (www.cnn.com, 2005, para. 2).

More recently, Wilkerson has charged that President Bush and Vice President Cheney are guilty of "high crimes and misdemeanors" concerning the Iraq war which should have been the basis for their impeachment (www .rawstory.com, 2007, p. 1). Wilkerson's charges (www.rawstory.com, 2007, p. 2) are based on his observation that President Bush and Vice President Cheney deliberately deceived the U.S. public about the threat posed by Iraq: "I think we went into this war for specious reasons. I think we went into this war not too much unlike the way we went into the Spanish American War with the Hearst press essentially goading the American public and the leadership into war. That was a different time in a different culture, in a different America. We're in a very different place today and I think we essentially got goaded into the war through some of the same means." Additionally, Wilkerson has stated that President Bush and Vice President Cheney did not know how to create accountability in their administration. In all likelihood, Bush and Cheney had no desire to encourage accountability because to do so would have limited their ability to abuse their official powers. In other words, if there had been accountability in the Bush administration, then the Iraq war would almost certainly have never have happened.

Even Scott McClellan, the former White House press secretary (2003–2006), who was long considered to be one of President G. W. Bush's most loyal assistants, has been harshly critical of his old boss. Although he was once the keeper of the party flame, McClellan (2008) now argues that the president was "not open and forthright" about the war and that the Bush administration relied on "propaganda" and "manipulating" public opinion in the run-up to the invasion of Iraq. McClellan (2008, p. 10) further states that President Bush "convinces himself to believe what suits his needs at the moment" and engages in "self-deception" to justify his political ends. In hindsight, McClellan says he came to view the Iraq war as a mistake by a president and advisors who were caught up in a grand and misguided plan to promote democracy in the Middle East by overturning Saddam Hussein's regime. McClellan (2008) says that President Bush and his aides became so wrapped up in pushing the argument for war that they simply ignored or attempted to debunk intelligence that did not support that argument. McClellan's disenchantment with the Bush administration upon learning that he had been deceived by his former boss is further discussed in chapter six.

These former Bush administration insiders and loyalists have provided powerful and persuasive accounts of the deceptions employed in the buildup to war. Their involvement or direct access to the Bush inner circle makes their charges against the administration even more compelling. Some of them, such as Scott McClellan, have been criticized for "cashing in" and telling their stories in exchange for lucrative publishing deals. This may be true but that does not mean their charges are incorrect. In response to McClellan, for example, the Bush administration did not deny his allegations. Instead, the Bush administration simply stated that the accusations in his book were "disturbing" and "not the Scott we knew." The accusations of these insiders confirm that the alleged threat was grossly exaggerated, if not fully fabricated, by the Bush administration prior to the invasion of Iraq. The testimonies of these former Bush administration loyalists, combined with other facts and information made public since the invasion, such as the final Senate Intelligence Committee report, help to establish the key criteria of a moral panic including concern, hostility, and disproportionality. Furthermore, that same post-invasion information bolsters an argument that a moral panic over Iraq was contrived by the Bush administration and fueled by the general media's overwhelming reliance on the "Iraq as evil" news frame in its reporting prior to the war.

## CONCLUSION

In order to be effective, any sales message must be repeated. As media critic Norman Solomon (www.usa.mediamonitors.net, 2006, p. 1) wrote: "Whether you are selling food from McDonald's or cars from General Motors or a war from the U.S. government, repetition is crucial for making propaganda stick. Bush's promoters will never tire of depicting the war on Iraq as a war on terrorism (and linking it to 9/11). And they certainly appreciate the ongoing assists from the news media." The findings of this research study fulfill the five criteria of a moral panic. Also, the actions of the Bush administration and the news media, and their combined influences on public opinion leading up to the invasion of Iraq, constitute an elite-engineered moral panic as conceptually defined (Goode & Ben-Yehuda, 1994). Based on the findings, it is reasonable to conclude that the first theoretical proposition is correct: The war in Iraq was legitimized by a moral panic engineered by the Bush administration, and fueled by the news media, over a nonobjective threat posed by the regime of Saddam Hussein. This threat was socially constructed through presidential rhetoric that was mass disseminated through the general news media.

Consistent with the news net perspective (Tuchman, 1978), an unwitting news media were complicit in the deception of the U.S. public by relying on the Bush administration to establish the pro-war news frame on Iraq that dominated the coverage leading up to the invasion. Stated differently, and to paraphrase former White House Chief of Staff Andy Card, the Bush administration's marketing campaign for the Iraq war, although false, deceptive, and coercive, was well timed and highly effective. In the next chapter, Millsian sociology on the higher immorality of the power elite is presented. Sociological perspectives on state crime and war crime are presented as well.

CHAPTER 5

# The Power Elite, State Crime, and War Crime

IN THIS CHAPTER the theoretical and methodological approaches used to examine the second of two central propositions in this book are discussed. The second proposition is: The Bush administration participated in elite deviance, state crimes, and war crimes. More specifically, the moral panic engineered by the Bush administration constitutes elite deviance, including moral harm to society, and the invasion and occupation of Iraq are state crimes and violations of international criminal law.

This proposition raises two related questions. First, by what standards can the actions of the Bush administration concerning Iraq be considered elite deviance? Second, by what standards can those same actions be considered either state crime or war crime? In this chapter the theoretical perspectives and specific evaluation criteria necessary to answer these two questions are presented. The chapter begins by explaining that the Bush administration's rhetoric and actions concerning Iraq after 9/11 will be examined from the perspective of Millsian sociology on the "higher immorality of the power elite" (Mills, 1956). This perspective facilitates an examination of whether the Bush administration committed elite deviance as contended. Later in the chapter, it is explained that the March 2003 invasion of Iraq (a sovereign nation that neither threatened nor provoked the United States) will be analyzed through the lens of state crime (see Kramer, Michalowski & Rothe, 2005). The chapter concludes by explaining that the invasion and occupation of Iraq will also be evaluated as war crimes in violation of international law, as defined by the Geneva Conventions of 1949, the Nuremberg Charter, and as prosecuted by the International Criminal Court in The Hague, Netherlands.

## THE HIGHER IMMORALITY OF THE POWER ELITE

An examination of the G. W. Bush administration's moral panic over Iraq from the Millsian perspective of elite wrongdoing (Mills, 1956; Simon, 2002) is the first step in testing the second proposition advanced in this book. Mills stated that acts of elite deviance that cause social harm, regardless of their criminality in a legal sense, are part of the higher immorality of the power elite. This begs a question. Just who are the power elite?

Mills (1956) observed that a small group of wealthy and powerful individuals controlled America's dominant institutions (i.e., political, economic, and military). More specifically, the governing elite in the United States are comprised of: (1) the highest political leaders, including the president and a few key cabinet members and advisors; (2) major corporate owners and directors; and (3) the highest ranking military officers. Mills called this group the power elite. Although the power elite constitute a close-knit group, these individuals are not part of a grand conspiracy that secretly manipulates world events in order to pursue their own diabolical self-interests. It is not a dictatorship and it does not rely on the physical torture of fellow citizens in order to maintain its dominant position in society. Significantly, the power elite do not have to resort to such extreme measures. Because of their control over the key institutions in U.S. society, including the mass media, the power elite need not resort to harsh physical coercion in order to promote their interests and achieve their goals.

Membership in the power elite, despite its relatively small size, is not closed to outsiders. Also, some of the power elite gain their status due at least in part to being born into prominent families. An example of this is President George W. Bush, the son of a wealthy oilman and former U.S. president. Bill Gates, the founder of Microsoft, leveraged family wealth and social connections to achieve elite status through business entrepreneurship. Another prominent contemporary member of the power elite group is Dick Cheney. He has held key positions in the federal government, including White House chief of staff under Gerald Ford, secretary of defense under George H. W. Bush and vice president under G. W. Bush. Cheney has also held key corporate positions, including chairman of Halliburton, a leading U.S. military contractor that now controls the pumping of oil and operates the pipelines in Iraq. Regardless of personal histories, Mills (1956) argued that membership in the power elite is limited to those few individuals in society who effectively control its political, economic, and military institutions. Interestingly, Mills was echoed in 1961 by President Eisenhower in his farewell address when he warned of the self-serving acts of the "military-industrial complex"—that is, his term for the power elite (Simon, 1995).

What really binds the power elite to one another are their mutual interests, social networks, and the adoption of elite ideology and values (Mills, 1956). The importance of social networks cannot be overstated for it is in those powerful, yet informal, networks that bonds are formed, elite values learned, and heritage shared (Falcon & Melendez, 2001). Although diversity is increasing in the United States, as demonstrated by the presidency of Barack

Obama, the majority of the power elite are still white, Anglo-Saxon, Protestant males. Members of the power elite attend the same private schools and universities, join the same clubs and fraternities, belong to the same churches and charities, and live in the same neighborhoods. They work and play together and they employ one another. White elites enjoy broad-based, informal social networks that provide access to information and referrals that result in preferential employment opportunities (Falcon & Melendez, 2001). Once inside of those formal organizations, privileged, white males are sponsored to the top of the hierarchy by older, white male mentors. This phenomenon, known as "homosocial reproduction," refers to the tendency of a homogeneous organization to reproduce itself by continually promoting the same types of individuals (Kanter, 1993). This process tends to exclude women and minorities while protecting the dominant white male status quo in the United States. The consequences of homosocial reproduction are profound because elite, white social networks ensure that the concentration of power and control over the key institutions of society remain in the hands of the privileged few.

A central contradiction of the power elite is that they frequently violate the very laws they are sworn to uphold. Why would individuals who are entrusted to occupy the "top command posts of society" (Mills, 1956) break the laws they help to create? Mills argued that bound by mutual interests, the power elite periodically commit acts of elite wrongdoing (e.g., dumping toxic waste) and enact policies (e.g., declaration of war) that are designed to perpetuate their power and to preserve their control over society. Mills stated that elite acts that cause either physical or social harm represent the higher immorality of the power elite. Mills argued that not only crime per se, but also governmental deeds that cause social harm, regardless of their criminality in a legal sense, should be included in the conceptual definition. Simon (2002) expanded upon Mills's concept of the higher immorality to include immoral or unethical acts in his concept of "elite deviance." He called such acts "moral harms": "Moral harms are the deviant behavior of elites (people who head governmental or corporate institutions) that form a negative role model that encourages deviance, distrust, cynicism, and/or alienation among non-elites" (Simon, 2002, p. 35).

Simon (1995, pp. 57–58) argued that "these violations [i.e., acts of elite deviance] take place in part because of the way corporate, political, and military intelligence institutions are structured: they are bureaucracies. Significantly, bureaucratic organizations are structured in ways that regularize crime and deviance." More specifically, bureaucracies are goal-oriented, amoral entities that exist to maximize profits and/or expand their own power. These goals encourage an *ends over means* mentality among the top commanders of bureaucracies. For example, the top executives of a public, for-profit corporation are well aware that the board of directors and shareholders are much more interested in meeting quarterly profit goals than they are in the actual decisions and actions required to meet those goals.

The higher immorality of the power elite is also possible because the elites do not have to win the moral consent of those over whom they hold power (Mills, 1956). Instead, a passive majority in society generally trusts that the few elites will act in the best interests of non-elites. Mills argued that this situation is fostered by anti-intellectualism and a fear of knowledge among the masses in modern society. As noted by critical theorists, an over-reliance or dependency on television news "sound bites" and media-disseminated elite rhetoric results in alienation among the masses, which can be exploited by the elites. In fact, Mills (1956, p. 355) foreshadowed Chomsky (2002) when he stated that "manipulation [of public opinion] and undebated decisions of power [have] replace[d] democratic authority" in contemporary society. Thus, Mills (1956, p. 343) concluded that the higher immorality is a "systematic feature of the American elite." Indeed, its general acceptance by the masses without critique is an essential feature of modern U.S. society.

As explained by critical criminology, the harmful actions of the power elite are generally not defined as criminal because they (the power elite) have control over the major institutions in U.S. society, including the criminal justice system (Chambliss, 1975). According to critical criminology, those in power define their deeds as normative while they define the actions of the powerless as deviant or criminal. Chambliss argued that "one way to resolve [human] conflicts . . . is to define some groups or classes of people as less than human" (1975, p. 151). The marginalization and stigmatization of disvalued individuals or groups helps to reinforce the superior position of those in power in society and helps to justify their actions. This argument finds support in the critical school's assertion that societal elites—i.e., those who control the technology of mass communication—manufacture the official governing ideology. This ideology includes definitions of right and wrong and also proclaims who is either good or evil. In short, the power elite both define who and what is criminal *and* also control the selective enforcement of those definitions.

Mills (1956) also argued that there is a profound lack of intellectual cultivation by political elites in modern society. In such an environment, political rhetoric or propaganda has supplanted intellectual debate (Chomsky, 2002). It has been long argued, for example, that President G. W. Bush actively discouraged intellectual debate among his key advisors throughout his administration (McClellan, 2008). Given the tremendous volume of Bush administration rhetoric or propaganda that preceded the U.S. invasion and occupation of Iraq, as well as Bush's aggressive rhetoric directed at Iran and North Korea, the insights offered by Mills five decades ago remain valid today. Mills's concept of the higher immorality of the power elite, as expanded by Simon (2002) into elite deviance, offers a compelling theoretical framework for examining the effects of a Bush administration-engineered moral panic in U.S. society.

Although the power elite are bound by mutual interests and social networks, they frequently squabble among themselves, as any hotly contested presidential election or corporate merger will demonstrate. According to Mills (1956), however, these differences are relatively minor and vastly overshadowed by a fundamental agreement on a "world view." This world view is comprised by a set of values, beliefs, and attitudes that shape and galvanize the power elite's agenda and prevent deep divisions from arising among them. In other words, the power elite have a set of shared global values, such as the expansion of Western capitalism, that trump minor differences and serve to unite them. Mills (1956, p. 276) explained that the "power elite is . . . frequently in some tension: it comes together only on certain coinciding points and only on certain occasions of 'crisis.'" In chapter six, it is argued that the Bush administration's framing of Iraq as a growing threat to the national security of the United States created such a crisis, and its engineering of a moral panic over Iraq can be understood as a manifestation of the higher immorality of the power elite.

Mills (1956) noted that the power elite establish the governing policy agenda in such vital areas as foreign policy and national security in the United States. This is because the power elite are the authors of the governing ideology in society. Mills also observed that the power elite have either direct or indirect control over the mass media that help to shape society's perceptions of the world. The power elite's framing of policy issues often becomes the dominant news frame on those issues due to the media's reliance on political leaders as news sources (Tuchman, 1978). Thus, the dominant news frame on important social problems in the media generally reflects the power elite's interests, agenda, and desired outcomes. Because the dominant news frame on an issue also defines reality for the majority of the audience, the general public does not directly influence the nature or content of fundamental polices, including the decision to declare war. As a result, the public's role in the policy-making process in modern U.S. society is largely symbolic—that is, voting in elections every two or four years (Mills, 1956). In summary, the Millsian lens of higher immorality facilitates an analysis of the *effects* of the Bush administration's elite-engineered moral panic over Iraq on the U.S. public. In chapter six, an argument is presented that the moral panic over Iraq created moral harm to U.S. society in the form of cynicism, fear, and alienation. Moreover, it is argued that the moral panic led to an unprovoked and unnecessary invasion of a foreign country.

## STATE CRIME

The second theoretical proposition also contends that President G. W. Bush and key members of his administration, including Vice President Dick Cheney and Secretary of Defense Donald Rumsfeld, participated in state crime. More specifically, it is argued that the March 2003 invasion and subsequent occupation of Iraq, which resulted from a Bush administration-engineered moral panic, constitute *state crimes* as defined in the scholarly literature. However, this raises an important question. Specifically, what is the definition of state crime? The answer to this question is not straightforward.

As argued by Clinard, Quinney, and Wildeman (1994, p. 145), "Governmental crime is difficult to analyze and define." They offer several reasons to support this conclusion. First, the traditional conceptualization of the government or state as the author and enforcer of the law tends to preclude the notion of the state as a law violator. Given the classical idea that the state is sovereign over the people, it logically follows that the state is above the law. From this perspective, the state's authority and obligation are to oversee and control the actions of the people and not itself (Clinard et al., 1994). As noted by Rothe and Friedrichs (2006, p. 150), the common argument was that "governments and their agencies do not commit crimes, but only because the criminal law does not take cognizance of them as criminal actors." As a result, both classical and contemporary criminologists have tended to focus on crimes *against* the state, as opposed to crimes *by* the state (Chambliss, 1975).

The second reason that state crime is difficult to analyze and define is that much governmental crime is shielded from the view of the public, and it is even shielded from the view of other supposed watchdog branches of government (Clinard et al., 1994). As noted by Simon (2002), illegal acts of the government are frequently the subject of elaborate cover-ups (e.g., President Nixon and the Watergate scandal) and lengthy investigations. Furthermore, state elites utilize the best defense attorneys, public relations firms, as well as scapegoats to protect or buffer themselves from scrutiny and/or prosecution. In addition, executive privilege and national security concerns are often invoked by governmental elites in order to justify their withholding of information not only from the public but also from the Congress and the judiciary (Simon, 1995). An example of this involved a declaration of executive privilege by President G. W. Bush and his refusal to let his political advisor, Karl Rove, comply with a Senate Judiciary Committee subpoena requiring Rove to testify under oath regarding his role in the alleged politically motivated firing of nine federal prosecutors in 2006 and 2007.

A third reason for the difficulty in analyzing and defining state crime is that the mass media also play a role in restricting information on such activities to the public. As previously discussed, the news media rely overwhelmingly on information they are provided with by governmental elites to define social problems (Tuchman, 1978; Clinard et al., 1994). In addition, Welch, Fenwick, and Roberts (1997) demonstrated that the relationship between state managers and the news media is symbiotic because state officials define crime for journalists at the same time they promote their own institutional agendas. Moreover, numerous studies suggest that political elites (especially presidents) and the news media play prominent roles in the construction of social problems and, as a result, in the generation and shaping of public concern and policy preferences regarding those problems (Beckett, 1994; Hawdon, 2001; Johnson, Wanta & Boudreau, 2004; Reinarman & Levine, 1989; Rothe & Muzzatti, 2004). Simon (2002) argued that this situation is exacerbated by the tremendous concentration of media ownership in the hands of a few giant conglomerates such as General Electric and Disney. More specifically, the major media conglomerates have powerful regulatory and profitability incentives to divert public attention away from their own infractions by deliberately ignoring elite deviance in their news coverage. By doing so, the major media conglomerates reinforce stereotypes and the status quo in society by portraying crime as largely a problem of the lower classes.

Because of these obstacles, the scholarly study of crimes of the state is relatively new to the field of criminology. Also, given that the interest in this topic is relatively new, much of the scholarly work has focused on simply defining state crime. Chambliss (1989) introduced the concept of "state-organized crime" in his frequently cited 1988 presidential address to the American Society of Criminology (ASC). Chambliss (1989, p. 184) characterized state-organized crime as "acts defined by laws as criminal and committed by state officials [actors] in pursuit of their jobs as representatives of the state." As argued by Kramer et al. (2005, p. 54), this definition has three important characteristics:

> First, it directs attention to the structural and organizational basis of state crime by emphasizing that these crimes are committed by state officials in furtherance of the organizational goals of the state. Second, it proposes that analyses of state crime must be grounded in a legal framework that enables us to clearly distinguish between legitimate and illegal uses of state power in the furtherance of state goals. Third, it relies on a conventional definition of law as legal prohibitions established by the nation-state in which the alleged crime was committed.

By choosing to define and discuss state-organized crime in his 1988 ASC presidential address, Chambliss used an important scholarly platform to present a powerful argument that state crime was a legitimate topic for criminological study. Chambliss was not the first, however, to call for more criminological attention to crimes of either the privileged and/or of the state.

Writing a few years prior to Chambliss's ASC address, another conflict theorist, Austin Turk (1982), examined the nature of political crime. He attempted to explain how and under what circumstances *international criminal law* prevails when political crimes are perpetrated by the state. Also, Sutherland's (1949) groundbreaking book on white collar crime arguably paved the way for the study of state crime despite the fact that he did not address crimes of the state per se. Significantly, Sutherland (1949) called attention to an overlooked but important area of crime—that is, crimes of privileged individuals within the context of legitimate occupations, and the crimes of corporations. As noted by Rothe and Friedrichs (2006, p. 149), Sutherland's "extension of the concept of crime *beyond its conventional parameters* did provide an important foundation, built upon by many later scholars, for the establishment of a criminology of crimes of the state" (emphasis added).

There has been a recent increase in scholarly interest in the definition, explanation, and control of state crime, particularly since the 1990s (Hogan, Long, Stretesky & Lynch, 2006). For example, Kauzlarich, Mullins, and Matthews (2003, p. 241) argued that state crime is "an explicit and distinct action by a state for the furtherance of its organizational goals which violates law or produces social injury." As previously mentioned, however, the idea of the state being liable for criminal behavior when the state itself defines and enforces the legal codes has met with considerable resistance within the field of criminology over the years. The considerable debate over using *legal codes* as the basis for defining state crime was well articulated by Barak (1991, p. 8): "The study of state crime is problematic because the concept itself is controversial, in part because of a debate over whether one should define crime in terms other than law codes of individual nations. Some argue that if a state obeys its own laws, it should be judged by no higher criterion." Responding to such criticism, alternative approaches have been proposed, from international legal codes, to human rights issues and the subjective perceptions or interpretations of the state's citizens (Barak, 1991; Friedrichs, 1996; Green & Ward, 2000; Kauzlarich & Kramer, 1998; Ross, 1995). For example, Green and Ward (2000) rely on labeling theory to argue that state crimes are only offenses when the actions in question are subjectively labeled as criminal by a majority of society within a particular context. From this perspective, the label of state crime reflects a social consensus on a particular state action. Aulette and Michalowski (1993) contend that acts of omission, such as the government failing to intervene to prevent certain harms, should also be included in the concept and definition of state crime.

Despite the controversy and numerous definitions, Chambliss's (1989) ASC presidential address offers the most "direct and immediate inspiration for more systematic attention to crimes of the state on the part of a number of criminologists" (Rothe & Friedrichs, 2006, p. 150). Chambliss was the first criminologist to directly address state crime and to position it as criminal acts committed by governmental elites within the context of their official state positions. In an expansion of the basic definition, Kramer and Michalowski (1990) proposed that "state-facilitated" crimes are actions of the state that either fail to constrain or enable criminal behavior. Chambliss eventually called for a resolution to the debate over a definition in the field of criminology. To end the debate, Chambliss (1995, p. 9) proposed a comprehensive definition of state crime that provides an international perspective: "State organized crimes, environmental crimes, crimes against humanity, human rights crimes, and the violations of international treaties increasingly must take center stage in criminology. . . . Criminologists must define crime as behavior that violates international agreements and principles established in the courts and treaties of international bodies."

Pursuant to Chambliss's call for an international perspective, there has been a recent movement in criminology to examine state crime within a broader framework of *International Humanitarian Law* or the law of armed conflicts (Green & Ward, 2004; Kramer et al., 2005). Some scholars argue that human rights violations can and should be incorporated within an international legalistic framework. In particular, Kramer et al. (2005, p. 57) presented a definition of state crime in their analysis of legal issues surrounding the 2003 U.S. invasion and occupation of Iraq that is integrated and comprehensive, yet parsimonious: "State crime is any action that *violates public international law, international criminal law, or domestic law* when these actions are committed by individuals acting in official or covert capacity as agents of the state pursuant to expressed or implied orders of the state, or resulting from state failure to exercise due diligence over the actions of its agents" (emphasis added). Because Kramer and colleagues were examining one of the key topics of this book, i.e., the legality of the U.S.-led invasion and occupation of Iraq, their definition of state crime provides an established and contextually relevant lens through which to analyze the actions of the Bush administration. As noted by Kramer et al. (2005, p. 57), their definition of state crime "recognizes that potential offenders under international or domestic law can be states qua states and/or officials using state power in pursuit of state goals." From this perspective, it does not matter whether the state itself considers the activities in question to be state crimes. Rather, to the extent that state-sponsored activities violate international law, they are criminal acts by definition. Therefore, similar to Kramer et al. (2005), the arguments presented in chapter six are grounded in a proposition that violations of international law that were perpetrated by the Bush administration in Iraq constitute state crimes.

In addition to a working definition of state crime to guide the analysis, it would be useful to have specific, empirical criteria for evaluating the acts of the Bush administration as state crimes (similar to Cohen's five criteria for evaluating moral panic). To this end, Kauzlarich et al. (2003) offered five criteria which they argue must be met in order for an act (or non-act) by the government to qualify as state crime. According to Kauzlarich et al. (2003, pp. 244–246), state crime:

1. Generates harm to individuals, groups, and property,
2. Is a product of action or inaction on behalf of the state or state agencies,
3. The action or inaction relates directly to an assigned or implied trust/ duty,
4. Is committed, or omitted, by a governmental agency, organization or representative,
5. Is done in the self-interest of (a) the state itself or (b) the elite groups controlling the state.

The guidelines provided by Kauzlarich and colleagues facilitate an analysis of the war in Iraq as state crime by providing five specific and empirical criteria that complement the definition of state crime employed in this book. Therefore, the five criteria are used in chapter six to guide an examination of the Bush administration's 2003 invasion of Iraq through the lens of state crime.

In summary, the definitions, concepts, and empirical guidelines provided by Kramer et al. (2005) and Kauzlarich et al. (2003) facilitate an examination of the proposition that the March 2003 invasion of Iraq—a sovereign nation that neither threatened nor provoked the United States—as well as the subsequent U.S. occupation of Iraq, constitute crimes of the state. It is contended here that violations of international law are state crimes by definition. Given the centrality of international law to this argument, war crimes and violations of international criminal law are discussed in the following section.

### WAR CRIME AND VIOLATIONS OF INTERNATIONAL CRIMINAL LAW

As stated at the beginning of this chapter, the second theoretical proposition posits that the invasion and occupation of Iraq are *war crimes* as defined by the Geneva Conventions of 1949, the Nuremberg Charter, and as prosecuted by the International Criminal Court. Generally, a war crime is defined as a punishable offense under international law, for violations of the laws of war by any person(s), whether military or civilian (Feldman, 2002). However, similar to state crime, the definition of war crime is subject to considerable debate among contemporary scholars, state and military officials, and legal historians. In fact, the concept of war crime has been debated for thousands of years. Therefore, a brief history of the ancient laws of war will serve as a useful introduction to contemporary international law.

There have been periodic attempts to limit and regulate wartime actions since the beginning of recorded history. This has included numerous attempts to codify the rules of appropriate military conduct. One of the earliest known of such attempts occurred in the sixth century BC when the Chinese warrior Sun Tzu suggested putting limits on the ways in which wars were conducted (Trombly, 2003). The notion of war crimes appeared again around 200 BC in the Hindu code of Manu. In 1305 AD, the Scottish freedom fighter and national hero Sir William Wallace was tried and executed in London for treason against England and for committing war crimes, specifically the murder of English civilians. More than three hundred years later, in 1625, the Dutch philosopher Hugo Grotius wrote the highly influential "On the Law of War and Peace," which focused on the humanitarian treatment of civilians during times of war (Trombly, 2003). Not until the last century and a half, however, has there been a significant and ongoing international effort to place constraints on warring parties. Surprisingly, not until the twenty-first century was a permanent international body established to prosecute alleged violators of international laws of war. Specifically, on July 1, 2002, a treaty-based court, called the International Criminal Court, was established in The Hague for the prosecution of war crimes committed on or after that date (Trombly, 2003). The significance of the fact that this event occurred during the first term of the G. W. Bush administration is discussed in chapter seven.

### The Geneva Conventions

At the heart of the concept of war crime is the idea that an individual can be held responsible for the actions of a nation or for a nation's soldiers (Feldman, 2002; Kafala, 2003). The bodies that together define crimes of war are the Geneva Conventions, the Nuremberg Charter, and the International Criminal Court located in The Hague (Feldman, 2002). However, the most significant and influential are the Geneva Conventions. Initiated by a Swiss businessman who founded the International Red Cross, Henri Dunant, the first Geneva Convention (or treaty) was signed in 1864 to protect the sick and the wounded in wartime. A committee of diplomats from sixteen nations, assisted by representatives of military medical services and humanitarian services, negotiated a treaty that specified four conditions during war time:

1. Ambulances, military hospitals, and the personnel serving with them are to be recognized as neutral and protected during conflict.
2. Citizens who assist the wounded are to be protected.

3. Wounded or sick combatants are to be collected and cared for by either side in a conflict.

4. The symbol of a red cross on a white background (the reverse of the Swiss flag in honor of the origin of this initiative) will serve as a protective emblem to identify medical personnel, equipment, and facilities (American Red Cross, 2001, p. 1).

The Geneva Convention of 1864 became the foundation of modern international humanitarian law, i.e., the laws of war (Feldman, 2002). Additionally, since its very inception, the International Red Cross has remained involved in the drafting and enforcement of the Geneva Conventions (Trombly, 2003).

Following the first Geneva Convention of 1864 were the treaties of 1899 which dealt with asphyxiating gases and expanding (or hollow tip) bullets. In 1907, thirteen separate international treaties were signed, followed in 1925 by the Geneva Gas Protocol, which prohibited the use of poisonous gases (responding to their extensive deployment in World War I) and the practice of bacteriological warfare. There were two more Geneva Conventions that dealt with the treatment of the wounded and prisoners of war in 1929. In 1949, following World War II, four additional Geneva Conventions extended protections to those shipwrecked, prisoners of war, and to civilians during wartime. In 1977, two additional protocols were added to the Geneva Conventions of 1949, which extended their protections to victims of civil wars. The Geneva Conventions thus encompass a body of laws that have evolved over time and that are still under construction (Kafala, 2003; Trombly, 2003).

In practice, the four Geneva Conventions of 1949 and the two additional protocols of 1977 represent the contemporary laws of war (Feldman, 2002). Collectively, they are known as The Geneva Conventions of August 12, 1949, and Protocols Additional to the Geneva Conventions of August 12, 1949 (American Red Cross, 2001). The first Geneva Convention of 1949 protects soldiers who are hors de combat (out of the battle). This includes soldiers who are either sick or wounded, as well as medical personnel. The second Geneva Convention of 1949 adapts the protections of the first Geneva Convention to reflect conditions at sea, including shipwrecked soldiers and hospital ships. The third Geneva Convention of 1949 establishes specific rules for the treatment of prisoners of war (POWs). It requires that POWs be treated humanely, adequately housed, and receive sufficient food, clothing, and medical care. Its provisions also establish guidelines on labor, discipline, recreation, and criminal trial. The fourth Geneva Convention of 1949 provides protection to civilians in areas of armed conflict and occupied territories.

Perhaps most important to the analysis of the Iraq war, including the invasion and occupation by the United States, is Article 147 of the *fourth* Geneva Convention. This defines war crime as:

> Willful killing, torture or inhumane treatment, including . . . willfully causing great suffering or serious injury to body or health, unlawful deportation or transfer or unlawful confinement of a protected person, compelling a protected person to serve in the forces of a hostile power, or willfully depriving a protected person of the rights of fair and regular trial . . . taking of hostages and extensive destruction and appropriation of property, not justified by military necessity and carried out unlawfully and wantonly (Kafala, 2003, p. 2).

According to international legal experts, the above statement provides the basic definition of war crimes (Kafala, 2003; Feldman, 2002). The Geneva Conventions apply in all cases of declared war, or in any other armed conflict between nations. They also apply in cases where a nation is partially or totally occupied by soldiers of another nation, even when there is no armed resistance to that occupation (American Red Cross, 2001). Nations that ratify the Geneva Conventions must abide by certain humanitarian principles and impose legal sanctions against those who violate them. Ratifying nations must "enact any legislation necessary to provide effective penal sanctions for persons committing or ordering to be committed any of the grave breaches" or violations of the Geneva Conventions (American Red Cross, 2001, p. 2). As testimony to their importance and influence, the four Geneva Conventions of 1949 have been signed by almost every nation in the world, including the United States (American Red Cross, 2001).

In 1977, two protocols, supplementary to the Geneva Conventions, were adopted by an international diplomatic conference in order to provide greater protection to victims of both international conflicts (Protocol I) and high-intensity internal armed conflicts, such as civil wars (Protocol II). Nearly two hundred nations have ratified one or both protocols, and they are under consideration by many other countries. Any nation that has ratified the Geneva Conventions but not the protocols is, nevertheless, bound by all provisions of the conventions (American Red Cross, 2001).

The United States has refused to ratify Protocol I which expands the Geneva Conventions' protections for the civilian population, as well as military and civilian medical workers in international armed conflicts (American Red Cross, 2001). Protocol I is a supplement to the Geneva Conventions and it is divided into three sections: (1) general provisions; (2) protections for the wounded, sick, and poor; and (3) protections for warfare combatants and prisoners of war. For example, it outlaws indiscriminate attacks on civilian populations and the destruction of food, water, and other materials needed for survival. Protocol I was adopted on June 8, 1977, by the Diplomatic Conference on the Reaffirmation and Development of the International Humanitarian Law. As of January 14, 2007, it had been ratified by 167 countries, with the notable exceptions of the United States, Iran, Israel, Pakistan, Afghanistan, and Iraq. However, it was signed by the United States, Iran, and Pakistan on December 12, 1977, with the *intention* of ratifying it (American Red Cross, 2001). Despite such intentions, the United States has yet to ratify Protocol I. The implications of this failure to ratify it are discussed in chapter six where the invasion and occupation of Iraq are examined through the critical lens of international criminal law.

### The Nuremberg Charter

Following World War II, the Allied victors and others in the world community set out to establish a legal framework to govern war that would minimize the likelihood of future armed conflict. The international legal framework governing war was also shaped by the Nuremberg Charter, a document that was created as a result of the post–World War II Nuremberg trials. The Nuremberg trials were a series of trials most notable for the prosecution of prominent members of the political, military, and economic leadership of Nazi Germany, including such infamous individuals as Rudolf Hess, Adolf Hitler's chief deputy (www.nuremberg.law.harvard.edu, 2008). The trials were held in Nuremberg, Germany, from 1945 to 1949 at the Nuremberg Palace of Justice. Approximately two hundred German defendants who were accused of war crimes were tried at Nuremberg throughout the four-year duration of the trials. The trials led to the execution of twelve Nazi leaders and the imprisonment of many others.

The legal basis for the Nuremberg trials was established by the London Charter, issued on August 8, 1945, which restricted the trial to the "punishment of the major war criminals of the European Axis countries" (www.nuremberg.law.harvard.edu, 2008, p. 2). The jurisdiction of the court was defined by the "Instrument of Surrender" that was signed by Germany on May 7, 1945. This instrument transferred political authority for Germany to the Allied Control Council. Because the Allied Control Council had sovereign power over Germany, it could choose to punish violations of international law, including the laws of war (www.nuremberg.law.harvard.edu, 2008).

The Nuremberg trials led to the creation of the Nuremberg Charter. Under the Nuremberg Charter, the supreme international crime is that of commencing a *war of aggression*, because it is the crime from which all war crimes follow (www.nuremberg.law.harvard.edu, 2008). Commencing a war of aggression includes the planning, preparing, initiating, or waging of a war of aggression, or a war in violation of international treaties, agreements, or assurances. Also, participating in a common plan or conspiracy for the accomplishment of any such act constitutes a war crime under the Nuremberg Charter. Furthermore, the Nuremberg Charter involves a list of seven key principles that collectively define international criminal law. The seven principles are as follows:

Principle I: Any person who commits an act that constitutes a crime under international law is responsible therefore and liable to punishment.

Principle II: The fact that internal law does not impose a penalty for an act that constitutes a crime under international law does not relieve the person who committed the act from responsibility under international law.

Principle III: The fact that a person who committed an act that constitutes a crime under international law acted as head of state or responsible government official does not relieve him from responsibility under international law.

Principle IV: The fact that a person acted pursuant to order of his government or of a superior does not relieve him from responsibility under international law provided a moral choice was in fact possible to him.

Principle V: Any person charged with a crime under international law has the right to a fair trial on the facts and law.

Principle VI: The crimes hereinafter set out are punishable under international law:

a) Crimes against peace:
   (i) Planning, preparation, initiation, or waging of a war of aggression or a war in violation of international treaties, agreements, or assurances.
   (ii) Participation in a common plan or conspiracy for the accomplishment of any of the acts mentioned under (i).
b) War crimes:
   Violations of the laws or customs of war that include, but are not limited to, murder, ill-treatment, or deportation to slave-labor, or for any other purpose, of civilian population of or in occupied territory, murder, or ill-treatment of prisoners of war, of persons on the seas, killing of hostages, plunder of public or private property, wanton destruction of cities, towns, or villages, or devastation not justified by military necessity.
c) Crimes against humanity:
   Murder, extermination, enslavement, deportation, and other inhuman acts done against any civilian population, or

persecutions on political, racial, or religious grounds, when such acts are done or such persecutions are carried on in execution of or in connection with any crime against peace or any war crime.

Principle VII: Complicity in the commission of a crime against peace, a war crime, or a crime against humanity as set forth in Principle VI is a crime under international law (www.nuremberg .law.harvard.edu, 2008, p. 1–2).

The International Law Commission, acting on the request of the United Nations General Assembly, produced a report in 1950 titled *Principles of International Law Recognized in the Charter of the Nuremberg Tribunal and in the Judgment of the Tribunal* (United Nations, 1950). The Nuremberg Principles were also adopted by the United Nations in 1950 and they have had a great influence on the laws of war. As explained by Henkin (1995, p. 111), "At Nuremberg, sitting in judgment on the recent past, the Allied victors declared *waging aggressive war to be a state crime* (under both treaty and customary law), as well as an individual crime by those who represented and acted for the aggressor states" (emphasis added). Kramer et al. (2005) explained that the Nuremberg principles helped to create an important new body of international rules—that is, international criminal law. Cassese (2003, p. 15) argued that international criminal law is "designed both to proscribe international crimes and to impose upon States the obligation to prosecute and punish at least some of those crimes."

Beyond obligating nations to punish war crimes, the Nuremberg Charter also led to numerous proposals by members of the international community after 1950 for the establishment of a permanent international criminal court. Those proposals were acted upon by the international community in the late twentieth century with the creation of the International Criminal Court, based in The Hague. Significantly, the Nuremberg trials established the only legal precedents for the cases tried at the world court (Cassese, 2003). A discussion of the International Criminal Court and its jurisdiction is provided in the following section.

### The International Criminal Court

The international community had long aspired to the establishment of a permanent international court and, in the twentieth century, reached consensus on definitions of genocide, crimes against humanity, and war crimes (Cassese, 2003; Kafala, 2003). As previously mentioned, in 2002, a treaty-based court, called the International Criminal Court (ICC), was established in The Hague, The Netherlands, for the prosecution of war crimes committed on or after that date. The ICC is the first-ever permanent international institution with jurisdiction to prosecute individuals responsible for the most serious crimes of concern to the international community. The ICC was established by the Rome Statute of the International Criminal Court, so named because it was adopted in Rome, Italy, on July 17, 1998, by the United Nations Diplomatic Conference of Plenipotentiaries on the Establishment of an International Criminal Court (www.un.org, 2008). The Rome statute is an international treaty, binding only on those states that formally express their consent to be bound by its provisions. Upon ratifying it, those states become formal "parties" to the Rome statute. The Rome statute came into force on July 1, 2002, after ratification by sixty countries. To date, 108 countries, with the notable exceptions of the United States and China, have become parties to the statute (www.un.org, 2008).

The ICC is an independent international organization, and it is not part of the United Nations system. However, the jurisdiction and functioning of the ICC are governed by the Rome statute, which is a treaty that was initiated by the United Nations. The ICC has jurisdiction over the most serious crimes of concern to the international community as a whole, such as genocide, crimes against humanity, and war crimes (www.un.org, 2008). Each of these crimes is clearly defined in the Rome statute and other relevant texts such as the Geneva Conventions. Similar to the Nuremberg Principles, the Rome statute clearly stipulates that acting in an official capacity as a head of state, member of government or parliament, or as an elected representative or public official in no way exempts a person from prosecution or criminal responsibility. Superiors or military commanders may be held responsible for criminal offenses committed by persons under their effective command and control or effective authority and control (www.un.org, 2008).

According to the Rome statute (www.un.org, 2008), the specific crimes of war that may be prosecuted by the ICC include:

A. Grave breaches of the Geneva Conventions, such as:
   1. Willful killing, or causing great suffering or serious injury to body or health
   2. Torture or inhumane treatment
   3. Unlawful wanton destruction or appropriation of property
   4. Forcing a prisoner of war to serve in the forces of a hostile power
   5. Depriving a prisoner of war of a fair trial
   6. Unlawful deportation, confinement, or transfer
   7. Taking hostages
B. The following acts as part of an international conflict:
   1. Directing attacks against civilians
   2. Directing attacks against humanitarian workers or U.N. peacekeepers

　　3. Killing a surrendered combatant
　　4. Misusing a flag of truce
　　5. Settlement of occupied territory
　　6. Deportation of inhabitants of occupied territory
　　7. Using poison weapons
　　8. Using civilians as shields
　　9. Using child soldiers
　C. The following acts as part of a noninternational conflict:
　　1. Murder, cruel or degrading treatment, and torture
　　2. Directing attacks against civilians, humanitarian workers, or U.N.
　　　peacekeepers
　　3. Taking hostages
　　4. Summary execution
　　5. Pillage
　　6. Rape, sexual slavery, forced prostitution, or forced pregnancy

However, the ICC only has jurisdiction over the above crimes where they are "part of a plan or policy or as part of a large-scale commission of such crimes" (Kafala, 2003, p. 2). Also, the ICC only tries those who are accused of the gravest crimes in violation of international law. Due to resource limitations, as the court is primarily funded by state parties, it is not able to bring to justice every person who has committed crimes of concern to the international community.

　　The ICC is intended to complement, not to replace, national criminal justice systems. In that regard, the ICC is a court of last resort (www.un.org, 2008). Proceedings before the ICC may be initiated by a state party, the prosecutor, or the United Nations Security Council. It will not act if a case is investigated or prosecuted by a national judicial system unless the national proceedings are not considered to be genuine, for example, if formal proceedings were undertaken solely to shield a person from criminal responsibility. Also, the ICC may exercise jurisdiction over international crimes only if they were committed on the territory of a state party or by one of its nationals. These conditions, however, do not apply if a situation is referred to the prosecutor by the United Nations Security Council, whose resolutions are binding on all U.N. member states, or if a state makes a declaration accepting the jurisdiction of the ICC.

　　The ICC prosecutor may start an investigation upon referral of situations in which there is a reasonable basis to believe that war crimes have been, or are being, committed (www.un.org, 2008). Such referrals must be made by a state party or the Security Council of the United Nations, acting to address a threat to international peace and security. In accordance with the "Rome

Statute and the Rules of Procedure and Evidence," the prosecutor must evaluate the material submitted to him/her before making the decision on whether or not to proceed. By mid-2008, three state parties had referred situations to the office of the prosecutor at the ICC. The U.N. Security Council had referred one situation to the prosecutor. In addition to state party and U.N. Security Council referrals, the prosecutor may also receive information on alleged crimes within the jurisdiction of the ICC provided by other sources, such as private individuals or nongovernmental organizations. The prosecutor must conduct a preliminary examination of such information in every case. If the prosecutor then decides that there is a reasonable basis to proceed with an investigation, he/she will request the ICC's pretrial chamber to authorize an investigation.

The ICC has received complaints about alleged crimes in at least 139 countries but, as of July 2008, the prosecutor had opened investigations into only four situations: (1) Uganda; (2) the Democratic Republic of the Congo; (3) the Central African Republic; and (4) Darfur, Sudan (www.un.org, 2008). By mid-2008, the ICC's detention unit housed five suspects: Thomas Lubanga, Germain Katanga, and Mathieu Ngudjolo Chui from Uganda; Jean-Pierre Bemba from the Central African Republic; and former Liberian President Charles Taylor. Taylor was being tried under the mandate and auspices of the Special Court for Sierra Leone, but his trial was being held in The Hague due to political and security concerns about holding the trial in Freetown, Sierra Leone (Goldstone, 2008).

Finally, in March, 2009, the prosecutor of the ICC issued an arrest warrant for Sudan's ruthless and tyrannical President, Omar Hassan al-Bashir. He was charged with genocide, crimes against humanity, and war crimes in Darfur. The decision to issue the arrest warrant was unanimously backed by the judges in The Hague. Nevertheless, taking action against a sitting head of state is most unusual. One has to go back to the cases of Slobodan Milosevic of Yugoslavia in 1999 and Charles Taylor of Liberia in 2003 to find the last times that international prosecutors charged a sitting head of state with war crimes (www.un.org, 2008). Milosevic was brought to trial for atrocity crimes but died in custody in 2006, before the trial could be concluded. Taylor was on trial in The Hague by mid-2008 for war crimes and crimes against humanity, as discussed. Although rare and controversial, the prosecution of elected presidents or heads of state falls within the jurisdiction of the ICC. Importantly, the 1998 Rome Statute of the International Court effectively removed head-of-state immunity for war crimes (www.un.org, 2008). The remote possibility and the implications of the G. W. Bush administration facing charges by the ICC for its actions in Iraq are discussed in chapter six.

CONCLUSION

This chapter outlined the theoretical perspectives, concepts, and specific criteria used to examine the proposition that the G. W. Bush administration committed elite deviance, state crime, and violations of international criminal law in the invasion and occupation of Iraq. The actual analyses of this proposition are presented in chapter six. To summarize, the Bush administration's engineering of a moral panic regarding Iraq is examined from the perspectives of Millsian sociology (Mills, 1956; Simon, 2002) to support an argument that the Bush administration perpetrated elite deviance. Also, the March 2003 invasion of Iraq is analyzed through the critical lens of state crime (Kauzlarich et al., 2003; Kramer et al., 2005). Finally, the invasion and occupation of Iraq are examined as violations of international criminal law, as established by the Geneva Conventions of 1949, the Nuremberg Charter, and as prosecuted by the International Criminal Court. The next chapter provides an analysis of the second major proposition of this book.

CHAPTER 6

# The Higher Immorality and Crimes
# of the Bush Administration

BY MID-2004 there were already allegations that the Bush administration had misled the U.S. public about the need to invade Iraq. Nevertheless, George W. Bush was reelected president in November of 2004. Mills (1956) argued that a passive and alienated U.S. public does not directly influence fundamental government policies such as the decision to go to war. Bush's reelection in 2004 indicates how effectively the moral panic over Iraq manipulated public attitudes and opinions concerning the alleged threat to national security. In this chapter, it is argued that the second theoretical proposition of this book is correct—that is, the Bush administration committed elite deviance, state crimes, and war crimes involving Iraq. The goals for this chapter are as follows:

1. To provide evidence that a moral panic engineered by the Bush administration and fueled by the U.S. news media, which was used by the Bush administration to justify the invasion of Iraq, can be understood as a manifestation of the "higher immorality of the power elite" (Mills, 1956).

2. To provide evidence that the 2003 invasion of Iraq constitutes state crime as defined by leading scholars (Kauzlarich, Mullins & Matthews, 2003; Kramer, Michalowski & Rothe, 2005).

3. To provide evidence that the U.S.-led invasion and occupation of Iraq are violations of international criminal law, as established by custom, charters, and treaties. The possibility of the G. W. Bush administration facing charges from the International Criminal Court for its actions in Iraq is also considered.

A detailed examination of each of these arguments is essential here because the culpability of the Bush administration for legal violations in Iraq is a central topic in the ongoing debate over the legitimacy and consequences of the Iraq war. These important issues are discussed in this chapter in the order outlined above.

## THE HIGHER IMMORALITY OF THE
## BUSH ADMINISTRATION

As discussed in the last chapter, Mills (1956) argued that the power elite, who are bound by mutual interests and who effectively control the economic, military, and political institutions in the United States, periodically commit acts of wrongdoing against society. Those acts of elite deviance include the enactment of harmful government policies such as the unnecessary declaration of war that is designed to reinforce the power elite's control over society. Mills (1956) argued that elite actions that cause social harm, regardless of the criminality of those actions in a legal sense, are part of the higher immorality of the power elite. From a Millsian perspective, the Bush administration's engineering of a moral panic over Iraq, using false and deceptive rhetoric in order to gain support for an unnecessary war, constitutes higher immorality.

Consistent with Mills's writings, it is argued here that an elite-engineered moral panic over Iraq after 9/11 provided a socially constructed crisis that benefited the power elite in the United States. Although perhaps not a crime in a legal sense, the moral panic was used to conceal the Bush administration's actual reasons for wanting to invade Iraq (which are addressed in chapter seven). Also, the moral panic was used to divert public attention and to channel the allocation of financial resources away from objectively harmful problems facing the United States that the Bush administration preferred not to address. Furthermore, the Bush administration caused moral harm to U.S. society by exploiting powerful, negative stereotypes of Arabs (Muslims) in its rhetoric toward Iraq which resulted in public fear and hatred, as well as cynicism and alienation. Finally, the moral panic led to an unprovoked and unnecessary invasion and occupation of Iraq. Empirical evidence is provided below in order to support each of these charges.

Compared to the rest of the world, the United States has staggeringly high military expenditures. By the end of the G. W. Bush administration, the world's military expenditures are estimated to have reached $1.4 trillion (www.globalissues.org, 2008). The United States accounted for almost half (48%) of the total, or $711 billion, in 2008. By comparison, China, ranked number two, represented just 8% of total military spending or $122 billion, while all of Europe comprised just 20% of the total or $289 billion. Russia represented 5% of total military expenditures or $70 billion. Together, the rest of the world comprised only 19%. Moreover, annual military expenditures more than doubled during the G. W. Bush administration. In 2001, Bush's first year in the White House, military expenditures totaled $335 billion. By 2008, the military budget exceeded $700 billion. Interestingly, the war in Iraq accounted for $130 billion of the $711 billion total spending in 2008. Therefore, although the Iraq war was responsible for a portion (approximately 35%) of the massive increase in military spending during the Bush administration, military spending completely unrelated to the Iraq war was actually responsible for the bulk of the increase between 2001 and 2008. So, what were the implications of the Bush administration's massive military spending?

In fiscal year 2007–2008, slightly more than 50% of all federal tax dollars went toward national defense (www.globalissues.org, 2008). In addition, more than half (52%) of the U.S. federal discretionary budget, or $482 billion, was allocated to national defense in 2008. The federal discretionary budget is the money that the U.S. president and Congress have direct control over and must allocate each year (www.nationalpriorities.org, 2008). This is different from mandatory spending—that is, the money that is spent in compliance with existing laws, such as social security benefits, Medicare, and paying the interest on the national debt. In comparison, only 6.3% of the federal discretionary budget or $58.6 billion was spent on education, and just 5.6% ($52.3 billion) was allocated to health care in 2008 (www.globalissues.org, 2008).

As previously discussed, spending on the Iraq war seriously damaged the U.S. economy—creating a staggering federal budget deficit—and draining funds that could have been used to address real problems and objective threats to U.S. society. By the end of 2008, the United States was facing an economic crisis, a healthcare crisis, a social security crisis, an energy crisis, a housing/mortgage crisis, and global warming. By choosing to invade and then occupy Iraq, the Bush administration directed valuable U.S. resources away from objectively harmful conditions and toward a socially constructed and benign threat to the United States. In fact, during its second term in the White House, the Bush administration spent as much each week in Iraq as it did *annually* in research and development on heart disease, the leading cause of death in the United States, which claims three-quarters of a million lives every year. At the same time, the cost of the Iraq war by mid-2008 could have purchased health care for more than half of the U.S. population and, more importantly, it could have funded health care for the nearly fifty million uninsured Americans, more than three times over.

In addition to its indifference to serious, chronic problems, the Bush administration was also slow to react in times of genuine crisis. For example, the Bush administration was broadly criticized for its slow and incompetent response to hurricane Katrina in 2005 in which more than twelve thousand U.S. citizens were made homeless. The Bush administration was accused of largely ignoring the plight of the victims of Katrina, who were desperately poor even before the disaster and who were mostly racial minorities, particularly African-Americans (D. Baker, 2008). Also, as previously discussed, the Bush administration emphatically denied that global warming, a well-documented health and environmental risk to the planet, was a serious, man-made problem. Even more disturbing, the Bush administration hid the facts that confirmed the dangers of global warming from the U.S. public (Revkin, 2008).

Although such behavior by the Bush administration may not be criminal in a legal sense, it nevertheless caused social harm. By deliberately deceiving the public about the genuine risks posed by global warming, neglecting the suffering victims of hurricane Katrina, and failing to address other serious threats such as the healthcare crisis, poverty, and the social security crisis, the Bush administration demonstrated the higher immorality of the power elite. The Bush administration's harmful actions and its equally harmful inactions constituted elite wrongdoing or moral harm, as defined by Mills, because they were unethical, immoral, and they placed large segments of U.S. society at risk. Such indifference toward human suffering and the possibility of real disaster in health care, for example, demonstrated the Bush administration's willingness to risk or sacrifice the well-being of U.S. citizens, which is central to Mills's concept of the higher immorality of the power elite.

The Bush administration's unprecedented military spending, particularly on the Iraq war, reflected its hegemonic approach to foreign policy and its self-serving agenda which included the rewarding of political allies among the power elite. A report issued by the Congressional Budget Office in mid-2008 revealed that $100 billion had been spent on private contractors in Iraq since the invasion began in 2003. That is a milestone that reflects the Bush administration's unprecedented level of dependence on private firms for help in the Iraq war (Risen, 2008). The report revealed that one out of every five dollars spent on the war had gone to contractors for the Pentagon and other government agencies. Incredibly, employees of private contractors actually outnumbered U.S. troops in Iraq. The Pentagon's reliance on outside contractors was far larger proportionately in Iraq than in any prior military conflict, and it fueled charges that such excessive outsourcing led to overbilling, fraud, and shoddy work that endangered and even killed U.S. troops and Iraqi civilians (Risen, 2008).

The Congressional Budget Office report also raised legal and ethical questions regarding the role of armed security contractors (essentially mercenaries) and whether the Bush administration relied too heavily on private armed forces in Iraq. By mid-2008, contractors in Iraq employed at least 180,000 people and effectively formed a second private army—that is, larger than the U.S. military force—and one whose roles and missions, and even casualties sustained and inflicted, were hidden from public view due to its privatization. That strategy allowed the Bush administration to hold down the number of military personnel sent to Iraq which helped it to avoid a draft. Given public animosity toward a military draft, the privatization approach likely propped up public support for the war, even as the death toll mounted in Iraq.

So, who benefited from massive federal spending on the Iraq war? The short answer is the power elite—in particular, friends of the G. W. Bush administration. For example, the Pentagon's reliance on private companies to support the Iraq war led to accusations of political favoritism by the Bush administration in the awarding of multibillion-dollar contracts, frequently without bids, which the Congressional Budget Office requires (Risen, 2008). For example, Kellogg, Brown & Root (KB&R), a subsidiary of Halliburton, the company run by Dick Cheney before he was vice president under G. W. Bush, was the largest Pentagon contractor in Iraq at the beginning of the war (Klein, 2003). After years of criticism and allegations of corruption and mis-management for its role in the war, Halliburton sold the KB&R unit, which continued to be the largest defense contractor in Iraq with forty thousand employees working there (Risen, 2008). Dina L. Rasor, an author and inde-pendent expert on contracting fraud, said she believed that the $100 billion cost of private contractors estimated by the Congressional Budget Office might be low since there were virtually no reliable audits of, or controls on, spending in Iraq, particularly during the first years of the war. Members of Congress responded to the report by calling for a special war-contracting committee like the panel that Harry S. Truman led in the Senate before he was selected to be Franklin D. Roosevelt's running mate in 1944 (Risen, 2008). Given the Bush administration's unprecedented reliance on private contractors, the absence of a bipartisan investigative committee on contract-ing in Iraq meant that more than $100 billion in U.S. tax dollars were awarded to groups such as Halliburton that were favored by the administra-tion and had almost no accountability or governmental oversight.

At the same time, soaring oil prices left the Iraqi government with a cumulative budget surplus of nearly $80 billion at the end of 2008, according to the Government Accountability Office (Glanz & Robertson, 2008). The same source reported that Iraqi oil revenue from 2005 to 2008 totaled $160 billion. Despite the Bush administration's promises that Iraqi oil profits would completely fund the country's reconstruction, less than $4 billion was spent by Iraq on its own reconstruction by mid-2008, while the United States had spent nearly $50 billion on such efforts. In another troubling sign, the U.S. Government Accountability Office reported that from 2005 to 2007, Iraq devoted only 1% of the operating expenses in its budget to maintaining reconstruction projects that had been started with American money. Senator Carl Levin, who was chairman of the Senate Armed Services Committee, said in a joint statement with Senator John Warner, Republican of Virginia, "It is inexcusable for U.S. taxpayers to continue to foot the bill for projects the Iraqis are fully capable of funding themselves . . . while Iraqi oil revenues pile up in the bank" (Glanz & Robertson, 2008, p. A14).

These two related problems—the reliance on private contractors and the failure to compel Iraq to fund its own reconstruction—demonstrated that the Bush administration not only lied to the U.S. public about the source of

funding for the war on Iraq and its reconstruction but also shirked its fiduciary responsibilities to U.S. taxpayers when spending the money. In essence,
the U.S. public first paid to blow up Iraq and then paid again to reconstruct
it. Much of the money was given to contractors who had no accountability or
oversight. The substantial privatization of the Iraq war meant that the roles
and actions of federally funded mercenaries or soldiers of fortune were largely
unmonitored and, therefore, unknown. The Pentagon's reliance on such
mercenaries—whose actions, including the killing and possible torture of
Iraqis, were unmonitored—further demonstrates the higher immorality of the
Bush administration. Moreover, the lies, mismanagement, and favoritism manifested in the allocation of federal tax dollars on Iraq caused harm to U.S. society, recognizing that far greater problems facing the country were ignored by
the Bush administration in favor of the war. That also demonstrated the Bush
administration's higher immorality.

There have been other subtle but significant negative effects of the moral
panic on the U.S. public, as well. For example, President Bush told
Americans after 9/11 that Iraq threatened them with the most horrible
weapons known to mankind. At the start of the invasion in 2003, two-thirds
of the U.S. public believed the framing of the Iraq threat by the Bush administration and news media while one-third of the public did not accept the
dominant, pro-war news frame. Public support for the war decreased dramatically over time as powerful evidence of the Bush administration's deceptions
concerning Iraq was made public, and as events in the war failed to deliver the
quick victory promised by the Bush administration.

As discussed in chapter four, by the fall of 2006, the majority of Americans
believed that President Bush had deceived them about the Iraqi threat.
Expanding on the work of Mills, Simon (2002) argued that such "elite
deviance" (i.e., President Bush lying to justify an unprovoked invasion of
another country) creates alienation among non-elites when they discover the
harmful actions of their leaders. What exactly is alienation and why is it
important? Marx (1844) defined alienation as the separation of things that nat-
urally belong together or to put antagonism between things that are properly
in harmony. In Marx's classic treatment, it refers to the alienation of people
from their *Gattungswesen* (usually translated as "species being" or "essence").
Marx believed that humans become self-realized through their labor. In his
critique of capitalism, Marx (1844) argued that capitalist workers have no
control of their labor and inevitably become alienated from themselves or
their "species being" as a result. Marx demonstrated, for example, how pro-
letarian workers were exploited and turned into "wage slaves" by bourgeoisie
industrialists in Europe during the nineteenth century.

Years later, critical theorists such as Lowenthal (1989) expanded on
Marx's concept of alienation by revealing that modern societal elites who

control the culture industry use it to disseminate false ideologies designed to confuse and oppress the general public. Critical theorists argue that public agitation instilled through the mass media creates an undesirable dependency on political elites who exploit public concern in order to justify their policies and legitimize their authority (Agger, 1978). Alienation leads a passive public to trust without question that political elites are acting in its best interests (D. R. Simon, 2002). Alienation is dangerous because an oppressed and uncritical society loses sight of itself. As discussed in chapter two, an oppressed society living in false consciousness is susceptible to manipulation, and it will allow the priorities and needs of the elites, including war, to become its own.

The concept of alienation helps to explain the U.S. public's general passivity upon learning that the Bush administration had been deceitful about the need to invade Iraq. President Bush was reelected in 2004 despite the failure to locate WMD in Iraq, as well as emerging evidence prior to the election that his administration had misled the U.S. public about the very existence of WMD in Iraq. Although by 2006 the U.S. public increasingly disapproved of the Bush administration's actions concerning Iraq, the majority of Americans did not demand accountability or call for impeachment despite their growing distrust of the administration. However, it could be argued that the 2006 midterm election results that returned the Congress to Democratic Party control expressed the public's growing dissatisfaction with the war in Iraq as the events there ran contrary to the prewar predictions of the Bush administration.

Mills argued that political elites are granted vast legitimacy and moral authority in modern society. This insight helps to explain the U.S. public's relative passivity and even willingness to reelect President Bush in 2004 after learning that Iraq did not have the WMD he had claimed. Many Americans continued to believe that the administration had acted in their best interests even after it was revealed that President Bush had misled them about the threat from Iraq. For the general public to believe otherwise would require a widespread recognition that an unjust and immoral man was the elected president and that would draw into question the existence of democratic authority in the United States. As explained by Mills, that sort of ontological inquiry is very unlikely on the part of the general public because fear of knowledge and anti-intellectualism are central features of modern U.S. society.

However, the public's reaction to the Iraq war was not universal. In fact, approximately 20% of the U.S. public still believed the dominant, prewar news frame of "Iraq as evil," even as G. W. Bush was preparing to leave office in late 2008. Significantly, it has been argued that public attitudes and opinions regarding war and presidential approval both vary at the individual level in society and that they are mediated by independent factors (Eschholz, Chiricos & Gertz, 2003). For example, Gartner (2008) found that social structures influence public opinion at the individual or micro level. Specifically, he demonstrated that familiarity with the victims of international violence influences support for war and presidential approval. Not surprisingly, Gartner found that those who lost a family member in Iraq were most likely to oppose the war. Significantly, he (2008, p. 694) also determined that "knowing a [Iraq war] casualty increases the likelihood a person will disapprove of the president, regardless of whether the loss is civilian or military and public support is high or low."

Although Gartner did not include an independent measure of "knowledge of presidential deception" in his study, it was conducted in 2006 or three years after the war began. By 2006, ample evidence of the Bush administration's distortions of intelligence on Iraq, including the first Senate Intelligence Committee Report, had already been released to the public. If experiences such as losing a loved one impact individual-level support for war and presidential approval, then it seems reasonable to assume that knowledge of presidential deception also influences support for war and presidential approval at the individual level. Stated differently, it is logical to argue that public reactions (such as alienation, frustration, and anger) to social issues have great variability in society based on mediating factors at the individual level.

Although micro-level analysis is not the focus of this book, it is important to recognize that there were many individual-level exceptions to the major macro-level argument made here that the U.S. public was generally passive and uncritical of the Bush administration's deceptions concerning Iraq due to its alienation. Clearly, not everyone remained passive or mute. Many Americans became angry and publicly protested the elite dishonesty. For example, Cindy Sheehan, a fifty-year-old from Vacaville, California, with little prior political experience became a passionate anti-war and anti-Bush activist after her son was killed in Iraq. She received national media attention when she sat in protest outside of President Bush's ranch in Crawford, Texas, and demanded a meeting with him in 2005. The White House denied her request, stating that Sheehan had discredited herself by calling for the president's impeachment (Gartner, 2008). Such an arrogant response from the Bush administration most likely increased Sheehan's frustration and anger.

Other individuals like the former Bush administration insider, Scott McClellan, reacted bitterly to personal betrayal. McClellan wrote a book and appeared on television news programs to condemn the administration after he learned that the Iraq war was sold to the public through deception. McClellan (2008), a longtime friend of G. W. Bush, who had worked for him since he was the governor of Texas and who was deputy press secretary during the buildup to the Iraq war, said his initial misgivings about a rush to invasion were offset by his affection for the president. "My beliefs were different then. I believed the president when he talked about the grave and gathering danger from Iraq," McClellan told NBC's *Today* show in May of 2008. McClellan

(2008) said he grew increasingly dismayed and disillusioned during 2006, his final year as White House press secretary. He pinpointed the unfolding of the C.I.A. leak case—that is, the vengeful leaking of the identity of C.I.A. operative, Valerie Wilson, by Karl Rove and Lewis "Scooter" Libby, and what it revealed about President Bush's role in releasing classified information about Iraq to the press—as his tipping point (McClellan, 2008). In hindsight, McClellan (2008, p. 37) states that the decision to invade Iraq was a "serious strategic blunder" but the biggest mistake made by the Bush administration was "a decision to turn away from candor and honesty when those qualities were most needed."

For Cindy Sheehan, the loss of her son was deeply personal and profoundly painful. That pain and anger no doubt fueled her subsequent anti-war and anti-Bush protest activities. Similarly, the reactions of insiders like McClellan seem to reflect disappointment, disillusionment, and anger. In all likelihood, McClellan expected more from his former boss, who was also a personal friend, and no doubt felt betrayed when he learned the truth about the Iraq war. In fact, McClellan (2008, p. 101) states that he was deceived by Bush and Cheney and deeply regrets being complicit in the White House's "carefully orchestrated campaign to shape and manipulate sources of public approval" in the march to the Iraq war.

It seems clear that the lies and deceptions of the Bush administration did more than simply manipulate public support for an unnecessary war. Those same deceptions created reactions such as alienation, cynicism, anger, and distrust in U.S. society when the public learned that it had been deceived by the Bush administration about Iraq. Those reactions had consequences at both the macro and micro levels of society. At the macro or structural level, alienation and passivity generally muted the possibility of a public outcry for accountability (let alone impeachment) despite widespread public disapproval of President Bush's handling of the Iraq war by 2006 (Mills, 1956; D. R. Simon, 2002). At the micro or individual level, great variability in reactions to the war and Bush were mediated by independent factors such as the loss of a loved one in the war, knowledge of the Bush administration's deceptions, and even experiences of personal betrayal (Eschholz et al., 2003; Gartner, 2008).

From a Millsian perspective, the negative consequences that resulted from the Bush administration's lies about Iraq, whether manifested at the macro or micro levels of society, further demonstrate the higher immorality of the Bush administration. The administration's deliberate deceptions about the alleged threat to U.S. national security from Iraq caused moral harm to society by creating anger, distrust, fear, cynicism, and alienation among nonelites. Thus, Mills's insights more than fifty years ago remain powerful and valid today because, now as then, the higher immorality is a systematic and institutionalized feature of the power elite, and the public's general acceptance of the higher immorality without meaningful critique is a central element of modern U.S. society.

The lies about a nonexistent Iraqi threat disseminated by the Bush administration after 9/11 did additional moral harm to the U.S. public. Specifically, the administration's punitive post-9/11 rhetoric promoted prejudice, fear, and hatred toward Arabs (Muslims), in general, and toward Iraqis, in particular. As previously discussed, moral panics typically arise when distorted mass media campaigns are used to create fear, reinforce stereotypes, and exacerbate pre-existing divisions in the world that are often based on race, ethnicity, and class (Goode & Ben-Yehuda, 1994). Consistent with that central tenet of the moral panic concept, President Bush's rhetoric concerning Saddam Hussein and his political regime following 9/11 built on negative, stereotypical images of Arabs in order to fuel public outrage toward them. Significantly, the stereotypes employed by the Bush administration were already established through more than twenty years of news media and popular culture portrayals of Arabs as evil, bloodthirsty, and animalistic terrorists (Entman, 2003).

From the perspective of communication theory and research (see Lowery & DeFleur, 1995), the framing of Saddam Hussein's regime as "evildoers" and "madmen" by President Bush after 9/11 interacted with established negative stereotypes of Arabs, in general, so as to prime hostile and retaliatory attitudes among the U.S. public toward the targeted group—that is, the Iraqi leadership. In an important study of post-9/11 presidential rhetoric, Merskin (2004) determined that the word choices and allusions used in the "carefully constructed" post-9/11 speeches of G. W. Bush closely resembled the accumulation of historically, politically, and culturally constructed negative words and images of Arabs in the public domain. Merskin (2004, p. 122) explains: "Depictions of Arab enemies in popular culture and employed by the media were mobilized by the Bush administration and fed to a receptive public. These carefully cultivated stereotypes, used to justify the invasion . . . and occupation of Iraq, were affirmed during the months following September 11, 2001, and reified by the time troops invaded Iraq in 2003."

In addition, President Bush used atrocity tales in his post-9/11 rhetoric to exploit negative stereotypes of Arabs and, thereby, bolster his case for invading Iraq. In his pre-invasion propaganda campaign, President Bush frequently referred to atrocities allegedly perpetrated by Saddam Hussein's army against the Iraqi people—in particular, the alleged use of chemical weapons against the Kurds (Merskin, 2004; Rothe & Muzzatti, 2004). Such atrocity tales were designed to prime or trigger moral outrage among Americans by interacting with and exploiting negative stereotypes of Arabs as cold-blooded killers. However, as noted by Kramer et al. (2005, p. 64): "President Bush failed to mention that these gassings occurred more than a decade earlier. By avoiding any periodization of Hussein's attacks on Kurdish villages, Bush helped to leave the impression in the minds of many Americans that these attacks were recent, and perhaps ongoing." Thus, President Bush misrepresented Iraqi history to the U.S. public. By giving the impression that the attacks were recent, the atrocity tales used by the Bush administration incited anger, reinforced racial stereotypes and primed prejudicial sentiments, particularly after 9/11, and helped to fuel a public fire that had been lit by the moral panic over Iraq. According to Chomsky (2005), this was part of a general and intentional misrepresentation of the case for attacking Iraq by the Bush administration in order to secure enduring public support for it.

In their model of enemy-image construction, Spillman and Spillman (1977) revealed a standard repertoire of propagandistic words such as "evil" and images that serve to dehumanize the "other" in the popular imagination and thus make a retaliatory response toward the common enemy seem both logical and natural. The Bush administration employed that standard repertoire and exploited pre-existing negative stereotypes of Arabs in order to define Iraqis as folk devils after 9/11. The administration also used atrocity tales to support its "evildoer" claims concerning Iraq. The Bush administration thus socially constructed Saddam Hussein and his followers as enemies of the United States in an elite-engineered moral panic that reinforced negative sentiments among the U.S. public toward all Arabs (Muslims).

In summary, from a Millsian sociological perspective, the Bush administration's engineering of a moral panic over Iraq in order to gain popular support for a war demonstrates its higher immorality. By manipulating public fears after 9/11, exploiting negative stereotypes of Arabs, and promoting racial hatred in its framing of Iraqis as evil, the Bush administration caused harm to U.S. society. Although not a crime in a strict legal sense, the moral panic caused moral harm to society by creating fear, distrust, cynicism, and alienation among the public. The Bush administration's moral panic diverted public attention and vital financial resources away from more serious problems and genuine risks to U.S. society, such as the growing healthcare crisis, economic crisis, global warming, and poverty. The lies, corruption, and irresponsibility in the Bush administration's allocation of U.S. tax dollars on the war and reconstruction of Iraq caused additional social harm to U.S. society. Finally, the moral panic itself led to an unprovoked and devastating attack on a sovereign state.

The Bush administration's higher immorality concerning Iraq was made possible because modern elites do not have to win the moral consent of those over whom they hold power. As explained by Mills, a passive U.S. public generally trusts that the power elite will act in its best interests. Arguably, that is what happened during the Bush administration's march to war in Iraq. Once the enemy image was established in the public's consciousness—that is, Iraq was framed as evil by the Bush administration—and the panic had reached its climax, the U.S. public generally wanted (expected) the folk devils, i.e., Saddam Hussein and his followers, to be eliminated. As originally explained by Cohen (1972), once a disvalued group is socially defined as folk devils, the elites then have the moral authority and even obligation to punish or eliminate them. Paradoxically, therefore, President Bush was fulfilling his moral obligation to society when he gave the order to invade Iraq, although he was actually eliminating a nonobjective threat that he had constructed.

## STATE CRIMES OF THE BUSH ADMINISTRATION

In addition to higher immorality, the second theoretical proposition in this book also contends that the Bush administration committed state crimes in the invasion and occupation of Iraq. As discussed in chapter five, this charge is based on the definition provided by Kramer et al. (2005, p. 57): "State crime is any action that *violates public international law, international criminal law, or domestic law* when these actions are committed by individuals acting in *official or covert capacity* as agents of the state pursuant to *expressed or implied orders* of the state, or resulting from state *failure to exercise due diligence* over the actions of its agents" [emphasis added].

Because Kramer and colleagues were analyzing legal issues related to the 2003 U.S. invasion and occupation of Iraq, their definition of state crime is relevant here for several reasons. First, this definition permits the invasion of Iraq, which was expressly ordered by President G. W. Bush and implemented by his key cabinet members, to be analyzed as a violation of both *domestic* and *international* law. Although it is argued here that a violation of international law is a state crime (Kramer et al., 2005) regardless of whether or not the state considers the action to be a crime, certain actions of the Bush administration discussed below did in fact violate U.S. law. Second, the Kramer et al. (2005) definition includes orders issued by the Bush administration to its subordinates that may have been *implied*, such as to disregard all evidence that would contradict a claim that Iraq possessed WMD. The definition also includes crimes of *omission*, such as the failure of the Bush administration to report Pentagon and C.I.A. doubts regarding the existence of WMD in Iraq to the U.S. public. Finally, the Kramer et al. (2005) definition also encompasses the *covert* engineering of a moral panic by the Bush administration which violated their due diligence (i.e., protection from physical, social, and moral harm) responsibilities to the public.

As discussed previously, there are five criteria that an act or non-act by the government must meet in order for it to qualify as a state crime (Kauzlarich et al., 2003, pp. 244–246):

1. Generates harm to individuals, groups, and property
2. Is a product of action or inaction on behalf of the state or state agencies

3. The action or inaction relates directly to an assigned or implied trust/duty
4. Is committed, or omitted, by a governmental agency, organization, or representative
5. Is done in the self-interest of (a) the state itself or (b) the elite groups controlling the state

Importantly, these five criteria both complement and provide empirical guidelines for applying the Kramer et al. (2005) definition of state crime. Therefore, these criteria guide the discussions and conclusions below.

The first type of state crime perpetrated by the Bush administration concerning Iraq was its deliberate fabrication of evidence against Iraq and the dissemination of that disinformation (i.e., false information or lies) to the U.S. public via the compliant and uncritical press. In fact, deceiving the U.S. public into believing that Iraq represented a dangerous and growing threat to national security was *the* state crime that preceded and facilitated all other state crimes of the Bush administration involving Iraq. As previously discussed, the Senate Intelligence Committee concluded that the Bush administration deliberately exaggerated the Iraqi threat to the U.S. public, and the Center for Public Integrity discovered nearly a thousand false statements by the Bush administration prior to the invasion concerning Iraq's alleged possession of WMD and links to al Qaeda.

Also, the Pulitzer Prize-winning journalist Ron Suskind (2008) presented two interlinking revelations that offer powerful evidence of deception and the fabrication of evidence by the Bush administration. First, Suskind revealed that more than three months before initiating the Iraq war President Bush and his top aides received information via the British government from Iraq's intelligence chief, Tahir Habbush, that Saddam Hussein had destroyed all of his weapons of mass destruction years earlier. The Bush administration "buried" the information from the Iraqi intelligence chief in its unrelenting march toward war. Second, Suskind revealed that after paying off Habbush, in the amount of $5 million, and resettling him in Jordan, White House officials used him to deceive the American people by forging a letter in his name, backdated to the summer of 2001, in which Habbush supposedly informed Saddam Hussein that he was training Mohammed Atta, soon to be the leader of the 9/11 terrorist attacks.

By the end of 2003, the Bush administration was already being criticized in many circles for its failure to find any WMD in Iraq. The Bush administration used the forged Habbush letter to establish a link between Iraq and the 9/11 attacks and, thereby, justify the Iraq war retroactively (Kellner, 2005). In December of 2003, the letter was leaked by the White House to an Iraqi politician and longtime C.I.A. informant, Ayad Allawi, who was soon to be

named the first interim prime minister of Iraq. Allawi then leaked the letter to
a prominent British journalist who published it on the front page of the *Daily
Telegraph*. From there, the forged letter made its way into the mainstream
U.S. news media where it received prominent treatment, and was claimed by
the Bush administration to provide proof of Iraq's involvement in 9/11
(Suskind, 2008).

It apparently did not matter to the Bush administration that such activity
by the president violates federal law and that it was expressly prohibited by
Congress in 1975, following similar practices by the administration of President
Richard Nixon (Altheide, 2002). In fact, it seems that the fabrication of intelligence and the spreading of disinformation via the news media were common practices of the G. W. Bush administration. For example, shortly after
the attacks of 9/11, the Orwellian sounding Office of Strategic Influence
(OSI) was established by the Bush administration in response to its concerns
that the United States was losing public support overseas for its war on terrorism, particularly in Islamic countries (Dao & Schmitt, 2002a). According
to information leaked to the press in February of 2002, the OSI had a "broad
mission ranging from 'black' campaigns that use disinformation and other
covert activities to 'white' public affairs that rely on truthful news releases"
(Dao & Schmitt, 2002a, p. A12). Apparently established to manipulate international public opinion by planting disinformation in foreign newspapers, the
OSI reported to Douglas Feith, the under secretary of defense, who reported
to Donald Rumsfeld. When confronted and questioned by the press about the
OSI, Secretary Rumsfeld initially denied that it existed. However, when it
became clear that press inquiries would not abate, on February 26, 2002,
Secretary of Defense Rumsfeld announced that the OSI was closing, telling
reporters that "the office has clearly been so damaged that it is pretty clear to
me that it could not function effectively. . . . So it is being shut down" (Dao &
Schmitt, 2002b, p. A6). The OSI obviously did exist after all. Moreover, it
has been alleged that the OSI was simply reorganized and reassigned, with all
its original functions intact, to the Bush administration's Office of Global
Communications (DeYoung, 2002).

The Bush administration's deliberate fabrication of evidence against Iraq,
and its dissemination of disinformation to the public via the press, meet the
five criteria of state crime. Specifically, the lies of the Bush administration
regarding Iraq harmed the U.S. public by creating fear, cynicism, and alienation, and promoting racial hatred. The duping of the U.S. public and news
media concerning the Iraqi threat resulted from deliberate deceptions perpetrated by the Bush administration in its official capacity and pursuant to its
assigned duties. Although the Bush administration steadfastly maintained that
it was acting in the interests of the public, the lies it disseminated created a
moral panic that served its self-interests, including: removing Saddam Hussein

from power, rewarding its political allies, and controlling Iraq's oil production (Muttitt, 2006). Furthermore, its lies concerning Iraq led to an unprovoked and illegal war. Thus, the deliberate deceptions perpetrated by the Bush administration, and its dissemination of disinformation to both domestic and international audiences, establish the five criteria of state crime. In chapter seven, the Bush administration's hidden agenda and its actual reasons for invading Iraq are discussed in more detail.

The second type of state crime perpetrated by the Bush administration involves the actual invasion and occupation of Iraq. It has been argued that the U.S. war on Iraq was unconstitutional (Bonifaz, 2004). The U.S. Constitution places the power to declare war solely in the United States Congress. As one may recall, the U.S. Congress never voted for the Iraq war. Instead, Congress voted for a resolution in October 2002 that unlawfully transferred to President G. W. Bush the decision-making power to launch a first-strike or "preemptive" invasion of Iraq. More specifically, Congress passed a resolution that stated: "The president is authorized to use the armed forces of the United States as he determines to be necessary and appropriate in order to (1) defend the national security of the United States against the continuing threat posed by Iraq; and (2) enforce all relevant United Nations Security Council resolutions regarding Iraq" (Bonifaz, 2004, p. 1).

Significantly, the U.S. Congress *cannot* transfer its exclusive power to declare war to the president. It is a nondelegable power held only by Congress. The transfer of power from Congress to the president and the use of that power to declare war on Iraq by President Bush were both illegal actions in violation of the U.S. Constitution. In fact, U.S. Senator Robert C. Byrd from West Virginia warned Congress prior to their vote on the resolution that the transfer of power was unconstitutional. Senator Byrd stated: "We are handing this over to the President of the United States. When we do that, we can put up a sign on the top of this Capitol, and we can say, 'Gone home. Gone fishing. Out of business.' I never thought I would see the day in these forty-four years I have been in this body . . . when we would cede this kind of power to any president" (Bonifaz, 2004, p. 2). A few years after the adoption of the Constitution, James Madison warned of such a situation when he said, "In no part of the U.S. Constitution is more wisdom to be found than in the clause which confides the question of war and peace to the legislature, and not to the president" (Bonifaz, 2004, p. 2).

The Iraq war was clearly in direct violation of the U.S. Constitution. As agents of the state, who were acting in official capacities and pursuant to their sworn duties, President Bush, who exercised illegal power by declaring an unprovoked war on Iraq, as well as the members of Congress who voted for an illegal transfer of power, violated domestic law. Thus, President Bush and the members of Congress who were complicit in his illegal declaration of war all knowingly committed state crime (Clark, 2006; Kramer et al., 2005). Furthermore, by not challenging the Bush administration's so-called evidence against Iraq prior to the invasion, an uncritical and compliant Congress was also a passive co-conspirator in the elite-engineered moral panic over Iraq.

As previously mentioned, Lawrence Wilkerson, Colin's Powell's former chief of staff, has stated that the Bush administration should have been held accountable for its violations of the Constitution concerning the Iraq war. Wilkerson has argued, for example, that President Bush and Vice President Cheney were far more deserving of impeachment than was President Bill Clinton. Specifically, Wilkerson (www.rawstory.com, 2007, p. 1) stated: "The language [in the Constitution] about impeachment is nice and precise—it's high crimes and misdemeanors. You compare Bill Clinton's peccadilloes [i.e., lying under oath about an extramarital affair] for which he was impeached to George Bush's high crimes and misdemeanors or Dick Cheney's high crimes and misdemeanors, and I think they pale in significance." Clarifying what he meant by high crimes and misdemeanors, Wilkerson stated that the U.S. public was duped into supporting an illegal war on Iraq through deliberate deceptions perpetrated by Bush and Cheney and their subordinates (www.rawstory.com, 2007). Although Wilkerson does not use the moral panic terminology per se, what he describes sounds very much like an elite-engineered moral panic launched by the Bush administration and reinforced by the U.S. news media. The research findings presented in chapter three of this book provide empirical support for Wilkerson's charges.

In addition to the illegality of a declaration of war by President Bush, certain events of the Iraq war also constitute state crimes. Most notable in this regard are the massive, unjustifiable military and civilian casualties in the war, particularly among Iraqis. By mid-2008, U.S. casualties totaled slightly more than forty-one hundred soldiers, while more than one million Iraqis had been killed (www.icasualties.org, 2008; Opinion Research Business, 2008). More than thirty thousand U.S. soldiers and countless Iraqis had also been wounded, many seriously (www.icasualties.org, 2008). In Baghdad alone, more than 40% of households had lost a family member.

The unjustifiable casualties resulting from the Bush administration's illegal war on Iraq meet the five criteria of state crime outlined by Kauzlarich et al. (2003). Specifically, the war caused grievous harm and loss of life to individuals, particularly Iraqis, as well as tremendous destruction of Iraqi property. The unnecessary carnage was the direct result of actions taken by the Bush administration. That action—an illegally declared war—was ordered by the president of the United States in his official capacity as commander and chief of the armed forces. Also, the action was authorized by President Bush allegedly in the best interests of the United States (i.e., national security), although it was actually orchestrated to satisfy the self-interests of the Bush administration. For example, insiders such as Clarke (2004) and McClellan (2008) have stated that removing Saddam Hussein from power in Iraq was a top priority of the Bush administration from its first days in the White House—i.e., eight months before the attacks of 9/11. Therefore, the tremendous cost of the Iraq war in terms of lives lost, human suffering, and property damage meet the five criteria of state crime. Furthermore, as explained later in this chapter, the Bush administration's invasion and occupation of Iraq violated international criminal laws. Accordingly, the actions of the Bush administration in Iraq constitute state crimes as defined by Kramer et al. (2005).

The misappropriation of federal funds on the war and reconstruction of Iraq, particularly the awarding of "no-bid" contracts to politically favored, private military contractors, constitutes the Bush administration's third and final type of state crime concerning Iraq. As previously discussed, the Bush administration's unprecedented reliance on private contractors in Iraq meant that more than $100 billion in federal funds were awarded to companies such as Halliburton that were favored by the administration—frequently without contract bidding, which Congress requires (Hogan, Long, Stretsky & Lynch, 2006). In addition, Halliburton itself was widely implicated in various contract abuses during the Iraq war, including overcharging the government for certain services and Halliburton executives receiving kickbacks from subcontractors (Hogan et al., 2006). Also, as previously discussed, the extensive privatization of the Iraq war by the Bush administration meant that the roles and actions of federally funded mercenaries or soldiers of fortune were largely unmonitored and, therefore, unknown.

The Bush administration's mismanagement, irresponsibility, and corruption in its allocation of federal funds on the war and reconstruction of Iraq meet the five criteria of state crime outlined by Kauzlarich et al. (2003). The Bush administration harmed the U.S. public by squandering billions of tax dollars on an illegal and unnecessary war while rewarding its political cronies with lucrative, no-bid military contracts. Such corruption was the result of actions taken by the Bush administration under the authority of the offices it held. Disturbingly, those corrupt actions were committed by the highest ranking officials in the U.S. government, allegedly in the best interest of the state. However, those corrupt deeds were actually committed by the Bush administration in its self-interest. Therefore, the misappropriation of federal funds on an illegal war and reconstruction of Iraq meet the five criteria of state crime. In addition, the Bush administration's violation of the laws of Congress in awarding no-bid contracts and failure to fulfill its fiduciary responsibility to taxpayers also constitute state crimes as defined by Kramer et al. (2005).

Finally, Kauzlarich et al. (2003) presented one additional metric for evaluating state crime that is useful in this discussion because it considers the role of elite ideology in state criminal activity. Specifically, the authors proposed a "complicity continuum" of state crime to accompany their five empirical criteria. The complicity continuum consists of four types of state crime arranged along two dimensions—that is (1) commission versus omission, and (2) explicit versus implicit. The first dimension distinguishes between acts of *commission* and acts of *omission* on the part of the state. At one end of the complicity continuum is commission and at the other end is omission. The second dimension distinguishes between *explicit* and *implicit* criminal acts on the part of the state. As explained by Kauzlarich et al. (2003, p. 246), the second dimension: "highlights how action or inaction relates to larger state goals such as legitimacy, hegemony, and elite ideology. . . . As one moves to the right of the continuum, the crimes are more likely to be a manifestation of specific, proximal, and material state goals. As one moves toward the left, the two categories of crime are more implicit, signifying a less direct or causally distal relationship between the crime and the state's goals." Moving from right to left, the four types of state crime on the continuum are: (1) commission-explicit; (2) commission-implicit; (3) omission-explicit; and (4) omission-implicit.

Based on the complicity continuum, the invasion of Iraq was a criminal act of commission by the Bush administration that explicitly or directly related to its post-9/11 ideology and rhetoric—that is, (1) Iraq was evil and possessed WMD; and (2) the terrorist attacks of 9/11 made preemptive war legitimate and necessary in order to protect the United States from evildoers (Kramer et al., 2005; Merskin, 2004). The Bush administration used its official capacities, as well as the authority and implied trust of the offices it held, to deliberately manipulate the U.S. public, and to launch an illegal war that it justified with lies. Therefore, the war on Iraq was a category one or commission-explicit state crime because a direct relationship existed between the crime itself (i.e., illegal war) and the policy rhetoric of the Bush administration. Also, this conclusion is consistent with the tenets of elite-engineered moral panic (Goode & Ben-Yehuda, 1994) which posit that political elites will deliberately manipulate public concerns and create folk devils in order to strengthen their authority and promote their ideology.

In summary, based on the various measures of state crime employed herein, the Bush administration committed numerous state crimes in the Iraq war. First, the deliberate deceptions regarding Iraq and the dissemination of disinformation through both domestic and international news media violated federal laws. Second, President G. W. Bush violated the U.S. Constitution by exercising a power that he did not legally possess when he declared war on Iraq in 2003. Also, the illegal war caused massive human casualties and a tremendous loss of Iraqi property. Such actions by the Bush administration constitute state crimes whether or not those actions violated U.S. law (Kramer et al., 2005). Third, the Bush administration's corruption and violations of domestic law in its allocation of federal funds on the war and reconstruction of Iraq also constitute state crimes. Finally, the Iraq war was a commission-explicit state crime as measured by the complicity continuum of Kauzlarich et al. (2003). An examination of the Bush administration's violations of international criminal law in the Iraq war is presented in the section below.

WAR CRIMES OF THE BUSH ADMINISTRATION

The second proposition of this book maintains that the administration of President G. W. Bush violated international laws and committed war crimes in the invasion and occupation of Iraq. More specifically, the March 19, 2003, U.S.-led invasion of Iraq violated international criminal law—in particular, the Nuremberg Charter of 1950, which the United States coauthored. Also, the killings, inhumane treatment of soldiers and civilians, and wanton destruction of property in Iraq that resulted from the war and occupation, constitute war crimes as defined by the four Geneva Conventions of 1949. Based on their authorization of those criminal acts, President G. W. Bush and key members of his administration, including Vice President Dick Cheney and former Secretary of Defense Donald Rumsfeld, can be considered war criminals (Clark, 2006). The possibility of their prosecution for war crimes by the International Criminal Court (ICC) in The Hague is considered at the end of this chapter.

Despite the Bush administration's claims to the contrary, there was no legal justification for the invasion of Iraq under international law (Ritter, 2003). The preemptive war on Iraq was a "war of aggression" under international criminal law because Iraq had neither attacked nor threatened to attack the United States prior to the invasion. As discussed previously, the expansion of international criminal law after World War II included the adoption of the Nuremberg Charter, which declared waging aggressive war to be a state crime under both treaty and customary law (Henkin, 1995). According to the Nuremberg Charter (Principle VI), the supreme international crime is that of commencing a *war of aggression* because it is the crime from which all war crimes follow (Clark, 2006; Kramer et al., 2005). Commencing a war of aggression includes the planning, preparing, initiating, or waging a war of aggression, or a war in violation of international treaties, agreements, or assurances. Significantly, legal scholar Amy Bartholomew (2006, p. 13) argued that the invasion of Iraq was a war of aggression according to the Nuremberg Charter, and thus violated international criminal law:

> The doctrine of "preventive war" is not recognized as a justification for war under international law. . . . The Bush Administration launched a full scale war against Iraq, a sovereign state; it did so not in self-defense or under the authorization of the United Nations Security Council. The Bush Administration knew prior to the 2003 invasion that Iraq had no

connection to Al Qaeda, was disarmed, had no weapons of mass destruction, and was incapable of mounting a credible defense much less an
attack on the United States. Accordingly, the Iraq war is an aggressive
war in violation of international law.

In the buildup to the invasion, the Bush administration consistently
asserted that Iraq possessed weapons of mass destruction that represented a
growing threat to U.S. security (Scheer , Scheer & Chaudry, 2003). The U.S.
public was told that preemptive action against Iraq was required in order to
eliminate impending disaster. It is now clear that such claims were false. It is
also clear that the Bush administration distorted and even manufactured evidence to support its call for war on Iraq (Bartholomew, 2006; Suskind, 2008).
The linkage between false claims made by the Bush administration and its war
of aggression is articulated by Ritter (2006, p. 13):

> The Bush administration steadfastly asserted only one justification for its
> invasion of Iraq: it claimed that Iraq had weapons of mass destruction.
> The Bush Administration fixed and manipulated intelligence on the
> existence of weapons of mass destruction in Iraq in order to mislead
> deliberately and persuade the United States population and their elected
> representatives to support the war of aggression. Accordingly, what the
> Bush Administration called intelligence to justify the invasion of Iraq was
> politically motivated propaganda deliberately concocted to prosecute a
> war of aggression.

Such distortion and fabrication of intelligence by the Bush administration in
the buildup to the Iraq war violated Article VI of the Nuremberg Charter,
which states that participating in a common plan or conspiracy for the accomplishment of a war of aggression constitutes a war crime (www.nuremberg
.law.harvard.edu, 2008). The Bush administration's prewar propaganda campaign, based on disinformation and lies, was part of a conspiracy to launch a
war of aggression against Iraq and thus violated international criminal law
(Ratner, 2002; Ritter, 2006).

As argued by Kramer et al. (2005), the invasion of Iraq was also a violation of the United Nations Charter of 1945, the highest treaty in the world,
which the U.S. Senate has ratified. Similar to the Nuremberg Charter, the
focus of the U.N. Charter is on the prohibition against waging a war of
aggression. The prohibition against aggressive war is articulated in Article 2(4)
of the U.N. Charter, which states that "All members shall refrain in their
international relations from the threat or use of force against the territorial
integrity or political independence of any state, or [behave] in any other manner inconsistent with the purposes of the United Nations" (Kramer et al.,
p. 58). Because the United States led an invasion of a sovereign state without

legal authorization from the international community, i.e., the United Nations Security Council, the invasion of Iraq is a prima facie violation of Article 2(4) of the U.N. Charter (Bartholomew, 2006; Kramer et al., 2005).

Refuting such claims, the Bush administration steadfastly maintained that the invasion of Iraq was justified on the basis of preemptive self-defense (Ritter, 2003). Exactly what is preemptive self-defense? In early 2002, soon after the attacks of 9/11, the Bush administration introduced a new national security strategy which stated that the United States could use preemptive force against perceived future threats to U.S. security (Ratner, 2002). Known as the "Bush doctrine," this new security strategy was used by the administration as an allegedly legal justification for invading Iraq. For example, when Secretary of Defense Rumsfeld testified before Congress on September 19, 2002, he "rejected the idea that a U.S. attack would violate international law and evoked a right of preemptive self-defense" (Kramer et al., 2005, p. 60). However, the Bush doctrine went far beyond any reasonable interpretation of preemptive self-defense, which would require that an actual attack was imminent or certain. Instead, the Bush doctrine was based on a much broader position that the United States was entitled to use force to eliminate any *possible* future threat to its national security, whether or not a threat was objective or imminent (Ratner, 2002; Ritter, 2003).

It should be noted that Article 51 of the U.N. Charter does recognize a state's "inherent right" to use force in self-defense. However, Article 51 limits a state's use of force in self-defense to when an armed attack is either launched against it or an attack is immediately threatened (Ratner, 2002). Clearly, the U.S.-led invasion of Iraq did not meet that standard and thus cannot be considered legal self-defense. Nevertheless, the Bush administration sought to preserve Chapter 51 self-defense protection for invading Iraq by falsely claiming that Iraq possessed WMD and that it was linked to al Qaeda and involved in the attacks of 9/11 (Kramer et al., 2005). However, Iraq had neither connections to al Qaeda nor WMD, and the Bush administration knew those facts prior to launching the invasion (Bartholomew, 2006; Clarke, 2004; Corn, 2003; Suskind, 2008). The self-defense argument was built on a foundation of deception. Therefore, any claims of self-defense by the Bush administration under Chapter 51 of the U.N. Charter as justification for the invasion of Iraq were baseless and untenable (Kramer et al., 2005; Ratner, 2002; Ritter, 2003).

However, even if Iraq had possessed WMD as the Bush administration charged, without an actual attack or an immediate threat to use them against the United States, there would still have been no justification for invading Iraq under Chapter 51 of the U.N. Charter (Kramer et al., 2005; Ratner, 2002). The mere possession of WMD does not constitute the threat of an attack, even if said weapons are in the hands of an enemy state (Ratner, 2002).

Article 51 prescribes the use of force in self-defense *only* when an attack against a country is imminent or certain. The mere possibility of a future attack from an enemy state using WMD does not constitute self-defense under Chapter 51. Furthermore, there was no authorization from the U.N. Security Council for the U.S.-led invasion of Iraq. Thus, even if Iraq had possessed WMD in 2003, in the absence of a clear plan to use those weapons against the United States, the preemptive strike would still have violated international law (Ratner, 2002; Ritter, 2003).

In addition to the unlawful invasion, the killing, torture, and inhumane treatment of Iraqi citizens and prisoners, and the wanton destruction of Iraqi property resulting from the occupation, constitute war crimes as defined by the four Geneva Conventions of 1949. As explained in chapter five, Article 147 of the fourth Geneva Convention of 1949 defines war crime as:

> Willful killing, torture or inhuman treatment, including . . . willfully causing great suffering or serious injury to body or health, unlawful deportation or transfer or unlawful confinement of a protected person, compelling a protected person to serve in the forces of a hostile power, or willfully depriving a protected person of the rights of fair and regular trial . . . taking of hostages and extensive destruction and appropriation of property, not justified by military necessity and carried out unlawfully and wantonly (Kafala, 2003, p. 2).

According to legal experts, the above statement provides the basic definition of war crimes under international law (Feldman, 2002; Greider, 2003). Significantly, those nations that have ratified the Geneva Conventions, including the United States, are sworn to refrain from the above actions in all cases of declared war or in any other armed conflict between nations.

Once the U.S.-led invasion forces became occupying powers in Iraq, they were obligated to abide by the Geneva Conventions. After major combat operations were declared over in Iraq, the U.N. Security Council passed Resolution 1483 which formally recognized that the United States and the United Kingdom occupied Iraq (Clark, 2006; Kramer et al., 2005). As occupiers, Resolution 1483 required them to "comply fully" with their obligations under the Geneva Conventions of 1949 and The Hague Regulations of 1907 which include the preservation of "public safety and order" (Greider, 2003). As explained by Kramer et al. (2005, p. 67), "Under the Fourth Geneva Convention, the occupying power [i.e., the United States and the United Kingdom] must ensure public safety and order, and guarantee the civilian population's fundamental rights to food, health care, education, work, and freedom of movement." Stated differently, the occupying power must respect the lives, well-being and property of civilians at all times. The failure to do so constitutes war crime.

It has been argued that the U.S.-led occupying powers in Iraq did indeed fail to meet their obligations as set forth in the Geneva Conventions (Clark, 2006; Greider, 2003; Kramer et al., 2005). For example, it has been revealed that the United States did virtually nothing to stop either the looting or wonton destruction of Iraqi property and important architecture that followed the fall of Saddam Hussein's political regime after the invasion (Clark, 2006). Perhaps the most grievous of the Bush administration's violations of the Geneva Conventions, however, was manifested in the loss of human life and injury to Iraqi civilians. By mid-2008, according to London-based Opinion Research Business and its research partner in Iraq, the Independent Institute for Administration and Civil Society Studies, the Iraqi death toll exceeded one million, including several hundred thousand civilians, while countless other Iraqis had been maimed or injured due to the war and occupation (Opinion Research Business, 2008). Also, indiscriminate missile attacks and the widespread use of banned weapons such as cluster bombs and napalm-like Mark 77 firebombs by the U.S. military in the invasion resulted in the deaths of countless Iraqi civilians without any discernable military gains (Clark, 2006; Human Rights Watch, 2003; Ritter, 2006).

The war crimes committed during the U.S. occupation of Iraq go further still. Numerous experts have charged that U.S. soldiers and private military contractors in the employment of the U.S. government attacked residential neighborhoods, invaded homes, arrested and detained civilians, and destroyed private property throughout the occupation of Iraq—all clear violations of the Geneva Conventions (Greider, 2003; Klein, 2003; Kramer et al., 2005; Ritter, 2006). Legal experts such as former U.S. Attorney General Ramsey Clark have harshly criticized the Bush administration's violations of international law in the occupation of Iraq. In his discussion of those violations, Clark (2006, p. 14) stated:

> Because the invasion of Iraq was the supreme war crime, the resultant occupation of Iraq itself is a war crime. The occupation consisted of additional war crimes such as: collective punishment upon the Iraqi people in the form of post invasion intentional and targeted attacks upon civilian populations, hospitals, medical centers, residential neighborhoods, electrical power stations and water purification facilities, the widespread use of torture against the Iraqi people, mass arrests and detention of civilians and civilian home demolitions, and the destruction and desecration of the cultural and archeological heritage of the Iraqi people.

Clark has argued that the Bush administration should have been held accountable for its violations of international law in the Iraq war, as did Lawrence Wilkerson, Colin Powell's former chief of staff. However, Clark was even more adamant than Wilkerson in his call for the impeachment of President

Bush and Vice President Cheney in 2005. Clark stated that President Bush and his cabinet were guilty of war crimes and he demanded that they be held accountable by Congress for their actions (www.democracynow.org, 2005). He contended that the failure to impeach them tarnished the moral integrity of the United States and its Constitution in front of the world audience.

It has been further charged that U.S.-led occupying forces in Iraq violated international law in their responses to the strong Iraqi insurgency that followed the fall of Saddam Hussein's government. In their relentless searches for insurgents, the occupying forces committed numerous war crimes such as taking hostages, killing demonstrators, destroying homes, and violating important cultural norms (including gender rules) and religious mores (Clark, 2006; Cohn, 2006; Kramer et al., 2005). Those actions by the occupying forces further provoked the insurgency and risked the security of Iraqi civilians. Moreover, detainees were held indefinitely by U.S. authorities without formal charges or access to lawyers (Kramer et al., 2005). The International Committee of the Red Cross (ICRC) claimed that nearly 99% of all those held by U.S. authorities at the infamous Abu Ghraib prison were wrongfully arrested, i.e., without probable cause that they had engaged in aggression against the occupying powers (ICRC, 2004). The torture and humiliation of Iraqi prisoners at Abu Ghraib by U.S. soldiers, which was documented in photos released by CBS's *60 Minutes II*, in 2004, violated both the Geneva Conventions and the U.N. Convention Against Torture of 1984 (Clark, 2006; Cohn, 2006).

How did the Bush administration justify its failure to provide certain protections to Iraqi citizens under the Geneva Conventions? As briefly discussed in the last chapter, the United States has signed but refuses to ratify Protocol I of the Geneva Conventions, which extends protections for the civilian population, as well as military and civilian medical workers, in international armed conflicts (American Red Cross, 2001). The primary objection of the Bush administration to Protocol I was that it would extend the 1949 Geneva Conventions' protections to individuals that it considered to be "unlawful combatants" (Greenhouse, 2008; Paust, 2002). Protocol I (Part III, Article 44, paragraph 3) clarifies and expands the definition of "lawful combatant" by stating that "combatants are obliged to distinguish themselves from the civilian population while they are engaged in an attack or in a military operation preparatory to an attack. Recognizing, however, that there are situations in armed conflicts where, owing to the nature of the hostilities an armed combatant cannot so distinguish himself, he shall retain his status as a combatant, provided that, in such situations, he carries his arms openly" (American Red Cross, 2001, p. 6). This is a significant extension of the laws of war because it appears to confer lawful combatant status on *guerrillas* (such as the insurgents in Iraq) who do not wear a military uniform that clearly distinguishes them from the civilian population (Feldman, 2002; Paust, 2002). Such individuals, despite their lack of uniform, are still entitled to the following protections under Protocol I (Part III, Article 44, paragraphs 4 and 5):

4.  A combatant who falls into the power of an adverse Party while failing to meet the requirements set forth in the second sentence of paragraph 3 shall forfeit his right to be a prisoner of war, but he shall, nevertheless, be given protections equivalent in all respects to those accorded to prisoners of war by the Third Convention [of 1949] and by this Protocol. This protection includes protections equivalent to those accorded to prisoners of war by the Third Convention in the case where such a person is tried and punished for any offences he has committed.

5.  Any combatant who falls into the power of an adverse Party while not engaged in an attack or in a military operation preparatory to an attack shall not forfeit his rights to be a combatant and a prisoner of war by virtue of his prior activities (American Red Cross, 2001, p. 6).

The international community generally accepts that the additional Geneva Conventions' protocols are obligatory on all parties worldwide. In fact, the protocols have become part of the customary international law (American Red Cross, 2001; Greenhouse, 2008). Despite an international consensus on the protocols, the G. W. Bush administration rejected the expanded definition of lawful combatant and the protections extended to such individuals under Protocol I. Ironically, the Bush administration's refusal to ratify Protocol I aligned the United States with two of President Bush's so-called axis of evil nations—Iraq and Iran—that also refused to ratify it.

In addition, the refusal of the Bush administration to ratify Protocol I had profound consequences beyond the war in Iraq. Specifically, the label of "unlawful enemy combatant" was central to the global war on terror which President Bush declared immediately after the terrorist attacks of 9/11. The label of unlawful enemy combatant was used by the Bush administration to deny habeas corpus rights to hundreds of so-called terrorist suspects who were confined indefinitely in the prison at Guantanamo Bay, Cuba (Greenhouse, 2008). Habeas corpus is the legal right of anyone being held by the U.S. government to challenge his/her confinement before a federal judge (Feldman, 2002; Paust, 2002). However, the U.S. Supreme Court dealt a serious blow to the Bush administration in June of 2008 by ruling that the detainees at Guantanamo Bay prison had a constitutional right to go to federal court and challenge their indefinite detention without having formal charges filed against them (Greenhouse, 2008). Subsequently, there were numerous calls from politicians, judges, legal scholars, and civil rights activists to shut down the prison at Guantanamo Bay. President Bush ignored such pleas and kept the prison open throughout his administration.

### WILL THE BUSH ADMINISTRATION FACE PROSECUTION FOR WAR CRIMES?

The Bush administration violated both the Nuremberg Charter and the U.N. Charter when it launched an invasion of Iraq in 2003. It also violated the Geneva Conventions of 1949 throughout the subsequent war and occupation of Iraq. So, this raises an important question: If members of the Bush administration violated international criminal law as argued here and by numerous scholars of international law, then why were they not charged with war crimes by the International Criminal Court during Bush's second term in office? After all, the 1998 Rome Treaty, which established the ICC, removed head-of-state immunity for war crimes.

The orchestrators of the illegal war on Iraq were not, and are not likely to be, prosecuted for bureaucratic and political reasons. First, no state has ever voluntarily agreed to subject itself to international prosecution and the United States almost certainly will not do so concerning Iraq (Cohn, 2006; Kafala, 2003). Second, as previously discussed, proceedings before the ICC may be initiated by a state party to the ICC, the ICC prosecutor, or the U.N. Security Council. Unless a referral is made by the U.N. Security Council, the ICC can exercise jurisdiction over international crimes *only* if they were committed on the territory of a state party or if they were committed by one of its signatory members. Therein lies the problem regarding the possible prosecution of the Bush administration for war crimes. The United States does not recognize the jurisdiction of the ICC as it has not signed the Rome statute. Similarly, Iraq does not recognize the authority of the ICC. Finally, as a permanent member of the U.N. Security Council, the United States has the ability to veto any move by the council to punish its illegal behavior (Kramer et al., 2005). Therefore, the G. W. Bush administration is almost invulnerable to international prosecution for its past actions concerning Iraq.

Significantly, the refusal of the U.S. to sign the Rome statute and recognize the authority of the ICC places it at odds with almost all of its staunchest international allies. Despite the fact that 108 nations, including most of Western Europe, Canada, Australia, and Japan, have signed the Rome statute, the United States and China have criticized the ICC and refused to either sign the Rome statute or permit the ICC to have jurisdiction over their citizens (Kafala, 2003; Paust, 2002). It is ironic that the U.S. government would be in agreement on this issue with China, a country the United States has frequently accused of human rights violations. Similarly, Iran, Iraq, and North Korea have not signed the Rome statute. Thus, the refusal to ratify the Rome statute and recognize the ICC aligns the United States with the G. W. Bush administration's axis of evil once again in rejecting international consensus on war crimes—similar to the refusal to ratify Protocol I of the Geneva Conventions.

Interestingly, the Bush administration justified its refusal to sign the Rome statute by claiming that the ICC could be used to pursue "politically motivated" prosecutions (Kafala, 2003). However, the Bush administration's argument against the ICC seems to be politically motivated itself. It is more likely that the Bush administration refused to recognize the ICC precisely because the court would make it accountable for pursuing its goal of removing Saddam Hussein and his Baath party from power in Iraq through force (Clarke, 2004; Cohn, 2006). The Bush administration's argument against the ICC was self-serving and it foreshadowed the actions of individuals who would seek to avoid prosecution for war crimes (Ritter, 2006). As argued by Michael Foucault, "Nothing is inherently political. On the contrary, everything *can* be politicized" (Deuber-Mankowsky, 2008, p. 135).

## CONCLUSION

In this chapter, evidence was provided that a moral panic over Iraq engineered by the Bush administration and supported by the news media can be understood as a manifestation of the higher immorality of the power elite. Evidence was provided that the Bush administration violated both domestic and international laws in the invasion and occupation of Iraq. Although it is argued here that a violation of international law is a state crime whether or not the state considers the action to be criminal, certain actions by the Bush administration did indeed violate the U.S. Constitution and federal laws. In particular, the illegally declared and unprovoked invasion of Iraq was a state crime. Also, the invasion of Iraq constituted a war of aggression that violated international laws as established by the Nuremberg Charter and the U.N. Charter. The subsequent occupation of Iraq involved war crimes and atrocities by the United States that violated the Geneva Conventions of 1949.

Based on the body of empirical evidence, it is concluded that the second proposition advanced in this book is accurate. Nevertheless, it is unlikely that either former President Bush or key members of his administration will ever be charged with war crimes by the international community. Because the United States is the dominant state (or 900-pound gorilla) in a hierarchical world order, members of the Bush administration enjoy both political and bureaucratic exemptions from prosecution under international laws. Chapter seven, the final chapter of this book, discusses the social and theoretical implications of the research findings presented here, and it also provides an examination of the Bush administration and the Iraq war within a socio-historical context.

CHAPTER 7

# What Are the Lessons of the Iraq War?

THE SPANISH PHILOSOPHER and poet George Santayana said, "Those who cannot remember the past are condemned to repeat it." The final chapter of this book discusses the contributions of the research to theory and it also presents a contextualized examination of the Bush administration's moral panic over Iraq. An important question guides the discussions presented in this chapter: What can we learn from the moral panic over Iraq about the power elite, the news media, and society in general? The chapter begins with a discussion of the contributions of the research to critical communication theory, introduced in chapter two, and the theoretic traditions that comprise it. Following that, alternative theoretical interpretations of the research findings are considered, and directions for future research on moral panic are offered. Later in the chapter, the moral panic over Iraq is examined in the social, political, and historical contexts in which it was engineered by the Bush administration with the support of the U.S. news media. This contextualized examination addresses important structural and historical antecedents to the elite-engineered moral panic over Iraq. The chapter concludes with a brief discussion of the future.

## THEORY IMPLICATIONS OF THE RESEARCH STUDY

The research findings outlined in this book support an integrated and interdisciplinary theoretic approach—that is, drawing upon critical sociology/criminology, communication theory, and social constructionism—to explain the elite-engineered model of moral panic. As introduced in chapter two, critical communication theory provides a more detailed and synthetic foundation for explaining how and why moral panics are engineered by political elites with the support of the news media, and the impact such panics have on public attitudes and opinions. The results of the research study provided empirical evidence that critical communication theory has explanatory value for the elite-engineered model of moral panic. Specifically, the results demonstrated that the combined forces of elite ideology (rhetoric) and news media coverage (framing) set the public agenda, shape public opinion, construct social problems, and create folk devils. The contributions of the research study to the various theoretic traditions that together comprise critical communication theory are considered below.

As discussed in chapter two, the Frankfurt School of critical sociology provides a basis for explaining how and why moral panics are successfully engineered by societal elites and the news media, and why the public generally accepts elite ideology as real and valid (Habermas, 1975). The central tenets of critical sociology were supported by the research findings presented in chapter three. Specifically, those results demonstrated that false elite ideology delivered through the culture industry can manipulate and oppress the public (Adorno, 1997). False ideology was reflected in the Bush administration's lies and disinformation regarding a "grave and gathering" threat from Iraq that the news media dutifully presented to the U.S. public. Additionally, the power of the media to influence public attitudes and beliefs was demonstrated by the general consensus concerning the Iraqi threat prior to the invasion which resulted from the massive dissemination of pro-war rhetoric in the news.

The findings of the research study support and extend the Frankfurt writers' insights regarding the creation of false consciousness in society (Habermas, 1975; Horkheimer, 1987). Specifically, false consciousness was demonstrated by Gallup polls in the increased public support for invading Iraq which mirrored the increased punitive rhetoric from the Bush administration in the news media. The Bush administration used its influence over the news media to deliver false ideology or disinformation concerning Iraq to U.S. society in order to manipulate public opinion and manufacture consent for war (Chomsky, 2005). Stated differently, the Bush administration used its unfettered access to the U.S. news media to present a false argument intended to convince the public that an invasion of Iraq was vital to national security. As discussed in chapter four, the "news net" perspective maintains that U.S. journalists are generally uncritical of authorities due to the occupational norms, roles, and bureaucratic practices of the news business (Tuchman, 1978). Therefore, reporters would have been very unlikely to question the sincerity or credibility of the Bush administration's pro-war argument. From the perspective of the news net, the news media followed routine procedures after 9/11 which meant that journalists obediently relied on Bush administration sources to frame the alleged threat to the United States from Iraq (Edelman, 1988). Thus, the news media were unquestioning partners in the Bush administration's moral panic over Iraq, which is consistent with critical theory.

As discussed in chapter two, critical theorists argue that false consciousness resulting from the adoption of elite ideology without debate is a defining element of advanced capitalist societies (Adorno, 1997; Agger, 1978; Habermas, 1975). An oppressed society living in false consciousness is susceptible to manipulation, and it will allow the priorities and needs of the elites, including war, to become its own. Arguably, false consciousness in U.S. society virtually eliminated the possibility of meaningful public debate over the legitimacy of the Bush doctrine of preemptive self-defense prior to the invasion (Altheide, 2006; Chomsky, 2005). Also, the results of the analyses of public opinion presented in chapter three indicated that the U.S. public generally accepted the Bush administration's false ideas concerning the Iraqi threat. Therefore, from the perspective of critical theory, a state of false consciousness in U.S. society facilitated the moral panic over Iraq.

The Marxian concept of alienation (or separation from one's "species being") can explain why a passive and uncritical U.S. public generally believed that the Bush administration acted in its best interests and, therefore, did not demand accountability when the administration's lies regarding Iraq were revealed. However, as discussed in chapter six, it is important to note that there were many individual-level exceptions to the major macro-level argument made here that the U.S. public was generally passive and uncritical of the Bush administration's lies concerning Iraq due to alienation. Clearly, not everyone remained passive or mute in response to the Bush administration's decision to invade Iraq. At the micro or individual level, great variability in reactions to both the war and President Bush were mediated by independent factors such as the loss of a loved one in the war, knowledge of the Bush administration's deceptions, and even experiences of personal betrayal (Eschholz, Chiricos & Gertz, 2003; Gartner, 2008).

Despite individual-level variations in society's response to the war, critical theory nevertheless offers great insights into how and why the Bush administration created a moral panic over Iraq with the passive cooperation of the news media. The elite-engineered moral panic increased the Bush administration's power and authority in U.S. society, and it also legitimized the Bush administration's decision to invade Iraq in the minds of Americans. The Bush administration's moral panic over Iraq increased U.S. society's dependency on it by creating fear and alienation among the general public (Agger, 1978; Altheide, 2006). In summary, critical sociology theory explains how and why the Bush administration engineered a moral panic over Iraq, and why the U.S. public generally believed that an unprovoked invasion of a sovereign nation was necessary, justified, and paradoxically, its own idea. Thus, the results of this study both support and expand upon the critical school of sociology.

This study also makes contributions to critical criminology theory. The Bush administration's labeling of Saddam Hussein and his followers as evildoers demonstrates Chambliss's (1975) critical criminology argument that those in power will often define a group or class of people as less than human in order to resolve conflicts in society and in order to justify their self-serving policies. As the research findings in chapter three demonstrated, the Bush administration used punitive rhetoric, particularly the word "evil," to define the regime of Saddam Hussein as folk devils in the moral panic over Iraq. The study supports and expands upon critical criminology theory by offering insights into how and why disvalued groups become defined as folk devils and targeted for punishment or elimination in elite-engineered moral panics.

The findings of the study also have important implications for communication theory. Communication theory provides information on the social construction of reality, how public opinion is established, and how public concern regarding an alleged threat can facilitate a moral panic. In particular, second-level agenda-setting theory provides insights into the processes by which specific attributes and dispositions are attached to issues by the news media that may facilitate a moral panic. Additionally, the communication mechanisms of framing and priming help to explain how political elites and the news media together can create public consensus regarding a moral panic and hostility toward the folk devils. As previously discussed, agenda-setting, framing, and priming were not directly tested in the study presented here. Nevertheless, the effects of those communication processes and mechanisms on U.S. society can be interpreted from the findings of the research presented in chapter three.

Consistent with the literature (Hawdon, 2001; Johnson, Wanta & Boudreau, 2004; Reinarman & Levine, 1989), the results of the study revealed that the president of the United States participates in the agenda-setting process and influences public opinion through the framing of an issue such as the alleged Iraqi threat, and the priming of dispositions regarding that issue. As previously discussed, President Bush's rhetoric toward Saddam Hussein and his political regime following the attacks of 9/11 was designed to incite public hostility toward Iraq by building on negative images of Arabs (Muslims) in the minds of Americans. Powerful stereotypes of Arabs already existed in the United States prior to the attacks of 9/11, as a result of two previous decades of negative media depictions of Arabs as evil, bloodthirsty terrorists (Merskin, 2004). The framing of Saddam Hussein and his followers as evildoers in the news media after 9/11 interacted with negative stereotypes of *all* Arabs so as to prime hostile public attitudes regarding the Bush administration's target (Entman, 2003; Lowery & DeFleur, 1995; Merskin, 2004). Stated differently, the Bush administration exploited pre-existing negative stereotypes of Arabs (Muslims) in the United States in order to define or label Iraqis as folk devils after the terrorist attacks of 9/11.

It has been argued that the symbolic language of political elites, which is dutifully reported by the news media, is at the heart of setting the agenda for public discourse (Edelman, 1988). Providing a powerful example of this,

Rothe and Muzzatti (2004) demonstrated that the U.S. news media unquestioningly framed the "global war on terror" after 9/11 according to the specifications set by the G. W. Bush administration. Importantly, however, the framing of Saddam Hussein/Iraq as evil was first presented by the administration of President George H. W. Bush, and it was established by the media as the dominant news frame on the 1990–1991 Persian Gulf War (Bennett & Paletz, 1994). Because the news frame of Saddam Hussein/Iraq as evil predated the events of 9/11, it was readily available to the G. W. Bush administration after the terrorist attacks.

From the perspective of news as frame (Tuchman, 1978), the news media were following normal journalistic routines after 9/11 when they relied overwhelmingly on G. W. Bush administration sources to define the Iraq issue for the U.S. audience. The results of this study reveal that the punitive, pro-war argument of the Bush administration concerning Iraq became the dominant news frame on Iraq, and as a result, that frame defined reality for the majority of the U.S. public. As argued by Kellner (2005, p. xvi), the "U.S. corporate media enabled the Bush administration's policy [on Iraq]." Although there were occasional counterclaims in the news media to dispute the pro-war argument, as demonstrated by the content analysis in this study, the dominant news frame leading up to the invasion was the Bush administration's "Iraq as evil" message.

The results of the study revealed that rhetorically powerful words used by the Bush administration in reference to Iraq such as "evil" and "threat" significantly increased public support for war. Prior communication research has demonstrated that the U.S. president's ability to prime public support for an issue is directly related to how much emphasis he places on that issue (Hawdon, 2001; Johnson et al., 2004). The findings here support that same conclusion by demonstrating that increased volume (or the sheer number) of news articles with quotes from President Bush regarding Iraq, over and above the effects of the tones of rhetoric used by him, increased public support for invading Iraq in Gallup polls. That is, increased emphasis on the Iraq issue by President Bush, independent of the tone of rhetoric he employed, primed public support for the invasion of Iraq.

In summary, the findings of the research study offer new insights into communication theory on media effects. The results extend the insights into media effects by demonstrating that the news media and the U.S. president together can set the public agenda, frame an issue, and prime dispositions in the direction of a moral panic (Hawdon, 2001; Johnson et al., 2004; Lowery & DeFleur, 1995). Although agenda-setting, framing, and priming were not tested directly in this study, the results nevertheless contribute to communication theory by suggesting that those processes apply to the news media's coverage of presidential rhetoric concerning an alleged threat from a foreign nation and, in particular, a presidential policy argument for war. Finally, from the perspective of news as frame, the general media were following normal journalistic routines and procedures after 9/11 when they relied on the Bush administration's depiction of Iraq as evil to establish the dominant news frame on Iraq.

The research study findings are also consistent with social constructionism and moral panic (Garland, 2008; Goode & Ben-Yehuda, 1994). From a social constructionist perspective, what makes a condition a social problem is the degree of felt concern by society about that condition, regardless of whether it is objectively harmful or whether it even exists. The findings presented in chapter three demonstrated that public opinion mirrored the pro-war rhetoric of the Bush administration. As discussed in chapter four, the Bush administration persistently claimed that Iraq represented a growing threat to U.S. security after 9/11, despite the fact that it knew with virtual certainty that Iraq did not possess the alleged weapons of mass destruction. This demonstrates that the so-called threat to the United States did not exist objectively. On the contrary, the threat was socially constructed by the Bush administration with the cooperation of the U.S. news media.

Therefore, the research findings demonstrated that even public consent for war can be manufactured or elite-engineered (Chomsky, 2005; Goode & Ben-Yehuda, 1994). Such manufactured consent was demonstrated in Gallup polls by increased public support for war following increased Bush administration rhetoric in the news media concerning the alleged Iraqi threat. In particular, the study revealed that increased punitive and communitarian rhetoric used in combination by the Bush administration (i.e., an increased number of news articles containing such quotes) prior to Gallup polls increased public support for invading Iraq.

Furthermore, the research findings are consistent with the social construction of evil, generally, and the labeling of folk devils in a moral panic, specifically. The word "evil," a key example of punitive rhetoric, increased the likelihood of public support for invading Iraq (independent of the source of the rhetoric) in three-month time lags prior to public opinion polls. Such findings demonstrate the unique rhetorical power of the word "evil"—that is, its considerable impact on public attitudes and opinion (Bromley, Shupe & Ventimiglia, 1979; Entman, 2003; Merskin, 2004; Rothe & Muzzatti, 2004). However, it has been argued that the power of the labeler also contributes to the perceived legitimacy and general acceptance of the "evil" label by the public (Bromley et al., 1979). Consistent with that argument, the results here demonstrated that the U.S. president can provide the necessary outlet for public concern that moral panics require, as evidenced by the impact of President Bush's punitive rhetoric, particularly his use of the word "evil," on public support for invading Iraq (Goode & Ben-Yehuda, 1994).

The implications of applying the label of "evil" to others are grave. Once a disvalued individual or group becomes defined as evil in a moral panic, those in power have the moral authority and even obligation to eliminate the folk devils (S. Cohen, 1972; Garland, 2008). This central element of moral panic was manifested in the Bush administration's militaristic response to the socially constructed evildoers in Iraq. The U.S. public generally believed the Bush administration's argument that Saddam Hussein and his followers were evil and, therefore, generally supported the president's choice to go to war. Furthermore, consistent with social constructionism and moral panic, many Americans even believed that the pre-emptive strike on Iraq was their own idea.

Becker (1968, p.142) referred to the practice of reductionism by political elites (e.g., the Bush administration's framing of Iraqis as folk devils) combined with the absence of critical reasoning in society when presented with false universals as "the demonic nature of evil in our time." In his writings on the structure of evil, Becker (1968, p. 142) warned that when "uncritical fictions" take control of society, without either responsible dissent or review of the *ends* of action, then "the world of ineluctable movement assumes its own laws." From that perspective, the alleged threat posed by Saddam Hussein and his political regime became a socially constructed crisis and moral imperative in the United States that justified ends over means. The Bush administration fulfilled its moral obligation to U.S. society by providing a self-serving solution to its own elite-engineered crisis—that is, the invasion of Iraq and removal of Saddam Hussein from power. As discussed, the Bush administration's unnecessary war on Iraq was initially embraced by the majority of Americans. However, public support for it eroded dramatically when the quick victory promised by the Bush administration failed to materialize and the U.S. death toll climbed.

Fish (2001) argued that the presentation of "false universals," such as the Bush administration's "good versus evil" foreign policy argument after 9/11, lay the foundation for annihilating an entire group of people. Fish (2001, p. A-19) stated:

> How many times have we heard these new mantras: "we have seen the face of evil"; "these are irrational madmen"; "we are at war against international terrorism." Each is at once inaccurate and unhelpful. We have not seen the face of evil; we have seen the face of an enemy who comes at us with a full roster of grievances, goals and strategies. If we reduce that enemy to "evil," we conjure up a shape-shifting demon, a wild-card moral anarchist beyond our comprehension and therefore beyond the reach of any counterstrategies.

Immediately following the attacks of 9/11, President Bush reduced the world to a dichotomy—good versus evil—and he used that dichotomy to frame the alleged threat from Iraq (Entman, 2003). According to Fish (2001), when one's opponent is framed as evil that opponent is stripped of all humanity and is assumed to be without reason or morality. From that simplistic perspective, it is foolish and even futile to attempt to communicate with an enemy who is inhuman. Thus, the reductionism inherent in the social construction of evil eliminates any possibility of recourse other than the complete destruction of the enemy. By mid-2008, more than one million Iraqis had died in the U.S.-led war and subsequent occupation (albeit not all at the hands of U.S. soldiers and mercenaries) in contrast to more than forty-one hundred Americans. The tremendous death toll of the Iraq war clearly demonstrates the terrible consequences of labeling one's opponent as evil.

As previously discussed, President Bush used atrocity tales in his punitive post-9/11 rhetoric to bolster the case for invading Iraq. In the months leading up to the invasion, he frequently referred to atrocities allegedly perpetrated by Saddam Hussein against the Iraqi people, such as the use of chemical weapons against the Kurds in northern Iraq prior to the Persian Gulf war (Merskin, 2004; Rothe & Muzzatti, 2004). Atrocity tales were used by President Bush to provide so-called evidence, regardless of whether the claims were true or false, to support the administration's argument that Saddam Hussein and his followers were evil and represented a growing threat to U.S. security (Bromley et al., 1979; Corn, 2003). The atrocity tales were designed to trigger hostility toward Iraq among the U.S. public. Stated differently, the atrocity tales were used to prime retaliatory sentiments among Americans who were hungry for revenge against all Arabs (Muslims) after the attacks of 9/11 (Kellner, 2005). Atrocity tales were thus an integral part of the propaganda campaign used by the Bush administration to manufacture public consent for the invasion of Iraq (Chomsky, 2005; Entman, 2003).

The findings of this study demonstrated that the war in Iraq was legitimized by a moral panic engineered by the Bush administration and reinforced by the news media, which manipulated public support for the invasion of Iraq. The research findings regarding presidential rhetoric support the moral panic literature (Hawdon, 2001; Johnson et al., 2004; Reinarman & Levine, 1989; Rothe & Muzzatti, 2004) which has demonstrated that the president of the United States participates in the social construction of reality and the elite engineering of moral panics. Furthermore, the findings revealed the primacy of the U.S. president as a source of ideology and as a public-agenda setter (Goode & Ben-Yehuda, 1994; Hawdon, 2001; Johnson et al., 2004; Kieve, 1994) because other individual sources and tones of rhetoric were *not* associated with support for invading Iraq once the effects of quotes from President Bush were taken into account. Most importantly, the results of the study demonstrated that the elite-engineered model of moral panic applies to the events following 9/11 that led up to the invasion of Iraq.

Thus, the findings of this study offer important contributions to the moral panic and social constructionism literatures by demonstrating that even public support for a war of aggression can be engineered by the president of the United States with the passive and routine assistance of the news media.

Additionally, this study expands the Millsian sociological literature on elite deviance by demonstrating that an elite-engineered moral panic can be understood as a manifestation of the higher immorality of the power elite. As explained in chapter six, the Bush administration's moral panic over Iraq created moral harm to society by creating cynicism, fear, and alienation among the U.S. public. Furthermore, this study expands the literature on state or government crime by revealing that the invasion and occupation of Iraq meet the necessary criteria of state crime established in the scholarly literature (see Kauzlarich, Mullins & Matthews, 2003). Finally, by examining the unprovoked military actions of the Bush administration against Iraq through the critical lens of international criminal law (as discussed in chapter six), this book expands the literature on war crimes.

In conclusion, the results of the research study supported the integrated theoretic approach introduced here—that is, critical communication theory—which combines perspectives and concepts from critical sociology (and criminology), communication theory, and social constructionism in order to explain elite-engineered moral panic. This integrated approach provides a more detailed and comprehensive foundation for explaining the elite-engineered model of moral panic than is provided in prior moral panic literature. Moreover, the findings of the study also offer important contributions to each of the theoretic traditions that comprise critical communication theory, and Millsian sociology, as well as the literatures on state crime and war crime.

### ALTERNATIVE EXPLANATIONS FOR THE RESEARCH FINDINGS

As argued throughout this book, the events leading up to the invasion of Iraq constitute an elite-engineered moral panic. However, it could be argued that those events and the results of the research are more consistent with the tenets of public arenas theory, or perhaps the grassroots model of moral panic, or risk society theory. As briefly discussed in chapter one, public arenas theory is a symbolic interactionist perspective that explains social problems as the products of a process of collective definition and interpretation (Hilgartner & Bosk, 1988). The theory maintains that many different social issues compete with each other for problem status in institutional arenas of public discourse at any given point in time. The important public arenas include governmental agencies, private foundations, and perhaps most important to this discussion, the mass media.

Public arenas theory contends that clear and unified images or frames of social problems are rarely disseminated to the public through the mass media. Instead, competing frames are presented in the media arena that offer different interpretations of the same social problem and vie for public acceptance. Significantly, public arenas theory recognizes that dominant frames generally prevail over minority ones in public discourse (Wilson, 1996). Public arenas theory further states that a situation does not become a social problem until it is labeled as such in the arenas of public discourse and social action. For example, national security competed with the economy for problem status in the United States following the terrorist attacks of 9/11. However, national security dominated the discourse in public arenas after 9/11, and it quickly became the leading social problem in the United States, according to public opinion polls (Rothe & Muzzatti, 2004).

The results of this study demonstrated that multiple frames on the Iraq issue were presented in the news media after 9/11, as public arenas theory would predict. For example, during the buildup to the invasion, the G. W. Bush administration's framing of Iraq as a serious and growing threat competed with the United Nation's counterframing of Iraq as a benign or even nonexistent threat. However, because the Bush administration was able to dominate the pre-invasion discourse concerning Iraq in important public arenas, particularly in the news media, its framing of the threat became the socially constructed reality that led to war.

The events leading up to the Iraq war were generally consistent with both public arenas theory and the elite-engineered model of moral panic. However, elite-engineered moral panic provides a more salient and comprehensive explanation of those events and of the motivations of the actors involved. That is because the emphasis of elite-engineered moral panic is on powerful elite actors in society who periodically construct social problems that are self-serving, while the emphasis of public arenas theory is on the causal role of the news media and other institutional arenas in defining social problems. Most importantly, elite-engineered moral panic is concerned with the motivations of elite actors in the construction of a social problem, while public arenas theory is focused more generally on how a situation becomes labeled a social problem in the institutions of public discourse.

As previously discussed, the results of this study revealed that different and competing frames of the Iraq issue were disseminated by official sources in the *New York Times* after 9/11, and that those competing sources and tones of rhetoric influenced public support for invading Iraq. However, it was also determined that no competing sources or tones of rhetoric were associated with support for invasion once the effects of quotes from President Bush (i.e., the source of the dominant frame) were taken into account. In particular, the results of the study demonstrated that counterclaims had no effect on public support for war once Bush's pro-war rhetoric was taken into account. That finding helps to explain why the public debate over the validity of the Bush doctrine of preemptive self-defense prior to the invasion was very limited and ineffectual (Kramer, Michalowski & Rothe, 2005; Rothe & Muzzatti, 2004).

Although the findings of the study generally support public arenas theory, the causal mechanisms behind the results are more consistent with the elite-engineered model of moral panic, particularly given the primacy of presidential rhetoric in the construction of the Iraqi threat. Stated differently, the Bush administration manufactured public consent for a war it chose to wage by presenting disinformation about the Iraqi threat to the U.S. public through the news media (Chomsky, 2005). That conclusion is much better explained by elite-engineered moral panic theory than by public arenas theory.

It might be argued that the temporal order argued in this book—that is, increased presidential rhetoric regarding the alleged Iraq threat preceded increased public support for invasion—is incorrect. Perhaps increased public concern regarding Iraq (and support for invasion) led to increased presidential rhetoric regarding the perceived threat. That alternative interpretation is consistent with the grassroots model of moral panic which argues "that panics originate with the general public; the concern about a particular threat is a widespread, genuinely felt—if mistaken—concern" (Goode & Ben-Yehuda, 1994, p. 127). Unlike the elite-engineered model of moral panic, i.e., a top-down approach in which elites orchestrate the panic from above, the grassroots model stipulates that the expression of concern in other spheres, including the media and polity, are really expressions of more widespread concern from the masses. As explained in chapter one, the grassroots model of moral panic is a bottom-up approach in which the masses, rather than the elites, initiate a panic in society.

The grassroots model of moral panic argues that political elites and the news media cannot fabricate public concern where none initially existed. It could perhaps be argued that public concern regarding Iraq prior to 9/11 (i.e., a fairly high level of support for invasion measured in Gallup polls) is consistent with the grassroots model. Interestingly, the first time Gallup asked Americans whether they favored invading Iraq (February 19, 2001) was seven months *before* the terrorist attacks of 9/11 but less than one month *after* the inauguration of President G. W. Bush on January 21, 2001. Exactly why Gallup chose to measure public support for invading Iraq for the first time just a few weeks after President Bush took office is an interesting question.

Arguably, there are only two plausible reasons why Gallup would have asked the U.S. public about Iraq immediately after President Bush took office. First, it is possible that the savvy folks at Gallup rightly suspected that Iraq was high on the Bush administration's short-term agenda and decided to gauge the public's support for an invasion. Second, it is also possible that the Bush administration contacted Gallup directly and asked it to measure the public's attitudes on Iraq to determine how much "marketing" (to quote Andy Card, G. W. Bush's chief of staff in the White House) would be required in order to sell an invasion to the U.S. public. Regardless of its reasoning, Gallup did not ask the same question again in a poll until shortly after the terrorist attacks of 9/11 seven months later. Importantly, the February 19, 2001, Gallup poll provided a pre-9/11 benchmark level of public support for invasion. Furthermore, it indicates that slightly more than half of the U.S. public supported the invasion of Iraq more than half a year before the events of 9/11. This relatively high level of support indicates that public concern and some consensus regarding the alleged threat from Iraq predated the terrorist attacks of 9/11 (S. Cohen, 2002). However, the relatively high pre-9/11 level of public support for invading Iraq was shaped in part by pervasive, stereotypical media portrayals (framing) throughout the 1980s and 1990s of Arabs, in general, as ruthless terrorists, as well as such depictions of Saddam Hussein and his regime, specifically, during the 1990–1991 Persian Gulf war (Altheide, 2006; Merskin, 2004; Rothe & Muzzatti, 2004). The pre-9/11 support for an invasion was also a social artifact of the Persian Gulf war—that is, it reflected a popular perception among the U.S. public that unfinished business remained at the end of the Gulf war (Scheer, 2003). The unfinished business was that Saddam Hussein and his followers were left in control of Iraq after the Gulf war. In fact, President George H. W. Bush was widely criticized by U.S. military leaders, conservative politicians, and segments of the U.S. public, after he left office in 1993, for not "finishing the job" in Iraq and for leaving Saddam Hussein in power (Cohn, 2006; Rothe & Muzzatti, 2004). The effects, on the early presidential agenda of G. W. Bush, of Saddam Hussein remaining in control of Iraq after the Persian Gulf war is discussed in the final section of this chapter.

Negative media stereotypes of Arabs (Muslims) in the decades prior to 9/11 created an important antecedent to the moral panic over Iraq. Specifically, a legacy of negative media framing of Arabs predisposed the U.S. public to punitive action toward Iraq even before the events of 9/11 (Merskin, 2004). The Bush administration effectively exploited that predisposition in the months following the terrorist attacks (Altheide, 2006; Entman, 2003). As previously discussed, the framing, by President Bush and the news media after 9/11, of Saddam Hussein and his followers as evildoers interacted with negative stereotypes of all Arabs in the United States, so as to prime hostile and retaliatory public attitudes toward Iraqis (Entman, 2003; Merskin, 2004). Punitive rhetoric by President Bush and other key administration sources toward Iraq increased dramatically after 9/11. By March 15, 2003, just four days prior to the invasion of Iraq, public support for it had peaked, and 70% of the U.S. population believed that Iraq was directly involved in the terrorist attacks of 9/11. In summary, the Bush administration used a successful propaganda campaign to link Iraq to the horrific but unrelated events of 9/11—in part by exploiting negative stereotypes of Arabs (Muslims)—and thus trigger hostility toward Iraq among Americans who were hungry for revenge after the terrorist attacks.

The elite-engineered model of moral panic is much more consistent with the events leading up to the invasion of Iraq than is the grassroots model. Furthermore, the findings of the research study support the elite-engineered model of moral panic. The results reveal that the temporal order argued here is correct—that is, increased pro-war rhetoric from the Bush administration regarding Iraq preceded increased public support for an invasion. Specifically, the analyses of public opinion, controlling for time-lagged effects, demonstrated that increased presidential rhetoric regarding the alleged Iraqi threat in various time periods *preceding* Gallup polls increased the likelihood of public support for an invasion. Therefore, the evidence clearly supports a conclusion that the Bush administration's inflammatory, pro-war rhetoric toward Iraq in the news media after 9/11 did engineer a moral panic in U.S. society.

Risk society theory offers another perspective on the events leading up to the Iraq war. According to the theory, risk society is seen as a condition or manifestation of late modern societies—particularly U.S. society. As briefly discussed in chapter one, it has been argued that the United States became a risk society following the attacks of 9/11 (Welch, 2006a, 2006b). Risk society theory states that immediately after the events of 9/11, U.S. society became hypersensitized to terrorist threats and hypervigilant concerning national security. From the perspective of risk society theory, the American public became preoccupied with national defense after 9/11 and it was likely to support state managers who not only offered assurances of security but also demonstrated a willingness to "kick some ass" among its enemies (Welch, 2006a, 2006b).

It has been argued that risk society and moral panic are complementary and mutually reinforcing theoretical perspectives (Welch, 2006b). However, it has been argued that moral panic theory is retrospective and episodic, while risk society theory addresses societal conditions that are more enduring (Welch, 2007). The elite-engineered model of moral panic posits that once societal elites frame an issue, all other interpretations of reality are critiqued through the lens of elite formulations (Goode & Ben-Yehuda, 1994). Risk society theory contends that Americans are highly susceptible to manipulation by governmental elites after 9/11 due to a heightened public fear of terrorism (Welch, 2006a, 2006b; Croft, 2006). As such, public fear can be manipulated in order to gain support for political candidates and policy initiatives. For example, the Republican candidate in the 2008 U.S. presidential election,

John McCain, attempted to manipulate public fears in his unsuccessful campaign against Barack Obama. McCain attempted to portray Obama as weak and ill-prepared to deal with national security challenges in times of war. That strategy might have succeeded if not for a global economic crisis prior to the election that, according to public opinion polls, usurped national security as the leading concern among Americans.

The Bush administration effectively tapped into social anxiety in the United States following 9/11 to manipulate public support for the invasion of Iraq. That is, the Bush administration deliberately linked the alleged Iraqi threat to 9/11 in order to exploit public fears and prime retaliatory sentiments among Americans who were hungry for revenge after the terrorist attacks. The central argument of this book is thus consistent with both risk society theory and the elite-engineered model of moral panic. In fact, the United States was highly susceptible to an elite-engineered moral panic over Iraq precisely because it had become a risk society following the 9/11 attacks (Croft, 2006). Stated differently, a post-9/11 risk society provided the contextual canvas on which an elite-engineered moral panic over Iraq could be readily painted by the Bush administration.

The risk society perspective is supported by Altheide (2006), who states that fear messages are so prominent in the news media—and so long-lasting—that there is almost a free-floating sense of fear that provides a baseline emotion for the U.S. audience. That condition was magnified by the wave of fear frames on terrorism that were presented in the news media after 9/11. According to Altheide (2006), a heightened level of fear over terrorism in the United States gave the government, i.e., the G. W. Bush administration, tremendous latitude to exercise its control over society and declare war on Iraq with little or no opposition from the major U.S. news media. This argument is further supported by Chomsky (2005), who states that societal consent for the invasion of Iraq was manufactured by the Bush administration after 9/11 through the dissemination of pro-war propaganda in the news media—that is, propaganda designed to induce fear and manipulate the U.S. public.

In conclusion, it is argued here that the elite-engineered model of moral panic is particularly relevant to the events and social conditions that both preceded and led up to the Iraq war. Specifically, elite-engineered moral panic effectively describes how the Bush administration used its influence over the news media in order to disseminate disinformation regarding an alleged Iraqi threat after 9/11 that created fear and contrived support for war among the U.S. public. The grassroots model of moral panic, public arenas theory, and risk society theory offer alternative perspectives on the events leading up to the Iraq war. However, the grassroots model of moral panic does not apply to the temporal order of those events. Public arenas theory and risk society theory are each complementary to the moral panic perspective in certain important regards—yet, the elite-engineered model of moral panic offers the most relevant and theoretically grounded explanation for the events preceding the Iraq war. In the section below, directions for future research on moral panic are briefly considered.

### DIRECTIONS FOR FUTURE RESEARCH

Although the research study presented in this book offers important contributions to critical communication theory, including the various theoretical traditions that comprise it, and the elite-engineered model of moral panic, the study also leaves several issues unaddressed that provide opportunities and directions for future research. First, the study only analyzed, through the lens of moral panic, the events leading up to the invasion of Iraq. Therefore, yet to be analyzed from a moral panic perspective are the effects of presidential rhetoric on public support for the Iraq war *after* the invasion began on March 19, 2003. This raises an important question: Do the post-invasion conditions, including presidential rhetoric and support for the Iraq war, correspond to the elite-engineered model of moral panic? This is an important research question that warrants consideration and empirical study.

As previously noted, public support for the invasion of Iraq peaked just prior to the first U.S. missile strikes in 2003. By December of 2006, nearly four years later, almost two-thirds (62%) of the U.S. public believed that the war was a mistake (Hutcheson, 2006). The erosion of public support for the war was likely driven by dramatic increases in the injury and death of U.S. soldiers in Iraq between 2005 and 2007. In addition, the moral panic perspective (see Hawdon, 2001) would predict that the diminution of public support for the war over time was associated with increases in reactive and rehabilitative presidential rhetoric combined with decreases in punitive and communitarian presidential rhetoric. In fact, important and substantive changes in the post-invasion rhetoric of the Bush administration concerning Iraq have been documented (Altheide, 2006; Iskandar, 2005; Rothe & Muzzatti, 2004). Specifically, the failure of the U.S. military to locate the alleged WMD forced the Bush administration to change its primary rationale for the Iraq war after the fact. As early as 2004, the Bush administration began to retroactively change the justification for the invasion from the threat of WMD to the liberation of the Iraqi people and the introduction of Western-style democracy to that country (Altheide, 2006; Suskind, 2008). Therefore, the dominant "Iraq as evil" news frame began to disappear in 2004. Consistent with the "news net" concept, the major news media followed normal journalistic routines and allowed the Bush administration to redefine the situation in Iraq (Tuchman, 1978). Stated differently, the U.S. news media dutifully reported the Bush administration's reframing of the Iraq war, which subsequently redefined reality for many Americans.

There is some evidence that President Bush's post-invasion rhetoric regarding Iraq was rehabilitative and reactive in tone as it focused on helping the Iraqi people (Hawdon, 2001; Kellner, 2005). However, analyses are required to provide empirical support for such a conclusion. Therefore, analyses of the Bush administration's rhetoric toward Iraq, as quoted in the *New York Times* after the invasion began, combined with analyses of the effects of the post-invasion presidential rhetoric on public support for the war, would comprise a valuable follow-up study to the prewar analyses presented here. Specifically, the post-invasion analyses would determine whether the elite-engineered model of moral panic can be applied to the events and conditions that transpired after the Iraq war began.

Also, consideration should be given to the appropriate or best time lags to use in the logistic regression analyses of public opinion (support for war) on volume and tone of presidential rhetoric. As discussed in chapter three, it is important to control for time-lagged effects of presidential rhetoric on public opinion in such studies (Beckett, 1994). However, there is also a dilemma in that regard. Specifically, sufficient time must be given for communication processes to occur but excessive time lags may have diminishing effects on public opinion. In the present study, for example, sources and tones of rhetoric seemed to have optimum effects on support for invasion in one-month and three-month lags preceding Gallup polls, while the five-month lag was rarely associated with increased public support. Further research is warranted on this issue, which may or may not yield similar findings to those produced here.

Second, as previously noted, one of the limitations of this research study was having only one data source of political rhetoric in the analyses. For both methodological and theoretical reasons, a replication of the analyses conducted in this study using alternative news media sources would contribute to the communication literature on media effects and, hopefully, demonstrate the reliability of this study. Such a replication study would involve the two sets of analyses conducted here—that is: (1) content analyses of pre- and post-9/11 presidential rhetoric (volume and tone by source) regarding Iraq; and (2) analyses of survey data (opinion polls) to examine the influences of the rhetoric on public support for invasion/war over time. It would be very interesting to conduct those analyses using a self-proclaimed, politically conservative newspaper such as the *Washington Times*. Because the *New York Times* is often considered to be liberal in tone and content, particularly by political conservatives (Scheer, 2003), it would be both theoretically and methodologically valuable to determine whether the two media sources produce similar results. Intuitively, one might expect a conservative news medium to be even more likely than a liberal news medium to promote the political agenda of President Bush and to embrace his post-9/11 framing of Iraq as evil. Therefore, it is possible that analyses using the *Washington Times* might produce even stronger support for the first proposition of this book than did analyses using the *New York Times*. In other words, the *New York Times* may actually have represented a worst-case scenario (medium) in which to test a central argument of this book.

Significantly, all of the major news media, not just the *New York Times*, followed normal journalistic routines after 9/11 and obediently relied on Bush administration sources to define the alleged threat to U.S. security from Iraq (Altheide, 2006; Entman, 2003; Kellner, 2005). It would be valuable to replicate this study using a network television news source such as CNN or Fox News, recognizing that powerful visual images of the 9/11 terrorist attacks were used by the Bush administration in its propaganda campaign to fuel the panic over Iraq. President Bush frequently invoked images of 9/11 in his daily television sound bites regarding the alleged Iraqi threat that were designed to trigger retaliatory sentiments among Americans who sought revenge for the terrorist attacks (Kellner, 2005; Mueller, 2006). Given the persuasive power of the visual medium (Iskandar, 2005), a television analysis would provide a cross-media comparison to the *New York Times* (Welch, Price & Yankey, 2002). In particular, an examination of the Fox News network's coverage of the Iraq issue after 9/11 would be compelling. The conservative political orientation of Fox News, and its support for the G. W. Bush administration and the Iraq war, are well established (Iskandar, 2005). Therefore, one would expect public support for invading Iraq to mirror Fox News's coverage, similar to the *Washington Times*'s coverage, due to the network's overwhelming reliance on the Bush administration to frame the alleged Iraqi threat for the U.S. audience.

Finally, future attention should be given to individual-level variations in media usage, including types of content, e.g., news versus dramatic programming, as discussed in chapter three. Given the theoretically informed assumption (see Nielsen & Bonn, 2008) that increased media usage at the individual level is associated with greater concern regarding the alleged threat posed by Iraq, an individual-level study of media usage and support for the Iraq war is warranted. However, a dataset that would facilitate such an analysis must first be identified. As previously noted, individual-level measures were not available from Gallup. If individual-level media usage and public opinion data are not available for a study of the Iraq war, then communication and moral panic research would benefit from an individual-level media usage analysis in another elite-engineered moral panic context such as the war on drugs in the United States.

## WHY DID THE BUSH ADMINISTRATION REALLY INVADE IRAQ?

Up to this point, this book has focused on the immoral and illegal actions of the Bush administration concerning Iraq and the consequences of those actions on the citizens of the United States and Iraq. Yet to be discussed in much detail are the Bush administration's real reasons for declaring war on Iraq in 2003. Did 9/11 create an opportunity for the Bush administration to pursue a hidden objective of invading Iraq by fraudulently linking that country to the terrorist attacks? As previously mentioned, Richard Clarke, the former chief counterterrorism advisor, revealed that President G. W. Bush asked him to find evidence that Saddam Hussein was connected to 9/11 within twenty-four hours of the terrorist attacks. It has also been argued that removing Saddam Hussein from power in Iraq was a top priority of the Bush administration from its very first days in the White House, i.e., eight months before the attacks of 9/11 (Clarke, 2004; Cohn, 2006; Ritter, 2006).

The key question is why did the Bush administration really target Iraq for conquest? More specifically, if the Bush administration knew with virtual certainty that Iraq did not pose an objective threat to U.S. security, then why did it declare the opposite to the U.S. public and launch a propaganda campaign to manufacture support for the invasion of Iraq? The answer to this question is important because it can establish the Bush administration's actual motivation(s) for war. In order to answer this question, it is necessary to examine the socio-historical context in which the moral panic over Iraq occurred. A contextualized analysis of the moral panic over Iraq reveals that President G. W. Bush's actual motivations for invading and occupying Iraq fall into one of two related categories: (1) Bush family legacy, and (2) geopolitical domination. Evidence to support this argument is provided below.

As previously mentioned, moral panics do not occur in a vacuum. That is, just because moral panics are "volatile and short-lived does not mean that they do not have structural or historical antecedents" (Goode & Ben-Yehuda, 1994, p. 39). In addition to the news framing, prior to 9/11, of Arabs (Muslims) as rogue terrorists, important structural and historical antecedents of the moral panic over Iraq include the Bush family's Middle East oil connections and businesses that facilitated two U.S. presidencies. In other words, the Bush family legacy provided important motivations for George W. Bush's engineering of a moral panic and declaration of war on Iraq.

A brief history of the Bush family in the United States is warranted. As long-term members of the power elite, the Bush family has profoundly influenced the affairs and policies of the United States. In fact, the Bushes have wielded vast and disproportionate amounts of power in the economic, military, and political spheres of the United States for a hundred years. It has been documented that the Bush family was deeply involved with "the mainstays of the twentieth-century American national security state: finance, oil and energy, the federal government [Congress and the Presidency] . . . and the CIA [George H. W. Bush is a former director], the National Security Agency, and the rest of the intelligence community" (Phillips, 2004, p. 215).

When Mills (1956) explained the dangers of concentrating vast power in the hands of a relatively few elites in society, he was referring to individuals and families such as the Bushes. In his 1961 farewell address, President Dwight D. Eisenhower warned of the same when he said that "we must guard against the acquisition of unwarranted influence, whether sought or unsought, by the military-industrial complex." Eisenhower's warning came decades late because the Bushes were fixtures in the U.S. military-industrial complex nearly fifty years prior to his farewell address.

The Bush family's business interests, particularly its interests in oil, established important structural antecedents and motivations for the war on Iraq. Kevin Phillips (2004), a former Republican strategist, explained that the Bush family fortune was started by G. W. Bush's great-grandfathers, the business entrepreneurs George Herbert Walker and Samuel Bush, both of whom were engaged in finance during and after World War I. By 1919, G. H. Walker was the president of Wall Street-based W. A. Harriman, which invested in oil, shipping, aviation, and manganese, partly in Russia and Germany, during the 1920s. Sam Bush ran an Ohio company, Buckeye Steel Castings, which produced armaments for the U.S. military and heavy equipment for the private sector. The family's ties to John D. Rockefeller and Standard Oil go back nearly a hundred years, when Rockefeller made Buckeye Steel Castings tremendously successful by convincing railroads that carried its oil to buy heavy equipment from Buckeye. George H. Walker helped refurbish the Soviet oil industry in the 1920s, and Prescott Bush (G. W. Bush's grandfather) acquired experience in the international oil business as a twenty-two-year director of Dresser Industries. George H. W. Bush worked for Dresser and ran his own offshore oil-drilling business, Zapata Offshore, prior to running for the Senate. George W. Bush mostly raised money from investors for oil businesses that failed prior to launching his own political career (Phillips, 2004).

Significantly, the Bush family's primary oil interests are located in the Middle East. In fact, the Bush family has had long-term financial ties with Middle Eastern countries, especially Saudi Arabia. As explained by Phillips (2004, p. 315), "No other political family in the United States has had anything remotely resembling the Bushes' four-decade relationship with the Saudi royal family and the oil sheikhs of the Persian Gulf." In fact, the Saudi royal family financed the debt in several of G. W. Bush's failed oil businesses. The Bush family's deep financial involvement in Middle East oil has focused its fortunes and its political agenda directly on the Persian Gulf (Phillips, 2004).

It is a matter of public record that the G. W. Bush administration was aligned with powerful multinational oil and gas companies (Muttitt, 2006; Phillips, 2004). For example, Enron Corporation, the giant energy company founded by a Bush-family friend, Kenneth Lay, was the largest contributor to G. W. Bush's political career. As a result, Ken Lay and his colleagues wielded tremendous influence over G. W. Bush's early presidential agenda and his energy policy (Phillips, 2004). Of course, that was prior to the "Enron scandal," involving corporate corruption and accounting fraud perpetrated by Lay and his executive staff, which destroyed the company and resulted in the criminal convictions of Lay and others in federal court.

As previously discussed, a relatively high level of public support for invading Iraq existed in the United States even before the attacks of 9/11. Consistent with the moral panic literature, the pre-9/11 public support for war was a social artifact of the Persian Gulf war, which did not remove Saddam Hussein from power in Iraq. President George H. W. Bush's decision to allow Saddam Hussein's political regime to remain in power at the conclusion of the war in 1991 was unpopular in many circles. Many high-ranking military leaders, conservative politicians, members of the press, and segments of the general public were harshly critical of the senior Bush's failure to remove Hussein. That social context established a final motivation for George W. Bush's invasion of Iraq, involving his family legacy.

It has been argued that George W. Bush was very critical of his own father for failing to "finish the job" in Iraq (R. Baker, 2004; Phillips, 2004). The son's frustration with his father in that regard was dramatically portrayed by the actor Josh Brolin in Oliver Stone's 2008 film *W*. In fact, eliminating Saddam Hussein became a priority for the younger Bush (Peterson, 2002). Two years before the 9/11 attacks, presidential candidate George W. Bush was already talking privately about the political benefits of attacking Iraq, according to his former ghostwriter, Mickey Herskowitz, who held many conversations with then-Texas governor G. W. Bush, in preparation for a planned autobiography (R. Baker, 2004). Herskowitz said that during their one-on-one meetings, G. W. Bush expressed frustration at being a lifelong underachiever in the shadow of an accomplished father. If elected president, the son saw the opportunity to emerge from that shadow by eliminating Saddam Hussein through military action and, thereby, complete his father's unfinished business in Iraq (R. Baker, 2004).

Clarke (2004) has stated that even before the attacks of 9/11, the G. W. Bush administration was distracted from efforts against Osama Bin Laden's al Qaeda organization by a "preoccupation" with Iraq and Saddam Hussein. Saddam Hussein was already targeted by G. W. Bush when he entered the White House in 2001, and the attacks of 9/11 created an opportunity for President Bush to eliminate Hussein by falsely linking the Iraqi leader to those catastrophic events (Clarke, 2004). Despite his claim that an invasion of Iraq was necessary due to its alleged ties to 9/11 and its alleged possession of WMD, Bush had personal motivations for war that were apparent. For example, during the buildup to the invasion, G. W. Bush personalized his argument for war, saying of the Iraqi leader, "He tried to kill my dad" (Peterson, 2002).

By removing Saddam Hussein from power in Iraq, the younger Bush avenged his father and also accomplished what his father had failed to do more than a decade earlier. Significantly, G. W. Bush created his own identity and legacy in the process. The implications of that legacy are discussed at the end of this chapter. Finally, the personal satisfaction G. W. Bush derived from defeating Saddam Hussein was symbolized by a souvenir that he kept in a study adjoining the Oval Office—that is, the pistol Hussein was holding when he was captured by U.S. forces in Iraq (www.news.bbc.co.uk, 2004).

Beyond the Bush family legacy, other motivations for the Iraq war were linked to the Bush administration's goal of geopolitical domination, including the control of energy. Shortly after taking office in 2001, Vice President Dick Cheney declared that "Middle East oil producers will remain central to world oil security. . . . [Therefore, the] Persian Gulf will be a primary focus of U.S. international energy policy" (Muttitt, 2006, p. 8). Under the supervision of Cheney, an "oil security" strategy was implemented in 2001 that was designed to pursue the Bush administration's energy goals through aggression (Phillips, 2004). To put the importance of the oil issue in perspective, the United States has only 5% of the world's population but uses 25% of the world's energy (Phillips, 2004). At the same time, Iraq possesses 10% of the world's oil reserves—the third largest such reserves on the planet (Muttitt, 2006). Iraq's massive oil reserves represented an inviting target to a G. W. Bush administration that was fixated on the domination and control of energy resources (Cohn, 2006). Therefore, the Bush administration declared war on Iraq and removed Saddam Hussein from power in order to take control of Iraq's oil production and massive reserves (Cohn, 2006; Ritter, 2006). Providing support for this argument is the amazing fact that the only public building that was protected by the U.S. military during the chaos that followed the overthrow of Saddam Hussein's government in 2003 was the one that housed the Iraqi Oil Ministry.

Key beneficiaries of the Iraq war were the giant U.S.-backed multinational oil companies and the private contractors that were favored by the Bush administration (Cohn, 2006). It has been charged that control of much of Iraq's oil wealth was handed over to U.S.-backed multinational oil companies through long-term contracts that will cost Iraq hundreds of billions of dollars over several decades (Muttitt, 2006). Known as production-sharing agreements (PSAs), such contracts are typically signed in secrecy and generally last for twenty-five to forty years. Significantly, they prevent a government such as Iraq from later altering the terms of the agreement. PSAs guarantee massive profits to foreign investors with rates of return between 50–150%. Such contracts were heavily promoted by the G. W. Bush administration, and they were also backed by senior figures in the Iraqi Oil Ministry after the collapse of Saddam Hussein's government (Muttitt, 2006). The invasion and occupation of Iraq provided the Bush administration with the power and authority to orchestrate such agreements and, thereby, gain access to a disproportionate share of the world's oil reserves through its political allies, i.e., the multinational oil companies (Cohn, 2006). At the same time, the Bush administration used the Iraq war to reward some of its other political allies such as Halliburton with lucrative no-bid security and reconstruction contracts. As previously discussed, the Bush administration's reliance on politically favored private contractors resulted in more than $100 billion in U.S. funds being awarded to groups that had little or no accountability or oversight.

It is clear that the invasion of Iraq was also motivated in part by the Bush administration's imperialist desire to achieve domination of the Middle East (Kramer et al., 2005). Disturbingly, the invasion of Iraq and the forced restructuring of its government were glaring examples of neocolonialism. As previously discussed, the Bush administration used the hegemonic and illegal "Bush doctrine" to justify the invasion of a sovereign nation that had neither attacked nor threatened the United States. In addition to its oil reserves, Iraq also provided the Bush administration with a strategic military location next to Iran, another member of its so-called axis of evil (Clark, 2006). If the Bush administration had decided to launch an attack on Iran, then a base of operations adjacent to it in Iraq would have provided a distinct military advantage. In summary, the invasion of Iraq was not done to promote civil society, as claimed by the Bush administration *after* it failed to locate the alleged WMD there. On the contrary, President G. W. Bush invaded Iraq in order to strengthen his family's Middle East oil interests, avenge his father, pursue geopolitical advantages, reward his political allies, and create his own legacy in the process.

CONCLUSION

The results of the study and the other empirical evidence presented in this book are consistent with the elite-engineered model of moral panic. That evidence also supports an integrated and interdisciplinary theoretical framework, i.e., critical communication theory, introduced here to provide a more comprehensive explanation of the elite-engineered model of moral panic. The findings of the study supported the theoretically based research predictions by demonstrating that even public consent for invading a sovereign nation can be elite-engineered by the U.S. president. Thus, as stated in the first proposition of this book, it is reasonable to conclude from the research findings that the war in Iraq was legitimized by a moral panic engineered by the G. W. Bush administration after 9/11, and fueled by the news media, over an allegedly grave and growing threat posed by the regime of Saddam Hussein.

The evidence also supports the second proposition of this book. Specifically, the moral panic over Iraq, which was built on a foundation of deception and lies, constitutes the higher immorality of the power elite, or more specifically, the Bush administration. Also, the Bush administration violated both domestic and international laws in the invasion and occupation of Iraq. In particular, the illegal declaration of war by President Bush and the unprovoked invasion of Iraq were state crimes. Furthermore, the invasion of Iraq was a war of aggression that violated international criminal law as established by the Nuremberg Charter and the U.N. Charter. The subsequent occupation of Iraq involved war crimes and atrocities that violated the Geneva Conventions of 1949. However, it is unlikely that either former President G. W. Bush or key members of his administration will ever be charged with war crimes by the International Criminal Court in The Hague because they enjoy both political and bureaucratic exemptions from such prosecution under international laws.

## WHAT'S PAST IS PROLOGUE: WILLIAM SHAKESPEARE

On November 3, 2004, President G. W. Bush and Vice President Dick Cheney were celebrating their relatively narrow reelection victory over the Democrat candidate John Kerry and his running mate, John Edwards. That night Dick Cheney announced to a cheering Republican audience, "If ever a man met his moment as leader of this country, that man is George W. Bush." President Bush responded to both Dick Cheney and the crowd as follows: "Our military has brought justice to the enemy [i.e., Saddam Hussein] and honor to America. We are entering a season of hope. We'll continue our economic progress. We'll reform our outdated tax code. We'll strengthen the Social Security for the next generation. We'll make public schools all they can be. And we will uphold our deepest values of family and faith."

Of course, none of the claims or promises he made in 2004 became the legacy of George W. Bush. Instead, the Bush legacy is an unprovoked and illegal war in Iraq which nearly crippled the U.S. economy and tarnished the United States' image worldwide. By the fall of 2008, the United States was still spending in excess of $10 billion every month in Iraq. Despite a significant reduction in violence in Baghdad, suicide bombings were still wreaking havoc in Iraq. There was still no law to apportion Iraq's oil revenues among the various ethnic, religious, and political factions in the country, and there was no law to determine the future of the disputed city of Kirkuk. Iraq remained a politically turbulent country with an uncertain future.

In the fall of 2008 critics argued that only a firm deadline and sound withdrawal plan for the occupying U.S. forces would enable and encourage Iraqi officials to implement political reforms that might stabilize Iraq (Levinson, 2008; Robertson & Oppel, 2008). In fact, the Iraqi cabinet sought an agreement before President Bush left office that would require all U.S. troops to exit Iraq by 2012 (Zoepf & Dagher, 2008). On November 28, 2008, after nearly a year of negotiations with the United States, Iraq's parliament signed a pact that required a full withdrawal of American troops by the end of 2011. The agreement represented a significant concession by the departing Bush administration because it had previously rejected setting any timetable for removing U.S. troops from Iraq.

The agreement also gave Iraq's parliament an expanded role in approving and overseeing U.S. military operations there. In particular, it required U.S. troops to obtain a warrant before searching homes or detaining Iraqis, except in active combat (Levinson, 2008). It also included a clear ban against the United States launching attacks on Iraq's neighbors from within its borders. The agreement gave Iraqi authorities the power to inspect all cargo arriving at U.S. bases in Iraq. The deal stipulated that U.S. troops and contractors who committed major crimes could face trial before an Iraqi court if the offenses were committed when U.S. troops were off duty and off base. Iraq's parliament sought such authority and jurisdiction because the Bush administration had previously insisted on the exclusive right to prosecute U.S. troops for virtually all offenses committed there, including those committed against Iraqi citizens—a serious violation of the Geneva Conventions. The 2008 agreement was G. W. Bush's final action in a war he had launched illegally nearly six full years earlier and that his successor would inherit.

On November 4, 2008, Barack Obama, a relatively less experienced senator (Democrat) from Illinois who promised the people of the United States hope and change, was elected the forty-fourth president of the United States in a decisive victory over his Republican opponent, Senator John McCain from Arizona. Barack Obama exhibited a thoughtful approach and poise throughout his campaign that inspired nearly sixty-seven million Americans to vote for him, including many first-time voters. His message of change resonated with Americans, who were disillusioned and alienated after eight years of deceit and failures by the Bush administration.

President Obama offered the promise of a new, more inclusive U.S. foreign policy—one freed from President Bush's aggressive and simplistic us–versus–them ideology. It was uncertain in the early spring of 2009 what the Obama presidency would mean to the world but his message of change was embraced globally, even by nations with a history of grievances toward the United States such as Syria, North Korea, and Iran. For example, shortly after the 2008 U.S. presidential election, Iranian President Mahmoud Ahmadinejad predicted that President Obama would replace Bush's oppressive foreign policies with an approach based on fairness and respect, and a lack of intervention (military or otherwise) in the affairs of sovereign nations. The Iranian president was responding to Barack Obama's campaign pledge to meet with adversarial heads of state in order to discuss their differences, without requiring preconditions for such meetings. In contrast, President G. W. Bush had refused to even meet with certain leaders such as Ahmadinejad unless he fulfilled preconditions established by the United States. Republican presidential candidate John McCain had advocated the same unilateral approach as Bush throughout his campaign. In fact, the hegemonic ideology of McCain was apparent even in his callous attempts at humor prior to the 2008 election. On the campaign trail, for example, McCain made an infamous gaffe when he sang "bomb, bomb Iran" to the melody of the Beach Boys' "Barbara Ann."

Although Barack Obama displayed many impressive skills throughout the 2008 presidential race, his decisive victory over McCain was in large part a reaction by American voters to the lies and corruption of the G. W. Bush administration. The moral panic engineered by the Bush administration was highly successful in garnering initial support for the invasion of Iraq, but it later triggered resentment among a substantial portion of the U.S. public when the Bush administration's prewar lies were revealed, and the war itself brought tremendous human suffering, loss of life, and staggering financial debt. The U.S. public's animosity toward Bush was manifested in his job approval rating, which dropped below 25% before he left office, as well as in Obama's decisive victory in the 2008 presidential election. Obama rode the tide of public dissatisfaction with President Bush and Vice President Cheney to become the first African-American to occupy the Oval Office. More specifically, the failures and deceit of the Bush administration interacted with a global economic crisis to create an environment in which the historic victory by Barack Obama could occur. Throughout this book the focus has been on how and why public attitudes and opinions in advanced capitalist societies can be manipulated by political elites, with the assistance of compliant news media, in order to fulfill mutually rewarding goals. Perhaps, however, the moral panic engineered by the Bush administration over Iraq taught at least a portion of the U.S. public the merits of an old saying: Fool me once, shame on you. Fool me twice, shame on me.

# Appendix

Table A.1

*Gallup Public Opinion Polls on Support for Invasion of Iraq*

Question: Do you favor or oppose sending American ground troops into Iraq to remove Saddam Hussein from power?

| Poll Date | Sample Size (n) | % Favor | % Oppose | % Don't Know/ Refuse |
|---|---|---|---|---|
| Feb 19–21, 01 | 1016 | 52.5 | 41.7 | 5.8 |
| Nov 26–27, 01 | 1025 | 73.9 | 20.3 | 5.7 |
| Jun 17–19, 02 | 519 | 59.3 | 33.1 | 7.5 |
| Aug 19–21, 02 | 802 | 52.7 | 40.7 | 6.5 |
| Sep 2–4, 02 | 1002 | 57.7 | 35.7 | 6.6 |
| Sep 5–8, 02 | 505 | 58.0 | 36.0 | 6.0 |
| Sep 13–16, 02 | 803 | 57.1 | 38.5 | 4.4 |
| Sep 20–22, 02 | 518 | 56.6 | 39.8 | 3.7 |
| Oct 3–6, 02 | 1501 | 53.3 | 39.9 | 6.8 |
| Oct 14–17, 02 | 504 | 56.0 | 37.0 | 7.0 |
| Oct 21–22, 02 | 1012 | 54.0 | 40.0 | 6.0 |
| Nov 8–10, 02 | 1015 | 58.7 | 35.3 | 6.0 |
| Nov 22–24, 02 | 1018 | 57.8 | 37.6 | 4.7 |
| Dec 9–10, 02 | 1009 | 55.0 | 38.9 | 6.1 |
| Dec 16–17, 02 | 479 | 57.9 | 34.6 | 7.5 |
| Dec 19–22, 02 | 501 | 53.2 | 38.1 | 8.6 |
| Jan 3–5, 03 | 487 | 56.5 | 38.9 | 4.5 |
| Jan 10–12, 03 | 1003 | 55.4 | 38.3 | 6.3 |
| Jan 23–25, 03 | 1000 | 52.5 | 43.0 | 4.6 |
| Jan 31–Feb 2, 03 | 1004 | 57.5 | 38.2 | 4.2 |

*(continued)*

*Appendix*

TABLE A.1   *Gallup Public Opinion Polls on Support for Invasion of Iraq*
*(continued)*

| Date | Sample Size (n) | % Favor | % Oppose | % Don't Know/ Refuse |
|------|-----------------|---------|----------|----------------------|
| Feb 7–9, 03 | 1000 | 63.4 | 33.4 | 3.2 |
| Feb 17–19, 03 | 1002 | 57.2 | 38.9 | 3.9 |
| Feb 24–26, 03 | 1003 | 59.2 | 36.5 | 4.3 |
| Mar 3–5, 03 | 1002 | 59.0 | 37.0 | 4.0 |
| Mar 14–15, 03 | 478 | 64.1 | 32.9 | 3.0 |

NOTE: There were twenty-five Gallup polls in which this question was asked between February 2001 and March 2003 (N=25). However, one poll (conducted on November 26, 2001) was excluded from the analysis as an extreme outlier that skewed the data. In this poll, which was the first conducted after the attacks of September 11, 2001, and was likely influenced by the emotional state of the public at that time, 73.9% of respondents favored the invasion of Iraq (ten percentage points higher than any subsequent poll). It was excluded as an aberration after a statistical analysis (one-sample $t$-test) failed to demonstrate a significant difference in the mean level of support for invasion, with or without the outlier.

TABLE A.2

*Names, Description, and Coding of Variables*

| Variable | Description | Coding |
|---|---|---|
| *1. Volume* | | |
| Source | Source of rhetoric in article | 1=Administration |
| | | 0=Nonadministration |
| Term | Administration term | 1=Bush |
| | | 0=Clinton |
| Multiple | Article contains multiple administration sources | 1=Yes |
| | | 0=No |
| Bush | Contains President George W. Bush quote | 1=Yes |
| | | 0=No |
| Cheney | Contains Vice President Dick Cheney quote | 1=Yes |
| | | 0=No |
| Rumsfeld | Contains Secretary of Defense Donald Rumsfeld quote | 1=Yes |
| | | 0=No |
| Powell | Contains Secretary of State Colin Powell quote | 1=Yes |
| | | 0=No |
| Rice | Contains National Security Advisor Condoleezza Rice quote | 1=Yes |
| | | 0=No |
| Ashcroft | Contains Attorney General John Ashcroft quote | 1=Yes |
| | | 0=No |
| Fleischer | Contains Press Secretary Ari Fleischer quote | 1=Yes |
| | | 0=No |
| Wolfowitz | Contains Deputy Secretary of Defense Paul Wolfowitz quote | 1=Yes |
| | | 0=No |
| Sr. Official | Contains unnamed senior administration official quote | 1=Yes |
| | | 0=No |
| Republican | Contains Republican policy maker quote (identified) | 1=Yes |
| | | 0=No |
| Democrat | Contains Democratic policy maker quote (identified) | 1=Yes |
| | | 0=No |
| Annan | Contains U.N. Secretary General Kofi Annan quote | 1=Yes |
| | | 0=No |
| Blix | Contains U.N. Chief Weapons Inspector Hans Blix quote | 1=Yes |
| | | 0=No |
| *2. Tone* | | |
| *Types* | | |
| Punitive | Article contains punitive rhetoric | 1=Yes |
| | | 0=No |
| Communitarian | Contains communitarian rhetoric | 1=Yes |
| | | 0=No |
| Reactive | Contains reactive rhetoric | 1=Yes |
| | | 0=No |

*(continued)*

TABLE A.2 *Names, Description, and Coding of Variables* (*continued*)

| Variable | Description | Coding |
|---|---|---|
| Rehabilitative | Contains rehabilitative rhetoric | 1 = Yes<br>0 = No |
| Indefinite | Contains indefinite rhetoric | 1 = Yes<br>0 = No |
| Counterclaim | Contains alternate view/<br>counterclaim rhetoric | 1 = Yes<br>0 = No |
| Combo Punitive/<br>Communitarian | Contains both punitive and<br>communitarian rhetoric | 1 = Yes<br>0 = No |
| Combo Punitive/<br>Indefinite | Contains both punitive and<br>indefinite rhetoric | 1 = Yes<br>0 = No |
| Combo Reactive/<br>Rehabilitative | Contains both reactive and<br>rehabilitative rhetoric | 1 = Yes<br>0 = No |
| Combo Indefinite/<br>Counterclaim | Contains both indefinite and<br>counterclaim rhetoric | 1 = Yes<br>0 = No |
| *Key Words* | | |
| "Evil" | Contains key word evil or evildoers | 1 = Yes<br>0 = No |
| "Terrorism" | Contains key word terrorism or terror | 1 = Yes<br>0 = No |
| "Sanctions" | Contains key word sanctions | 1 = Yes<br>0 = No |
| "WMD" | Contains key phrase weapons<br>of mass destruction | 1 = Yes<br>0 = No |
| "Threat" | Contains key word threat | 1 = Yes<br>0 = No |
| *Time Lags* | Sum of articles with particular tone<br>in two-week, one-month,<br>three-month, and five-month lags<br>preceding Gallup polls | 1 = Yes<br>0 = No |
| *3. Time* | | |
| Post-9/11 | Timeframe 9/12/01–3/18/03 versus<br>3/1/00–9/11/01 | 1 = Yes<br>0 = No |
| Concurrent | one-month and three-month time<br>intervals in chronological order | 1 = Yes<br>0 = No |
| *4. Public Opinion* | | |
| Gallup Poll | Percentage of U.S. population<br>supporting invasion of Iraq | 1 = Same or higher<br>than previous poll<br>0 = Lower than<br>previous poll |

NOTE: Each article in the analysis may contain multiple sources of rhetoric (e.g., President Bush and Kofi Annan) and multiple types/tones of rhetoric (e.g., punitive and indefinite).

# Bibliography

Adorno, T. W. (1997). Opinion delusion society. (H. W. Pickford., Trans.). *Yale Journal of Criticism, 10.2*, 227–245.

Agger, B. (1978). *Western Marxism: An introduction.* Santa Monica, CA: Goodyear.

Altheide, D. (2002). *Creating fear: News and the construction of crisis.* New York: Aldine de Gruyter.

—— (2006). Terrorism and the politics of fear. *Cultural Studies ⇔ Critical Methodologies, 6*, 415–439.

American Red Cross (2001). *A summary of the Geneva conventions and additional protocols.* Washington, D.C.: American Red Cross.

Aulette, J., & Michalowski, R. (1993). Fire in hamlet: A case study of state-corporate crime. In K. Tunnel (Ed.), *Political crime in contemporary America* (pp. 171–206). New York: Garland.

Baker, D. (2008, July 31). A cloudy forecast for the U.S. economy. *The Guardian.* Retrieved from www.guardian.co.uk.

Baker, R. (2004). Exclusive: Bush wanted to invade Iraq if elected in 2000. Retrieved October 28, 2008, from www.gnn.tv/print/761/Exclusive_Bush/20042710.

Barak, G. (1988). Newsmaking criminology: Reflections on the media, intellectuals, and crime. *Justice Quarterly, 5*(4), 565–587.

—— (1991). *Crimes by the capitalist state: An introduction to state criminality.* Albany, NY: State University of New York Press.

Barkan, S. E., & Cohn, S. E. (2005). Why whites favor more money to fight crime: The role of racial prejudice. *Social Problems, 52*(2), 300–314.

Barstow, D. (2008a, April 20). Message machine: Behind TV analysts, Pentagon's hidden hand courting ex-officers tied to military contractors. *New York Times*, p. A1.

Barstow, D. (2008b, November 30). One man's military-industrial-media complex message machine. *New York Times*, p. A1.

Bartholomew, A. (2006). *International commission of inquiry on crimes against humanity committed by the Bush administration of the United States.* [Testimony]. New York: Bush Crimes Commission.

Becker, E. (1968). *The structure of evil: An essay on the unification of the science of man.* New York: G. Braziller.

Beckett, K. (1994). Setting the public agenda: "Street crime" and drug use in American politics. *Social Problems, 41*(3), 425–447.

Bennett, W. L., & Paletz, D. L. (Eds.). (1994). *The media, public opinion, and U.S. foreign policy in the Gulf war.* Chicago, IL: University of Chicago Press.

Berger, P. L., & Luckmann, T. (1966). *The social construction of reality: A treatise in the sociology of knowledge.* New York: Anchor Books.

Best, J. 1994. *Troubling children: Studies of children and social problems*. New York: Aldine de Gruyter.

Blow, C. M. (2008, July 26). Americans move to the middle. *New York Times*, p. A17.

Blumer, H. (1971). Social problems as collective behavior. *Social Problems, 18*, 298–306.

Bonifaz, J. C. (2004). The first lie. Retrieved September 4, 2008, from www .commondreams.org/cgi-bin/print.cgi?file=/views04/0128–08.htm.

Bromley, D. G., Shupe, A. D., Jr., & Ventimiglia, J. C. (1979). Atrocity tales, the Unification Church, and the social construction of evil. *Journal of Communication, 29*(3), 42–53.

Burns, R., & Crawford, C. (1999). School shootings: The media and public fear: Ingredients for a moral panic. *Crime, Law and Social Change, 32*(2), 147–168.

Cassese, A. (2003). *International criminal law*. Oxford: Oxford University Press.

Chambliss, W. J. (1975). Toward a political economy of crime. *Theory and Society, 2*, 149–170.

—— (1988). *Exploring criminology*. New York: Macmillan.

—— (1989). State organized crime. *Criminology, 27*(2), 183–208.

—— (1995). Commentary by William J. Chambliss. *Society of Social Problems Newsletter, 26*(1), 9.

Chambliss, W. J., & Mankoff, M. (1976). *Whose law? What order?* New York: John Wiley.

Chiricos, T., Eschholz, S., & Gertz, M. (1997). Crime, news and fear of crime: Toward an identification of audience effects. *Social Problems, 44*, 342–357.

Chiricos, T., Padgett, K., & Gertz, M. (2000). Fear, TV news and the reality of crime. *Criminology, 38*, 755–785.

Clark, R. (2006). *International commission of inquiry on crimes against humanity committed by the Bush administration of the United States*. [Testimony]. New York: Bush Crimes Commission.

Clarke, R. A. (2004). *Against all enemies: Inside America's war on terror*. Detroit: Free Press.

Clinard, M. B., Quinney, R., & Wildeman, J. (1994). *Criminal behavior systems (3rd ed.)*. Cincinnati, OH: Anderson.

Chomsky, N. (2002). *Media control: The spectacular achievements of propaganda*. New York: Seven Stories Press.

—— (2005). Global ethics, American foreign policy and the academic as activist: An interview with Noam Chomsky. *Journal of Global Ethics, 1*(2), 197–205.

—— (2007). Foreword. In D. Downes, P. Rock, C. Chinkin & C. Gearty (Eds.), *Crime, social control and human rights: Essays in honour of Stanley Cohen*. Cullompton (Devon) UK: Willan Publishing.

Cohen, B. (1963). *The press and foreign policy*. Princeton, NJ: Princeton University Press.

Cohen, J. (1992). A power primer. *Psychological Bulletin, 112*(1), 155–159.

Cohen, S. (1972). *Folk devils and moral panics: The creation of the mods and rockers*. London: MacGibbon & Kee.

—— (2001). *States of denial: Knowing about atrocities and suffering*. Cambridge: Polity.

—— (2002). *Folk devils and moral panics: The creation of the mods and rockers (3rd ed.)*. New York: Routledge.

Cohn, M. (2006). Bush on trial for crimes against humanity. Retrieved September 24, 2008, from www.truthout.org/article/bush-trial-crimes-against-humanity.

Corn, D. (2003). *The lies of George W. Bush: Mastering the politics of deception*. New York: Crown Publishers.

Coyle, M. J. (2004). *Finding and defining evil: The social construction of crime as evil.* Paper presented at the American Society of Criminology annual conference. Nashville, TN, November 19.

Croft, S. (2006). *Culture, crisis and America's war on terror.* Cambridge: Cambridge University Press.

Dao, J., & Schmitt, E. (2002a, February 19). Pentagon readies efforts to sway sentiment abroad. *New York Times*, p. A12.

Dao, J., & Schmitt, E. (2002b, February 27). A "damaged" information office is declared closed by Rumsfeld. *New York Times*, p. A6.

Davis, N. J., & Stasz, C. (1990). *Social control of deviance: A critical perspective.* New York: McGraw-Hill.

Deuber-Mankowsky, A. (2008). Nothing is political, everything can be politicized: On the concept of the political in Michel Foucault and Carl Schmitt. *Telos, 142*(Spring), 135–161.

DeYoung, K. (2002, July 30). Bush to create formal office to shape U.S. image abroad. *Washington Post*, p. A3.

Edelman, M. (1988). *Constructing the political spectacle.* Chicago, IL: University of Chicago Press.

Elliott, S. (2002, September 15). Madison Avenue never rests. *New York Times*, Week in Review, p. 4.

Entman, R. W. (1993). Framing: Toward clarification of a fractured paradigm. *Journal of Communication, 43*(4), 51–58.

—— (2003). Cascading activation: Contesting the White House's frame after 9/11. *Political Communication, 20*, 415–432.

Eschholz, S., Chiricos, T., & Gertz, M. (2003). Television and fear of crime: Program types, audience traits, and the mediating effect of perceived neighborhood racial composition. *Social Problems, 50*, 395–415.

Ewing, C. P., & Aubrey, M. (1987). Battered woman and public opinion: Some realities about the myths. *Journal of Family Violence, 2*(3), 257–263.

Falcon, L., & Melendez, E. (2001). The social context of job searching for racial groups in urban centers. In A. O'Connor, C. Tilly & L. Bobo (Eds.), *Urban inequality: Evidence from four cities* (pp. 341–371). New York: Sage.

Feldman, N. (2002). Choices of law, choices of war. *Harvard Journal of Law & Public Policy, 25*(2), 457–485.

Fish, C. (2001, October 15). Condemnation without absolutes. *New York Times*, Opinion, p. 32.

Friedrichs, D. O. (1996). *Trusted criminals: White collar crime in contemporary society.* Belmont, CA: Wadsworth.

Gallup (2003). Iraq. *The Gallup poll* (March 14–15). Gallup Organization, Princeton, NJ.

—— (2006). *The Gallup panel.* Gallup Organization, Princeton, NJ.

Garland, D. (2008). On the concept of moral panic. *Crime, Media, Culture, 4*(1), 9–30.

Gartner, S. S. (2008). Ties to the dead: Connections to Iraq war and 9/11 casualties and disapproval of the president. *American Sociological Review, 73*(4), 690–695.

Gerbner, G., & Gross, L. (1976). Living with television: The violence profile. *Journal of Communication, 26*, 173–199.

Glanz, J., & Robertson, C. (2008, August 6). As Iraq surplus rises, little goes into rebuilding. *New York Times*, p. A12.

Goldstone, R. (2008, July 15). Catching a war criminal in the act. *New York Times*, p. A19.

Gonzenbach, W. J. (1996). *The media, the president, and public opinion: A longitudinal analysis of the drug issue, 1984–1991.* Mahwah, NJ: Lawrence Erlbaum.

Goode, E., & Ben-Yehuda, N. (1994). *Moral panics: The social construction of deviance.* Cambridge, MA: Blackwell.

Goodman, E. (2006, December 18). U.S. occupation: Stay or leave? Ask the Iraqis. *Miami Herald*, p. 29A.

Green, P., & Ward, T. (2000). State crime, human rights, and the limits of criminology. *Social Justice, 27*(1), 101.

—— (2004). *State crime: Governments, violence and corruption.* London: Pluto Press.

Greenhouse, L. (2008, June 13). Justices, 5–4, back detainee appeals for Guantanamo. *New York Times*, p. A1.

Greider, W. (2003, November 17). Occupiers and the law. *The Nation*, pp. 5–6.

Habermas, J. (1975). *Legitimation crisis.* Boston: Beacon Press.

Hall, S., Critcher, C., Jefferson, T., Clarke, J., & Roberts, B. (1978). *Policing the crisis: Mugging, the state, and law and order.* London: Macmillan.

Hartung, W. 2004. *How much are you making on the war Daddy? A quick and dirty guide to war profiteering in the Bush administration.* New York: Nation Books.

Hawdon, J. E. (2001). The role of presidential rhetoric in the creation of a moral panic: Reagan, Bush, and the war on drugs. *Deviant Behavior, 22*(5), 419–445.

Henkin, L. (1995). *International law: Politics and values.* Dordrecht, The Netherlands: Martinus Nijhoff.

Herman, E. S., & Chomsky, N. (1988). *Manufacturing consent: The political economy of the mass media.* New York: Pantheon Books.

Hilgartner, S., & Bosk, C. L. (1988). The rise and fall of social problems: A public arenas model. *American Journal of Sociology, 94*(1), 53–78.

Hogan, M. J., Long, M. A., Stretesky, P. B., & Lynch, M. J. (2006). Campaign contributions, post-war reconstruction contracts, and state crime. *Deviant Behavior, 27*(3), 269–297.

Horkheimer, M. (1987). Foreword. In L. Lowenthal, *False prophets: Studies in authoritarianism.* Communication in Society, Vol. 3 (pp. 1–3). New Brunswick, NJ: Transaction Books.

Human Rights Watch (2003). *Off target: The conduct of the war and civilian casualties in Iraq.* New York: Human Rights Watch.

Humphries, D., & Caringella-MacDonald, S. (1990). Murdered mothers, missing wives: Reconsidering female victimization. *Social Justice, 17*(2), 71–89.

Hutcheson, R. (2006, December 22). Will Bush heed polls' Iraq view? *Miami Herald*, p. 1A.

Hutcheson, R., & Talev, M. (2007, February 15). Bush accuses Iran of deadly meddling in Iraq. *Miami Herald*, p. 1A.

ICRC (2004). *Report of the International Committee of the Red Cross (ICRC) on the treatment by the coalition forces of prisoners of war and other protected persons by the Geneva Conventions in Iraq during arrest, internment and interrogation.* Geneva: ICRC.

Iskandar, A. (2005). "The great American bubble": Fox News channel, the "mirage" of objectivity, and the isolation of American public opinion. In L. Artz and Y. R. Kamalipour (Eds.), *Bring 'em on* (pp. 155–174). Lanham, MD: Rowman & Littlefield.

Jarecki, E. (2006). *Why we fight.* Sony Pictures, Los Angeles, CA.

Jay, M. (1973). *The dialectical imagination.* Boston: Little, Brown.

Johnson, T. J., Wanta, W., & Boudreau, T. (2004). Drug peddlers: How four presidents attempted to influence media and public concern on the drug issue. *Atlantic Journal of Communication, 12*(4), 177–199.

Kafala, T. (2003). What is war crime? Retrieved January 25, 2008, from www.newsvote .bbc.co.uk.

Kant, I. (1965). *Critique of pure reason*. (Norman Kemp Smith, Trans.). New York: St. Martin's Press. (Original work published 1781).

Kanter, R. M. (1993). *Men and women of the corporation*. New York: Perseus Books.

Kauzlarich, D., & Kramer, R. C. (1998). *Crimes of the American nuclear state: At home and abroad*. Boston: Northeastern University Press.

Kauzlarich, D., Mullins, C. W., & Matthews, R. A. (2003). A complicity continuum of state crime. *Contemporary Justice Review, 6*, 241–254.

Kellner, D. (1990). *Television and the crisis of democracy*. Boulder, CO: Westview Press.

—— (2005). Foreword: The Bush administration's march to war. In L. Artz & Y. R. Kamalipour (Eds.), *Bring 'em on* (pp. vii–xvii). Lanham, MD: Rowman & Littlefield.

Kieve, A. (1994). *The modern presidency and crisis rhetoric*. Westport, CT: Praeger.

Kiousis, S. (2003). Job approval and favorability: The impact of media attention to the Monica Lewinsky scandal on public opinion of President Bill Clinton. *Mass Communication & Society, 6*(4), 435–452.

Klein, N. (2003, November 24). Bring Halliburton home. *The Nation*, p. 10.

Koch, J. W. (1998). Political rhetoric and political persuasion: The changing structure of citizens' preferences on health insurance during policy debate. *Public Opinion Quarterly, 62*(2), 209–229.

Kramer, R., & Michalowski, R. (1990). *Toward an integrated theory of state-corporate crime*. Paper presented at the American Society of Criminology. Baltimore, MD.

Kramer, R., Michalowski, R., & Rothe, D. (2005). The supreme international crime: How the U.S. war in Iraq threatens the rule of law. *Social Justice, 32*(2), 52–81.

Krugman, P. (2007, September 7). Time to take a stand. *New York Times*, p. A29.

Lang, G. E., & Lang, K. (1983). *The battle for public opinion: The president, the press, and the polls during Watergate*. New York: Columbia University Press.

Levinson, C. (2008, November 17). Iraq deal draft: U.S. troops out in 3 years. *USA Today*, p. 1A.

Lowenthal, L. (1989). *Critical theory and Frankfurt theorists: Lectures, correspondence, conversations*. Communication in Society, Vol. 4. New Brunswick, NJ: Transaction Books.

Lowery, S. A., & DeFleur, M. L. (1995). *Milestones in mass communications research: Media effects* (3rd ed.). New York: Longman.

Marcuse, H. (1964). *One-dimensional man*. Boston: Beacon Press.

Marx, K. (1959). *Economic and philosophical manuscripts*. Moscow: Progressive Publishers. (Original work published 1844).

Maxwell, K. A., Huxford, J., Borum, C., & Hornik, R. (2000). Covering domestic violence: How the O. J. Simpson case shaped reporting of violence in the news media. *Journalism & Mass Communications Quarterly, 77*(2), 258–272.

Mazzetti, M. (2007, December 3). U.S. says Iran ended atomic arms work. *New York Times*, p. A17.

Mazzetti, M., & Rohde, D. (2008, June 30). Amid U.S. policy disputes, al Qaeda grows in Pakistan. *New York Times*, p. A1.

Mazzetti, M., & Shane, S. (2008, June 6). Bush overstated evidence on Iraq, senators report. *New York Times*, p. A1.

McClellan, S. (2008). *What happened: Inside the Bush White House and Washington's culture of deception*. New York: Perseus Books.

McCombs, M. E., & Shaw, D. L. (1972). The agenda-setting function of mass media. *Public Opinion Quarterly*, summer, 176–187.

McCorkle, R. C., & Miethe, T. D. (1998). The political and organizational response to gangs: An examination of a "moral panic" in Nevada. *Justice Quarterly, 15*(1), 41–64.

——— (2001). *Panic: Rhetoric and reality in the war on street gangs.* Saddle River, NJ: Prentice-Hall.

McLuhan, M. 1964. *Understanding media: The extension of man.* New York: McGraw-Hill.

Mediamark Research Inc. (2005). Syndicated audience data: New York Times. New York, NY.

Merskin, D. (2004). The construction of Arabs as enemies: Post-September 11 discourse of George W. Bush. *Mass Communication & Society, 7*(2), 157–175.

Michalowski, R. 2009. Power, crime and criminology in the new imperial age. *Crime, Law, and Social Change, 51.* In press.

Mills, C. W. (1956). *The power elite.* New York: Oxford University Press.

Moore, D. W. (2006). Public polarized over Iraq. *The Gallup Poll* (February 2). Gallup Organization, Princeton, NJ.

Mueller, J. (2006). *Overblown: How politicians and the terrorism industry inflate national security threats, and why we believe them.* New York: Free Press.

Muttitt, G. (2006). *Crude designs: The rip-off of Iraq's oil wealth.* London: Dane Publishing.

Nielsen (2005). Nielsen NetRatings (October). A. C. Nielsen. New York, NY.

Nielsen, A. L., & Bonn, S. (2008). Media exposure and attitudes toward drug addiction, 1975–2004. *Deviant Behavior, 29,* 726–752.

Opinion Research Business (2008). More than one million Iraqis dead since 2003 invasion: study. Retrieved August 2 from http://www.news.yahoo.com/s/afp/20080130/wl_mideast_afp/iraqunrestconflicttoll_080130213209_ylt=AkGAI03.sbL_t881uZfb t3tX6GMA.

Oxford English Dictionary (1971). Oxford: Clarendon Press.

Pagano, M., & Gauvreau, K. (2000). *Principles of biostatistics.* Pacific Grove, CA: Duxbury.

Paust, J. J. (2002). *There is no need to revise the laws of war in light of September 11th.* Washington, D.C.: American Society of International Law.

Peterson, S. (2002). Hussein may dodge U.S. hunt. Retrieved October 28, 2008, from www.globalsecurity.org/org/news/2002/021011-iraq1.htm.

Phillips, K. (2004). *American dynasty: Aristocracy, fortune, and the politics of deceit in the White House.* New York: Penguin.

Quinney, R. (1970). *The social reality of crime.* Boston: Little, Brown.

Ratner, M. (2002). The United Nations Charter and the use of force against Iraq. Retrieved September 12, 2008, from www.lawyersagainstthewar.org/legalarticles/ratner.html.

Reinarman, C., & Levine, H. (1989). Crack in context: Politics and media in the making of a drug scare. *Contemporary Drug Problems, 16,* 535–577.

Revkin, A. C. (2008, July 9). Cheney's office said to edit draft testimony on warming. *New York Times,* p. A12.

Risen, J. (2008, August 12). Use of contractors in Iraq costs billions, report says. *New York Times,* p. A11.

Ritter, S. (2003). *Frontier justice: Weapons of mass destruction and the bushwhacking of America.* New York: Context Books.

——— (2006). *International commission of inquiry on crimes against humanity committed by the Bush administration of the United States.* [Testimony]. New York: Bush Crimes Commission.

Robertson, C., & Oppel, R. A. (2008, August 7). Iraq parliament fails to approve an election law. *New York Times*, p. A1.

Ross, J. (1995). *Controlling state crime: An introduction.* New York: Transaction Publishers.

Rothe, D. L., & Friedrichs, D. O. (2006). The state of the criminology of crimes of the state. *Social Justice, 33*(1), 147–161.

Rothe, D. L., & Muzzatti, S. L. (2004). Enemies everywhere: Terrorism, moral panic, and U.S. civil society. *Critical Criminology, 12*(3), 327–350.

Satter, R. G. (2007, January 18). Five minutes to doomsday, top scientists say. *Miami Herald*, p. 17A.

Scheer, C. (2003). *Ten appalling lies we were told about Iraq.* AlterNet. Retrieved September 18, 2004, from http://www.alternet.org/story/16274/.

Scheer, C., Scheer, R., & Chaudry L. (2003). *The five biggest lies Bush told us about Iraq.* New York: Seven Stories Press.

Semple, K., & Lehren, A. W. (2008, August 7). Five hundred: Deadly U.S. milestone in Afghan war. *New York Times*, p. A1.

Simon, D. R. (1995). *Social problems & the sociological imagination.* New York: McGraw-Hill.

—— (2002). *Elite deviance* (7th ed.). Boston: Allyn & Bacon.

Simon, J., & Feeley, M. M. (1995). True crime: The new penology and public discourse on crime. In T. G. Blomberg & S. Cohen (Eds.), *Punishment and social control: Essays in honor of Sheldon L. Messinger* (pp. 147–180). New York: Aldine de Gruyter.

Singer, P. W., 2003. *Corporate warriors: The rise of the privatized military industry.* Ithaca: Cornell University Press.

Sniffen, M. J. (2007, January 30). Ex-Bush spokesman takes stand in C.I.A. leak trial. *Miami Herald*, p. 6A.

Solomon, N. (2006). Propaganda play. Retrieved August 7, 2008, from www.usa.mediamonitors.net/content/view/full/2365/.

Spiegel, P. (2006, November 4). Perle says he should not have backed the Iraq war. *Los Angeles Times*, p. A11.

Spillman, K. R., & Spillman, K. (1977). Some sociological and psychological aspects of "images of the enemy." In R. Fiebig-von Hase & U. Lehmkuhl (Eds.), *Enemy images in American history* (pp. 43–64). Providence, RI: Berghahn Books.

Stevenson, B. (1948) Attributed to Senator Hiram Johnson, remarks in the Senate, 1918. *The Macmillan book of proverbs, maxims, and famous phrases* (p. 2445). New York: Macmillan.

Strobel, W. P., & Talev, M. (2006, September 9). Senate panel: Hussein rebuffed bin Laden. *Miami Herald*, p. 16A.

Suskind, R. (2008). *The way of the world.* New York: HarperCollins.

Sutherland, E. (1949). *White collar crime.* New York: Holt, Rinehart & Winston.

Trombly, M. (2003). A brief history of the laws of war. Retrieved January 20, 2008, from www.spj.org/gc-history.asp.

Tuchman, G. (1978). *Making news: A study in the social construction of reality.* New York: Free Press.

Turk, A. (1982). *Political criminality.* Thousand Oaks, CA: Sage.

United Nations (1950). Principles of international law recognized in the charter of the Nuremberg tribunal and in the judgment of the tribunal. *Yearbook of the International Law Commission, 2,* 1–3.

Victor, J. S. (1994). Fundamentalist religions and the moral crusade against Satanism: The social construction of deviant behavior. *Deviant Behavior, 15*(3), 305–334.

www.americanheart.org (2007). Advocacy news. Retrieved January 30 from www.americanheart.org/presenter.jhtml?identifier=3011323.

www.answers.com (2006). September 11 attacks. Retrieved February 4 from www.answers.com/topics/september-11-attacks.

www.avert.org (2007). USA HIV & AIDS cases by deaths and year. Retrieved January 30 from www.avert.org/usastaty.htm.

www.cdc.gov (2007). Tobacco-related mortality. Retrieved January 30 from www.cdc.gov/tobacco/factsheets/Tobacco_Related_Mortality_factsheet.htm.

www.cnn.com (2005). Former aide: Powell WMD speech "lowest point in my life." Retrieved August 19, 2008, from www.cnn.com/2005/WORLD/meast/08/19/powell.un/.

www.corporations.org (2007). Media reform information center. Retrieved March 16 from www.corporations.org/media/.

www.democracynow.org (2005). Former U.S. attorney general Ramsey Clark calls for Bush impeachment. Retrieved September 24, 2008, from www.democracynow .org/2005/1/21/former_u_s_attorney_general_ramsey.

—— (2009). "Exclusive . . . Pentagon Pundits: New York Times Reporter David Barstow Wins Pulitzer Prize for Exposing Military's Pro-War Propaganda Media Campaign." May 8.

www.globalissues.org (2008). World military spending. Retrieved August 18 from www.globalissues.org/geopolitics/armstrade/spending.asp.

www.icasualties.org (2008). Iraq coalition casualty count. Retrieved August 6.

www.infoplease.com (2007). Ten leading causes of death in the U.S. Retrieved January 30 from www.infoplease.com/ipa/A0005110.html.

www.nationalpriorities.org (2008). Cost of Iraq war. Retrieved July 31 from www.nationalpriorities.org/index.php?option=com_wrapper&Itemid=182.

www.nchc.org (2007). Health insurance coverage. Retrieved January 30 from www.nchc.org/facts/coverage.html.

www.news.bbc.co.uk (2004). Bush has Saddam gun as souvenir. Retrieved October 31, 2008, from www.news.bbc.co.uk/go/pr/fr/-/1/hi/world/middle_east/3762641.stm.

www.nrdc.org (2007). The Bush administration's global warming policies. Retrieved February 1 from www.nrdc.org/globalWarming/bushinx.asp.

www.nuremberg.law.harvard.edu (2008). Nuremberg trials project. Retrieved January 25.

www.publicintegrity.org (2008). The war card report. Retrieved August 7 from www.publicintegrity.org/blog/entry/333/.

www.rawstory.com (2007). Former Powell aide says Bush, Cheney guilty of "high crimes." Retrieved August 19, 2008, from www.rawstory.com/printstory.php ?story=6032.

www.tobaccofreekids.org (2007). Federal cigarette excise tax revenue. Retrieved February 3.

www.un.org (2008). International criminal court. Retrieved June 1 from www .cyberschoolbus.un.org/treaties/criminal.asp.

www.usa.mediamonitors.net (2006). Solomon, N., November 11. Retrieved January 25, 2008.

Wanta, W., Golan, G., & Lee, C. (2004). Agenda setting and international news: Media influence on public perceptions of foreign nations. *Journalism & Mass Communication Quarterly, 81*(2), 364–377.

Webster's College Dictionary (1997). New York: Random House.

Welch, M. (2000). *Flag burning: Moral panic and the criminalization of protest*. New York: Aldine de Gruyter.

—— (2004). Quiet constructions in the war on terror: Subjecting asylum seekers to unnecessary detention. *Social Justice, 31*(1/2), 113–129.

—— (2006a). *Scapegoats of September 11th: Hate crimes and state crimes in the war on terror*. New Brunswick, NJ: Rutgers University Press.

——(2006b). Seeking a safer society: America's anxiety in the war on terror. *Security Journal, 19*(2), 93–109.

—— (2007, February 14). Personal correspondence.

Welch, M., Fenwick, M., & Roberts, M. (1997). Primary definitions of crime and moral panic: A content analysis of experts' quotes in feature newspaper articles on crime. *Journal of Research in Crime and Delinquency, 34*(4), 474–494.

Welch, M., Price, E. A., & Yankey, N. (2002). Moral panic over youth violence: Wilding and the manufacture of menace in the media. *Youth & Society, 34*(1), 3–30.

Wilson, G. (1996). Toward a revised framework for examining beliefs about the causes of poverty. *Sociological Quarterly, 37*(3), 413–428.

Woodward, C. (2008, May 30). Ex-aide says he initially gave Bush benefit of doubt on war logic. *Star-Ledger*, p. A3.

Young, J. (1971). The role of the police as amplifiers of deviance, negotiators of drug control as seen in Notting Hill. In S. Cohen (Ed.), *Images of deviance* (pp. 27–61). Harmondsworth, UK: Penguin Books.

Zoepf, K., & Dagher, S. (2008, November 9). Iraq gives religious minorities fewer seats than the U.N. suggested. *New York Times*, p. A25.

# Index

# About the Author

Scott A. Bonn is an assistant professor of sociology at Drew University in Madison, New Jersey. He received his doctorate in sociology at the University of Miami, Florida. Scott teaches courses in criminology, sociology of deviance, media and crime, and research methods. His primary research interests include white-collar crime, state crime, public agenda-setting, and media effects on society. He has over twenty years of corporate experience as an advertising and media executive, including vice president at NBC television network and executive vice president at SonicNet, an award-winning Internet start-up company sold to MTV networks. He resides in Manhattan, New York.

Available titles in the Critical Issues in Crime and Society series:

CPSIA information can be obtained at www.ICGtesting.com
Printed in the USA
270341BV00003B/29/P